I0223568

GRAMMAR

OF

DIVINITY

"There exist a number of detailed histories of the early Church and its passionate theological debates. What sets Brian Orr's book apart is the amazing love of God that shines through. Orr loves God—the true, simple, infinite, glorious God who is Three and One. His love of God gives his discussion of theological debates an unusual readability—his prose reflects his own excitement, his own wonder in speaking about the wondrous Holy One who is Father, Son, and Holy Spirit. Scripture and metaphysics come together here in a theological page-turner!"

— Matthew Levering, *James N. Jr. and Mary D. Perry Chair of Theology, Mundelein Seminary*

"Brian Orr has authored a marvelous book. Following upon and flowing from Scripture, he treats how the Fathers of the Church treated the mysteries of the Christian faith. His clear examination of these great theologians is insightful and creative. What the Fathers have to say comes alive, and one cannot help but grow in admiration as to what they taught, and also to grow in love for the truth that they proclaim."

— Thomas G. Weinandy, *OFM, Capuchin College*

"The doctrine of God is fruitful ground for exegesis and systematization, for the essence of eternal life is knowing God through His Son Jesus Christ (John 17:3). It is precisely this doctrine—as it has been articulated over the past two millennia—that has come under sustained attack in recent years. Drawing from such fields as patristics, grammar, and philosophy, Orr ably defends classical theism by demonstrating that the early church fathers justifiably (and selectively) appropriated the language and categories of Greek philosophy as a metaphysical framework for speaking analogically about God, the great I AM who is simultaneously incomprehensible, yet knowable, and mysterious, yet revealed. Above all, we see in this work how the early church fathers used extra-biblical terminology and concepts to *clarify* rather than to *contradict* the divine grammar of the sacred Scriptures. Here, then, is a compelling contribution to the growing body of literature in defense of this great tradition."

— Dr. Joel R. Beeke, *Puritan Reformed Theological Seminary, Grand Rapids, Michigan*

GRAMMAR
OF
DIVINITY

*Divine Simplicity and the Development of Metaphysical Language
in the First Four Centuries*

BRIAN J. ORR

KP KINGDOM PRESS

Apple Valley | California

Kingdom Press
13722 Delaware Road
Apple Valley, Ca 92307
Kingdompressbooks.com

© 2024 Brian J. Orr
All rights reserved.
Published 2024

ISBN: 979-8-218-52102-8

Name: Orr, Brian J., author.
Title: Grammar of Divinity: Divine Simplicity and the Development of Metaphysical
Language in the First Four Centuries.

Cover images: Dublin, CBL BP II, fol. 61 (P46), inscription to 2 Corinthians (with page
number above). ©The Trustees of the Chester Beatty Library, Dublin; "The First Council of
Nicaea" – Fresco in Stavropoleos Church, Bucharest (Romania).

Cover design and typesetting: Brian J. Orr

Except for brief quotations in critical publications or reviews, no part of this book may be
reproduced in any manner without prior written permission from the author/publisher.

Unless otherwise noted, all Scripture quotations are taken from the Christian Standard
Bible®, Copyright © 2020 by Holman Bible Publishers.

Scripture quotations marked KJV have been taken from the King James Version® public
domain. Scripture quotations marked RSV have been taken from the Revised Standard
Version. 1971. Oak Harbor, WA: Logos Research Systems, Inc.

For Paul Helm,

who opened my eyes to a classical view of God

and championed my cause in defending it

Contents

ACKNOWLEDGMENTS

I would like to thank Paul Helm, who was one of my doctoral supervisors at London School of Theology. It was a blessing and honor to be one of his last doctoral students. My classical-theism awakening occurred early on in my studies during a conversation we had about divine impassibility. Paul asked me which version I affirmed, and I was dumbfounded because I thought there was only one position, which, for me at the time, was not a classical model. He explained the various perspectives and suggested some books to read, which I devoured a few days later on my ten-hour flight from London to California. It was one of the more profound moments (and has continued ever since) in my Christian life, contemplating the grandeur and majesty of the God of heaven and earth.

Kevin Vanhoozer was vary gracious in giving up some of his valuable time to read a few chapters and offer suggestions to clarify certain statements. Tom Weinandy provided structural help to parts of the book and was a sounding board for the title. Heartfelt thanks are due to my endorsers for breaking away from their extremely busy schedules and deadlines to read my manuscript and issue such generous remarks about it.

Rachel Feinstein applied her scrutinous eye to the manuscript catching typos and missing words, which I overlooked after so many readings of the draft. Oh, the tiresome work of editing! Thank you Rachel!

I would like to thank Credomag.com for permission to adapt material for Part 4: The Post Nicene Era, Gregory of Nyssa, from: "The Grammar of Divinity (On Theology): A Logically and Thoroughly Biblical Account of the Divine Nature." *https://credomag.com/article/the-grammar-of-divinity-on-theology/.* December 5, 2023, Volume 14, Issue 13.

And to my greatest earthly treasure, my one-flesh partner, Myndi, I am so thankful for your enthusiasm and support.

. . . To him be the glory forever. Amen.

ENGLISH TRANSLATIONS OF
THE EARLY CHURCH FATHERS

Unless otherwise noted, all English translations of the early church fathers are from:

The Apostolic Fathers: Greek Texts and English Translations, Revised. Edited by Michael W. Holmes. Grand Rapids, MI: Baker Academic, 1999.

The Ante-Nicene Fathers. Edited by Alexander Roberts, James Donaldson, and A. Cleveland Coxe. 10 vols. Buffalo, NY: Christian Literature Company, 1885.

A Select Library of the Nicene and Post-Nicene Fathers of the Christian Church. Edited by Philip Schaff. 1st Series. 14 vols. New York: Christian Literature Company, 1887.

A Select Library of the Nicene and Post-Nicene Fathers of the Christian Church. Edited by Philip Schaff and Henry Wace. 2nd Series. 14 vols. New York: Christian Literature Company, 1895.

GLOSSARY

I have included a glossary[1] of theological/metaphysical terms. To indicate to the reader that a term is in the glossary, the term will appear in small capital letters and in bold. Ex: **THEOLOGY (*THEOLOGIA*)**

---

[1] The definitions of terms in the glossary were adapted from Gilles Emery, *The Trinity: An Introduction to Catholic Doctrine on the Triune God*, Thomistic Ressourcement Series (Washington, D.C.: Catholic University of America Press, 2012), 199–203.

PREFACE

The book you have in your hands started as an investigation into the definitive statement made by Richard Muller in his *Post-Reformation Reformed Dogmatics*, Volume 3:

> The doctrine of divine simplicity is among the normative assumptions of theology from the time of the church fathers, to the age of the great medieval scholastic systems, to the era of Reformation and post-Reformation theology, and indeed, on into the succeeding era of late orthodoxy and rationalism.[1]

My doctoral studies heavily engaged the doctrine of God. During this period (2016–2020), the doctrine of divine simplicity was a controversial topic in modern academic literature (and still is), so I wanted to understand the concept better. It was during this time that I stumbled upon Richard Muller's statement (above). Intrigued, I conducted a comprehensive search for terms such as divine simplicity, simple, divine ESSENCE, and other related terms in the *Ante-Nicene* and *Nicene and Post-Nicene Fathers* (*ANF* and *NPNF*) series and other modern English translations. As I read, I wrote expositions of each theologian to better understand the development of divine simplicity and how each theologian utilized it in Divine contemplation.

---

[1] Richard A. Muller, *Post-Reformation Reformed Dogmatics: The Rise and Development of Reformed Orthodoxy, ca. 1520 to ca. 1725*, 2nd ed. (Grand Rapids, MI: Baker Academic, 2003), 3:39.

I read and wrote for the next few years, while also writing my dissertation; it was an integral part of my work. But as I was reading and writing, my investigation of divine simplicity expanded as I began to see the development of divine grammar in formulating the doctrine of God, the Trinity, and Christ. I say *grammar* because the theological debates during the first four hundred years were not about logic (not that we should not devise sound, logical arguments). There was a communication problem—a problem of *grammar*. The early church fathers lacked specific metaphysical terminology to speak about the triune God. The pagan philosophers could ruminate how they wanted. But the fathers were bound to scriptural revelation. Therefore, theological language must not detract from God's Word, from the gospel. It must conform with "the pattern of sound words" (2Ti 1:13). Thus, the vocabulary and concepts must correctly declare the content of Scripture. Once the terms are established, no matter where or when the divine truths of Scripture are taught, they must *always* carry the precise meaning from when they were established (I do understand this is a debatable point).[2] Theology matters; thus, words matter.

As to the structure of the work, the Introduction and Part 1 establish the trajectory and scope of the project. I did not intend to delve deeply into the historical aspects of my investigation, so the work lacks that cohesive element from figure to figure. However, my expositions *surge* from the *heat* of the polemical environment, where the forging of a divine grammar took shape. Once I get into the exposition, for the most part, each figure stands alone. I stay close to the primary sources and only bring a few outside voices into the discussion. The expositions get longer and more in depth as the divine grammar develops and divine simplicity takes shape. So, my expositions of the early apostolic figures (up to Clement of Alexandria) are brief. I have junction points where I pause and interject short statements about the Councils of Nicaea, Constantinople, and Chalcedon; they are the capstones of the Church's theological development.

This study began as a journey through the fathers to satisfy my intellectual curiosity. However, my exploration did much more; it led me to soul-soaring adulation of our infinitely glorious and sublime Creator. The fathers wed Scripture and metaphysics in a symbiotic relationship

---

[2] However, my statement does not mean *ecclesia reformata, semper reformanda secundum verbi Dei* ("the church reformed, and always in need of being reformed according to the Word of God") ceases.

that, in turn, brings the heart and mind into a *sanctified* symbiosis, giving the eyes of the soul a glimpse of the beatific reality awaiting us when we get to behold our Creator face-to-face.

It is my hope that this book will be a helpful resource for anyone interested (or skeptical) about the significant role divine simplicity—and the grammar underlying it—played in formulating the *Christian* doctrine of God. But more importantly, my prayer is that your time spent reading this work will lead you to extol, alongside the early church fathers, our blessed triune God.

> PRAISE GOD, FROM WHOM ALL BLESSINGS FLOW;
> PRAISE HIM, ALL CREATURES HERE BELOW;
> PRAISE HIM ABOVE, YE HEAV'NLY HOST;
> PRAISE FATHER, SON, AND HOLY GHOST.

INTRODUCTION

The triune God has revealed himself in creation, in Holy Scripture, and most gloriously in the person of Jesus Christ. The incomprehensible God of the universe decided to speak. The Infinite became finite so the finite could know the Infinite. In a divine movement without parallel, the Uncreated brought created being into existence with time and space. His purpose? To have loving fellowship with creatures he made for his glory, to perfect them after the image of his beloved Son, our Lord Jesus Christ, bringing them to fulfillment according to his purpose for them.

The late theologian John Webster writes that God's triune revelation in time and space, his divine works *ad extra* "repeat or externalize God's immanent being"[1]—God *in se*. Creatures have no window into the Divine essence.[2] Moses could only see the back of God—whatever God's *back* might be. There is no creaturely way to apprehend the direct

---

[1] J B. (John Bainbridge) Webster, "Perfection and Presence - 'God with US' According to the Christian Confession," ed. David M. Goetz (Presented at the The Kantzer Lectures, Trinity Evangelical Divinity School, 2007), 173, https://henrycenter.tiu.edu/kantzer-lectures-in-revealed-theology/past-lectures- publications/john-webster-perfection-presence/.

[2] Thomas F. Torrance, *The Mediation of Christ*, Revised. (Colorado Springs, CO: Helmers & Howers, 1992), 109, would see this statement needing a bit of nuance, writing, "The cross was a window into the very heart of God, for in and behind the cross, it was God the Father himself who paid the cost of our salvation."

essence of God. However, we need to engage in discourse about it. But how do we engage in discourse regarding a reality in which nothing we say correlates directly? The purpose of God's external works is to lift our hearts, minds, and souls to gaze on the beauty of the Lord all the days of our lives (Ps 27:4). But we need a divine *grammar*, so we can contemplate his beauty, NATURE, character, attributes, and purpose. What words can describe the essence of God? What conceptual framework allows us to speak of God in a manner that adequately extols his glory and keeps us from breaking the first and second commandments? The greatest challenge for the early church writers was articulating a conceptual THEOLOGIA about the God of the Bible while remaining grounded in the biblical text.[3] In his monumental work, *The Search for the Christian Doctrine of God: The Arian Controversy, 318–381*, R.P.C Hanson captures the issue at hand:

> ... the theologians of the Christian Church were slowly driven to a realization that the deepest questions which face Christianity *cannot be answered in purely biblical language, because the questions are about the meaning of biblical language itself.*[4]

Early Christian theologians could not formulate language about God's essence comparatively, competitively, or contrastively to contingent reality, as the pagan modes of religion. God is not like creatures; therefore, our expressions and first principles about God must ensure *that* (Creator/creature) distinction guides our discourse.[5] So, where do we begin? For the early church, and notably for Augustine, that journey started at the Burning Bush of Exodus 3:14.

I. THE BURNING BUSH EXPERIENCE

Exodus 3 records Moses' calling, where God reveals himself to him in a flame of fire on a burning bush at Mt. Horeb. Moses was astonished that the bush was not burning up. As he got closer to it, God called out to

---

[3] *Theologia* and *oikonomia* will be contrastive terms, the former denoting the inner being of God *ad intra*, God as he is in himself—*in se*, and the latter, denoting the outer works *ad extra*, God's working externally from himself in time and space. See "Glossary."

[4] R. P. C. Hanson, *The Search for the Christian Doctrine of God: The Arian Controversy, 318-381* (Grand Rapids, MI: Baker Academic, 2006), xx–xxi. (Emphasis added).

[5] Such nomenclature is termed *apophatic* or negative theology, specifically stating what God is *not* since we cannot say what God *is*.

him: "Remove your sandals, for the place where you are standing is holy ground" (Ex 3:5). God then tells Moses that he is the God of Abraham, Isaac, and Jacob and that he has heard his people's cries and is going to deliver them from their oppressors. Therefore, he is going to send Moses to lead his people out of Egypt (Ex 3:10). But Moses asks a question: "If I go to the Israelites and say to them, 'The God of your fathers has sent me to you,' and they ask me, 'What is his name?' what should I tell them?" (Ex 3:13). And God replied to Moses:

> "I AM WHO I AM. This is what you are to say to the Israelites: I AM has sent me to you." God also said to Moses, "Say this to the Israelites: The Lord, the God of your fathers, the God of Abraham, the God of Isaac, and the God of Jacob, has sent me to you. This is my name forever; this is how I am to be remembered in every generation (Ex 3:14–5).

He identifies himself in three names: אלאים, יהוה, היה ("I AM," "LORD," "God"). What do these names mean? In Hebrew, "I AM" is היה *hayah*. It is a verb, not a noun. And, connecting it to the name Lord, it becomes יהוה (YHWH) or, in syllabic form, *Yahweh*. But the verb *hayah* simply means *to be* or *to have the quality of being*. And אלאים, "God," is *Elohim*. It speaks to the *what* or the *nature* of the Lord, as the supernatural being who created the cosmos, who rules and governs it. He is Israel's object of worship. *Yahweh*, the personal name of God, appears 6,828 times in the Old Testament and is God's name forever. It is the personal name of the covenant God, who is not only the transcendent Creator of all things but also the immanent Deity, who has made a people for himself for his glory. It is *this* name that becomes the foundation of all theology.

Yahweh functions as the starting point of man's contemplation of the divine nature and character of the God of the universe. The Creator of heaven and earth has revealed himself to his creation. Pagan notions of deity are widespread. But, in the grand revealing of I AM to Moses, humanity has a starting place to conceptualize a *who*-and-*what* understanding of God. The Lord's manifestation at the burning bush reveals many interesting facts about God. Moses had already mentioned his astonishment that the fire had not consumed the bush. How does fire not consume a bush? How does a fire continue to burn without "burning" up a material source needed to keep the fire burning? How does a voice manifest itself from a fire that does not have vocal cords? In this scenario, we have *philosophical* and *metaphysical* challenges to explain *what* God is.[6] Man's ability to comprehend and describe that nature and being of God is the aim of man's desire to relate to an infinite God *who is*.

II. Theological Metaphysics

Due to our limitations as human creatures, our language to describe God is also limited. Everyone operates under presuppositions when seeing and describing *what* and *how* the world is. These presuppositions carry over into our "God-talk." When we try to explain what is real, we engage in metaphysics. Metaphysics is a branch of philosophy that deals with the nature of reality—*what is real*. *Metaphysics* means "beyond" or "after" physics. I think of it as describing *what is* "behind the mask" of what I see, know, and experience. So, when describing God, we are attempting to make *analogical* inroads into the true nature of Divinity.

While the finite cannot fully comprehend the infinite, we can grasp some truths about the nature and character of God through revelation. Within this study of describing what is real, we enter the study of being, *ontology*, which is closely related or can be seen synonymously with *metaphysics*. Ontology and metaphysics attempt to understand what is real with *being* as the basic level of our metaphysical reality. However, not everyone holds to the same metaphysical understanding. What makes theological inquiry and discourse challenging is that we are trying to describe and understand the spiritual reality of God, who is Spirit (Jn 4:24), exists eternally, is omnipresent, omniscient, and omnipotent. We are physical creatures (psychosomatic unity), and God is Spirit. So, when reading Scripture, the spiritual reality communicated to us is steeped in metaphor.

Metaphor becomes the *copula* to communicating spiritual truths. Copula is the grammatical name to describe the linking verb: *is*. Jesus *is* Lord. Brian *is* human. So, in saying that God *is* light, what does that communicate about God? However, metaphors can run amuck when interpreters of Scripture absolutize a metaphorical depiction of God, making it the *root* metaphor of one's entire concept of God. For example, the Bible presents God as Creator, Judge, Savior, Lord, Father, King, Love, Light, Truth, etc., to name a few. The danger then is letting one's personal experience of God function as the foundation and lens through

---

[6] Regardless of the grammar we utilize, God-talk is analogical when it comes to speaking of the Divine essence.

which one sees God and interprets Scripture. This would be a root metaphor, which can become idolatrous.

A root metaphor shapes and guides an interpreter's hermeneutic because "it functions underneath full consciousness at the worldview level and defines what is considered axiomatic, valuable and criteriological."[7] For example, if one latches onto God as a parental figure (e.g., as is the tendency in open/relational theism), one tends to interpret passages about God's nature, character, and divine activity through a parental-familial lens. The interpreter, then, tends to downplay or avoid biblical texts that contradict or bear great tension on the God-as-parent metaphor, resulting in a lop-sided view of God and that of the redemptive story presented in Scripture.[8] To avoid metaphorical ambivalence, the interpreter must test his presuppositions with the primary documents of his Faith—Holy Scripture. He must reflect upon the different presuppositions of others who have come before him and who surround him.[9]

Theological metaphysics is central to what we say and think about God. All interpreters of Scripture make decisions based on a theological metaphysic. A theological metaphysic is the reality one sees regarding the nature and being of God. Craig Carter's definition is instructive: *theological metaphysics* "is the account of the ontological nature of reality that emerges from the theological descriptions of God and the world found in the Bible."[10] We all have metaphysical presuppositions; the goal is to let Scripture shape them. Classical theism[11] has a philosophical

---

[7] Amos Yong, "Divine Omniscience and Future Contingents: Weighing the Presuppositional Issues in the Contemporary Debate," *Evangelical Review of Theology* 26, no. 3 (July 2002): 243.

[8] For example, using a God-as-parent metaphor may cause one to interpret passages that speak of eternal judgment and eternal hell as symbolic or dismiss them altogether because they are not becoming of a God who is a loving parent to all his children.

[9] Paul Helm, "Understanding Scholarly Presuppositions: A Crucial Tool for Research," *Tyndale Bulletin* 44, no. 1 (May 1993): 143.

[10] Craig A. Carter, *Interpreting Scripture with the Great Tradition: Recovering the Genius of Premodern Exegesis* (Grand Rapids, MI: Baker Academic, 2018), 63.

[11] *Classical theism* asserts that God is *a se*, simple, transcendent, omnipotent, omniscient, omnipresent, omnibenevolent, immutable, impassible, and timelessly eternal. He is the sovereign Lord over his creation, having created it *from himself* (*ex nihilo*). He has decreed every event—past, present, and future—and fulfills all things according to the council of his will.

foundation grounded in biblical exegesis. And it is *theological metaphysics* that more accurately represents this relationship.[12]

John's prologue (1:1–18) is a helpful unit for expressing this attribution.[13] When John writes that the Word was with God and *is* God, having created all things, designating that the Word is not part of the *created* order (1:1–3), we are tasked with conceptualizing a metaphysical reality from which the Word comes.[14] Then, when John says that "in him was life" (1:4), profound ontological implications follow that are antithetical to a material understanding of the world. This was Augustine's dilemma in his early days when moving from Manichaeism to Christianity.[15]

Manichaeism lacked an ontological conception of God that distinguished between God and the material universe. Cosmic dualism was its solution. However, it created an ontological paradox.[16] The problem for Augustine was trying "to conceive of God as both *real* and also as *not* in any way part of the material universe."[17] It was not until he came to understand, through Platonism, the concept of *spiritual substance* that his exegesis then had a platform on which to stand. He could now say that God is a real *thing*, a spiritual SUBSTANCE, but not a *material* thing like the created universe. However, Platonic thought[18]

---

[12] The next two paragraphs come from Brian J. Orr, *A Classical Response to Relational Theism: A Reformed Evangelical Critique of Thomas Jay Oord's Evangelical Process Theology* (Eugene, OR: Wipf and Stock Publishers, 2022), 121–2.

[13] Some of the material in the following section is adapted from "Chapter 3 – The Theological Metaphysics of the Great Tradition" in Carter, *Interpreting Scripture*, 61–91.

[14] That is not to say that God comes into a material world; rather, the designation is merely conceptual. He is everywhere present. Even then, to say God is "everywhere present" is a creaturely construct, thus we inadvertently limit the infinite essence of God.

[15] See his thoughts on this in *Confessions*, books 7 and 5.

[16] Carter, *Interpreting Scripture*, 68.

[17] Carter, *Interpreting Scripture*, 69.

[18] Foundational to Greek Philosophy is the assertion that there was/is *one* first principle of all things. The discussion of first principle generated a second claim that if there is One it will not be many; it cannot have parts or be 'whole.' However, this One possesses the attributes of being and yet its possession of more than one attribute "pluralizes the subject," thus making it more than one. From the One, which is self-existent and the Cause of all, and is not a body, Plato sought to demonstrate that all bodily movements originate with the soul, with the One being an incorporeal substance (spirit). And this led to the argument of the *one* first mover in Aristotle, who concluded that motion always exists and cannot cease, something eternal, a necessary

only enabled him to perceive God from afar. Holy Scripture revealed the triune God, manifested as Father, Son, and Spirit.[19] Scripture revealed the glorious Christ as fully God, entering his creation, taking on flesh, dying in the flesh, and being resurrected by the eternal Spirit in glory.[20] Such words are meaningless if there is no ontological distinction between God and the universe. Only a God who is a spiritual substance could be perfect, immutable, and eternal, thus establishing the basis for Augustine's (and that of the Great Tradition, i.e., classical theism) theological metaphysics.[21]

The Great Tradition describes the tradition that unites exegesis, metaphysics, and dogma as found in the early church. This tradition's metaphysical foundation is that of Christian Platonism, most notably known in the works of Augustine. Craig Carter writes, "Christian Platonism . . . was developed in order to express the metaphysical implications of the doctrine of God that emerged from the pro-Nicene scriptural exegesis in the fourth century, and as a result, the exegesis, the dogma, and the metaphysics are all intertwined together."[22] As we will

---

first mover that first initiates motion, who is unmoved must exist. And this unmoved mover is the cause of all things; it exists by necessity. And because its existence is necessary it is necessarily good. Osborn, *The Emergence of Christian Theology*, 39–46. Aristotle writes, "The first mover, then, exists of necessity; and in so far as it exists by necessity, its mode of being is good, and it is in this sense a first principle. . . . On such a principle, then, depend the heavens and the world of nature. And it is a life such as the best which we enjoy, and enjoy for but a short time (for it is ever in this state, which we cannot be), since, its actuality is also pleasure. . . . Moreover, life belongs to God. For the actuality of thought is life, and God is that actuality; and the essential actuality of God is life most good and eternal. We hold, then, that God is a living being, eternal, most good; and therefore life and a continuous eternal existence belong to God; for that is what God is." Aristotle, *Metaphysics*, 1072b. The concept of a transcendent First Principle, as the ground of all existence and the cause of all matter, to be labeled God was developed in later Platonism, which appealed to later Christianity because of the parallel sentiment that God would not be the God of the Bible if he were not the source of all being and matter. Osborn, 48–9.

[19] For an excellent work on an early church interpretive approach to the doctrine of the Trinity, see Matthew W. Bates, *The Birth of the Trinity: Jesus, God, and Spirit in New Testament and Early Christian Interpretations of the Old Testament* (Oxford University Press, 2016).

[20] Augustine, *Confessions*, 7.9. Augustine lists a host of christological texts (e.g., Jn 1:1–14; Ph 2:6–11; Ro 5:6; 8:32) that had a great significance in his understanding of the Word, his incarnation, and redemptive work.

[21] Carter, *Interpreting Scripture*, 70.

[22] Carter, *Interpreting Scripture*, xiii.

see, "Metaphysics cannot be ignored without exegesis and doctrine being negatively affected."[23] The early church, dominantly manifested in the Augustinian-Thomistic theological tradition, arrived at its theological metaphysic through contemplation of God's special revelation in Holy Scripture. The Holy Spirit needs to guide our thinking and shaping of doctrine, and we must always put philosophy in its proper place as the "hand-maiden" to theology.

III. GOD'S LANGUAGE OF CREATION — ROMANS 1:19–20

Paul's introduction in his letter to the church in Rome lays bare that God's wrath is stored up for all mankind. God's wrath is just because humanity, whom God made for himself, has rejected its maker. All of humanity is ungodly; humanity has suppressed[24] the knowledge of God, even though God has made himself clearly known; in fact, he *has shown himself* to them (Ro 1:19). Paul indicates the clarity in God's revelation of himself: ". . . his invisible attributes, that is, his eternal power and divine nature, have been clearly seen since the creation of the world, *being understood through what he has made.* As a result, people are without excuse" (emphasis added). Man's rejection of God began after the Fall in the Garden and continues to permeate the hearts and wills of every man, woman, and child. The power of sin keeps humanity in bondage to godlessness and idolatry, to which the Scripture says God has given mankind over (Ro 1:24), resulting in every human being bearing the penalty of death and eternal destruction.

In looking back at *how* God has revealed himself, Paul writes that God revealed his *invisible attributes,* his *eternal power* and *divine nature,* to humanity through what he has created—the material reality in which all created beings/things exist. Thus, we can know something about God through cause and effect.[25] What does it mean to say one is *divine* and

---

[23] Carter, *Interpreting Scripture,* xv.

[24] The Greek word for "suppress" in this verse is the participle *katechontōn*, which expresses that man's suppression of God is an ongoing active work whereby mankind is preventing itself from accepting the knowledge of God. It is a willful suppression of the truth of God, which makes sense considering other biblical passages that depict the depraved, God-hating nature of man (cf. Ro 3:11–18).

[25] By way of cause and effect, the doctrine of *creatio ex nihilo* establishes the metaphysical foundation for language to speak of God, that of analogical predication, the manner of attributing characteristics to a subject to produce a truth statement. The challenge in theological discourse is in predicating attributes of God to his infinite

eternal? The grammar of Paul's statement demonstrates that God's *invisible attributes* are his eternal power and divine nature. The Greek word for *invisible* is *aoratos*, which means *not being subject to being seen, unseen, invisible, of God.*[26] The invisible God made himself *clear* to humanity so it would know his divine nature and eternal power. The invisible Creator brings about a visible creation so that he can be *clearly* perceived. Calvin writes, "God is in himself invisible; but as his majesty shines forth in his works and in his creatures everywhere, men ought in these to acknowledge him for they clear set forth their Maker."[27] While we have all fallen into sin because of Adam (Ro 5:12), every person is without excuse because he willingly rejects the truth of God. Therefore, he is accountable.

IV. Conclusion

It is essential to see that God has made himself known, yet he is incomprehensible.[28] And in what he manifested to us, we can formulate a grammar to discourse about the nature and being of God. I will get into more detail about that later. A few key texts that speak about the divine nature will function as our backdrop as we observe the development of the church's language about God's essence. From Holy Scripture, the church has described God as Spirit (Jn 4:24), eternal (Ps 90:2), immutable (Ps 102:26, 27), omnipresent (Je 23:24), omniscient (Ps 147:5), omni-sapient (all-wise) (Ro 16:27), omnipotent (Jb 26:15), holy (Ex 15:11), all-good (Mk 10:18), omnibenevolent (1Jn 4:8), and sovereign over his creation (Ps 103:19). These are just a sampling of

---

being. Further related, is how we demonstrate God's nature/characteristics in relation to human nature. The Christian tradition applies a form of analogy, whereby we make judgments about God's nature in proportion to human nature and vise-versa. Because of the Creator–creature distinction it would be improper to state God and man share characteristics identically because God is not a creature and cannot have creaturely properties. For example, God's knowledge is causal, which means he does not learn knowledge; rather, he is the cause of knowledge, which he imparts to creatures. Learning is a creaturely property. Therefore, because of that distinction, we have to say man's knowledge is like God's knowledge in an analogous, or similar, way.

[26] "ἀόρατος," in *BDAG*.

[27] John Calvin, *Commentary on the Epistle of Paul the Apostle to the Romans*, trans. John Owen (Bellingham, WA: Logos Bible Software, 2010), 70.

[28] cf. Ps 145:3; Ro 11:33–34; cf. Jb 42:1–6; Ps 139:6, 17–18; 147:5; Is 57:15; 1Co 2:10–11; 1Ti 6:13–16.

passages to support these ascriptions of God. We will identify more as we move through our study of a divine grammar.

Other vital aspects of discussion pertain to the doctrine of the Trinity, the deity of Christ, and the deity of the Holy Spirit. We believe in one God, yet there are three who the Scripture attributes with the full divinity of God. How is Jesus fully God and fully man? Is the Spirit a person or a force? The first four centuries were a turbulent time for the church in that it was constantly involved in heated doctrinal discussions with eternal significance.

Our excursion begins with the apostolic fathers, on the tail-end of the NT church era, traversing into the Ante-Nicene, Nicene, and Post-Nicene eras concluding our study with Cyril of Alexandria. We will look at the grammatical development in the metaphysical thought about God deployed in theological discourse. But first, it is important we grasp the philosophical landscape of the early church, where metaphysical roots sprouted, blooming into a conceptual, Christian divine grammar.

1

THE *ONE*, FIRST PRINCIPLE

Greek Philosophy—*the spoils of it*—supported a foundational conceptual scheme during the birth of church doctrine that provided a manner of speaking about God's essence, which developed further as later theological discourse gained analytic precision. While modern critics of classical theism attempt to discredit it as a biblically valid theological model, asserting that the early church fathers took Greek philosophy—wholesale—into classical theism, they were mistaken.[1] The fathers were quite critical of pagan philosophy, only appropriating that which functioned as a supportive metaphysical framework to articulate biblical truths.

The concept of the *first* PRINCIPLE of all things is the foundation of Greek philosophy. This *first principle* was not a 'god' but an 'it.' Aristotle categorized early philosophers into those who saw that everything derived from "it" and those who did not. The first principle, while having variation in exposition, is commonly understood as "*the first point from which a thing either is or comes to be and is known.*" And this first point is the beginning of a thing, the nature and essence of a thing, the element of a thing, the thought and will of a thing, and the final cause of a

---

[1] For a compelling argument refuting this claim, see, "The Case Against the Theory of Theology's Fall into Hellenistic Philosophy," in Paul L. Gavrilyuk, *The Suffering of the Impassible God: The Dialectics of Patristic Thought* (Oxford University Press, 2006), 21–46.

thing—"for the good and the beautiful are the beginning of both of the knowledge and of the movement of many things."[2]

Ancient Philosophy understood the complexity yet the simplicity of reality. In saying there is a first principle of all things presented the puzzling concept of the *One and the Many*, which Christian theology also needed to consider. Among the Greeks, discrepancies arose in that some overstressed one aspect over the other, thus losing the grounding principle. Therefore, "Christianity found Greek philosophy unserviceable as a prime resource for delineating the inner nature of God, the doctrines of creation and incarnation, and the relationship of God to man and the cosmos."[3] But, to jump ahead to the conclusion, the early church fathers' emphasis on the Logos as the creative source of all reality—i.e., metaphysical framework of substance and being—"metaphysically guaranteed the general possibility of the correspondence of divine and human thought about God, the world, and other selves, and did so by avoiding pantheism."[4]

But the *One-and-the-Many* framework led to the question of whether there are one or many gods. Plato did not think this was important. He argued that all bodily movements must depend on a previous movement, as in cause and effect. However, the chain of events of physical causation would flounder into infinite regress, so Plato said the cause of a physical body's movement stems from the soul, which generates its movement and is responsible for the movement of the entire cosmos.[5] The soul is prior to the body and can exist without a body (*Laws*. 896c). It is the cause of the good and the bad in things and all aspects of morality. It dwells in all things and controls all things that require movement; thus, it is the cause of all things; it "drives all things in Heaven and earth and sea by its own motions" (896d, e.).

A similar argument of an all controlling, divine soul led Aristotle to the *One*, First Mover. He said, "Since change must always exist without failing, there must be a first agent of change (or perhaps more than one) which is eternal and unchanging."[6] Something eternal, which is impervious

[2] Aristotle, *The Metaphysics*, 1013a.
[3] Carl F. H. Henry, *God, Revelation and Authority*, Logos edition. (Crossway, 1999), 5.168.
[4] Henry, *God, Revelation and Authority*, 5.168.
[5] *Laws*, Plato, *Plato in Twelve Volumes*, trans. R. G. Bury (Cambridge, MA: Harvard University Press; London, William Heinemann Ltd., 1967), 896a.
[6] Aristotle, *Physics*, 1st ed., (Oxford University Press, 2008), 258b.

to and utterly free *from* change, must exist to initiate change in something else (*Ph.* 258b). Aristotle notes that things can exist and not exist, even in "self-changers" that follow this process, there must be "something which includes them all and is separate from every one of them, and it is this that is responsible for some things existing and other things not existing, and for the continuity of change" (*Ph.* 258b). And this is what Aristotle called the Prime Mover or Unmoved Mover.

Advancing on Plato's concept of the source of motion, Aristotle writes:

> There is something which is eternally moved with an unceasing motion, and that circular motion. . . . Therefore, the 'ultimate heaven' must be eternal. Then there is also something which moves it. And since that which is moved while it moves is intermediate, there is something which moves without being moved; something eternal which is both substance and actuality. (*Metaph.* 1072a)

And this mover, who is both substance and actuality, is the first principle. The first principle is necessarily existent and is necessarily good (1072b). I will let Aristotle carry on as he arrives at his glorious conclusion of God, though he could not link it to the God of the Bible. Aristotle's conclusion provided an ontological framework, which the early church fathers (critically) adopted, as the metaphysical foundation and grammar to express the unique, transcendent God revealed in creation and Scripture. He writes:

> And the first principle must always be in this state (though we cannot) since its actuality is also pleasure. (And for this reason, waking sensation and thinking are most pleasant, and hopes and memories are pleasant because of them.) Now thinking in itself is concerned with that which is in itself best, and thinking in the highest sense with that which is in the highest sense best. And thought thinks itself through participation in the object of thought; for it becomes an object of thought by the act of apprehension and thinking, so that thought and the object of thought are the same, because that which is receptive of the object of thought, i.e. essence, is thought. And it actually functions when it possesses this object. Hence it is actuality rather than potentiality that is held to be the divine possession of rational thought, and its active contemplation is that which is most pleasant and best. If, then, the happiness which God always enjoys is as great as that which

we enjoy sometimes, it is marvelous; and if it is greater, this is still more marvelous. Nevertheless, it is so. Moreover, life belongs to God. For the actuality of thought is life, and God is that actuality; and the essential actuality of God is life most good and eternal. *We hold, then, that God is a living being, eternal, most good; and therefore, life and a continuous eternal existence belong to God; for that is what God is* (1072b, emphasis added).

Aristotle's conclusion about God as the One and the Monad as Mind, which contemplates the ideas, is the "central theme in later Platonism, that the ideas exist in the divine mind." The transcendent First Principle, also termed God, finds its appeal in later Christian thought: God would not be God if he were not the source of all being and the cause of all matter.[7]

The doctrine of God as One is connected to the idea of God as pure being, from which the doctrines of divine simplicity and immutability are drawn. The Monad as Mind implies that the One is the source of all; therefore, the One is "unoriginate" or "ingenerate," expressing that the One does not have a beginning or end, is independent of other beings, and is the source and ultimate cause of all that exists. "He Who Is" suggests that the One is a timeless, unchanging being.[8] And we can recognize this concept in Scripture, as recorded in John's Revelation, when he writes, ". . . from the one who is, who was, and who is to come" (1:4). With a Platonic metaphysic (e.g., Plato's *Republic*, 2:380–1), the early church fathers, almost without exception, had a framework to establish that God is a changeless being, all-powerful, and cannot suffer change from anyone or anything within or without himself. He cannot change for the better or become worse because he is the perfect being. Platonic metaphysics provided the substance and grammar to discuss the God of John's Revelation, "He Who Is."

I. Essentials of Platonism

For Plato, the one grand idea or theory is that of Forms. Forms are the Ideas from which all material things originate. They are objective truths, eternal realities, that ground material reality. These Ideas are more

---

[7] Osborn, *The Emergence of Christian Theology*, 48, 49.

[8] Christopher Stead, *Philosophy in Christian Antiquity* (Cambridge University Press, 1996), 128.

significant than what we can see. We see the shadows of an eternal, spiritual reality, which should leave us in awe and wonder. There are more things in heaven and earth than we can see; thus, "the essential point of Platonism: moreness, transcendence, another *kind* of reality outside our cave."[9] Modern thought wants to squash this reality so that by reducing the complex to the simple, mankind can conquer it. He retains control because he can scientifically analyze and comprehend *it* (i.e., the shadow of immaterial reality). Plato sought to be defeated by the greater reality, which he (and we) have no control over. Humanity exists *in* the Ideas; they are not psychological constructs, as the modern project claims. Behind the shadows sits an ordered, intelligible metaphysical reality of universals and particulars that exist within themselves. For example, the color green is always green, independent of *things* that have the color green. Goodness and Justice exist in themselves, even if humanity ceases to exist, even if there were no created universe. The laws of logic and $2 + 2 = 4$ are always true regardless of a material reality. But, the things that have been created "are *images* or reflections of their Forms, or essences, or Platonic ideas; they are like them or analogous to them. . . . We live in the Shadowlands. The whole world we see is an image of the world we do not see."[10]

What is the crucial difference between Plato and modern/ contemporary philosophy? Ethics. Plato valued ethics like rocks; they are objectively real and unchangeable. Modern philosophy sees ethics like artwork: *we* create them, and the social and cultural influx produces variations. The Platonic world is vast; the modern world is narrow. Plato's large world, outside of the cave, reveals what the modern world wants to run from: a loss of control. Plato's world of universals means that there are subjective and objective distinctions. The modern paradigm (Kreeft is referring to Freud) says that what is "real" or "true" comes down to preference or rationalizing our desires.[11] And therefore, what is real is subjective. But, if there are no objective reasons to believe

---

[9] Peter Kreeft, *The Platonic Tradition* (South Bend, IN: St. Augustine's Press, 2018), 5. *Cave* is a reference to Plato's most famous passage in *The Republic*, the parable of the cave, where he points to the light outside the cave that reveals a greater reality than what is directly around us in our caves.

[10] Kreeft, *The Platonic Tradition*, 7.

[11] Kreeft, *The Platonic Tradition*, 12. Freud, cited in Kreeft, said: "the one and only thing he is certain of is that of all our reasoning is only rationalizing our desires" (from *Civilization and Its Discontents*).

something is real and objective, then there is no reason for anyone to believe anything at all. The challenge to this way of thinking is: *who is* Freud to determine my beliefs based on his rationalizing? *Why* should I let his reasoning, which only rationalizes his desires, infringe upon my beliefs? "If reason is only subjective, then that piece of reason is only subjective too: it's only subjective that it's only subjective. If refutes itself. It commits rational suicide."[12] Therefore, reason must be anchored to an objective reality, principle, or truth; otherwise, we have no standard of judgment.

Modern thought determines that the distinction between man and beast is *reason*. But modern thought defines *reason* differently compared to how Plato defines it. While modern thought defines reason as man's ability to be intelligent, clever, and calculated, Plato defined reason as one having wisdom, understanding, and insight into the Forms. This use of *reason*, Plato divided into four categories or levels, "faculties in the soul."[13] The first level of knowledge is "reason answering to the highest," which is direct insight to the eternal reality, "the unchangeable qualitative form of Beauty or Human Nature or Life;" this knowledge makes man human, separating him from animals or computers.[14] The second level of knowledge is "understanding," where one attains knowledge through logic and deductive reasoning, deriving quantitative truths dependent on logic, where conclusions depend on their premises. The third level is "faith or conviction," through "direct sense experience," where one believes what he assumes without the need to prove it. This is where our objective sense of reality meets actual material objects. And the fourth level is "the perception of shadows," which is second-hand knowledge from opinions, reflections, and/or images of real things.

Plato's order of knowledge outlines the ascent of discovery from the mere shadows we see before our eyes to the reality of universals that we can only apprehend with our minds. "We can understand eternal, necessary truths. We can know the essential Natures of things. That's what it is to get out of the cave."[15] Plato posited that we can know objective truths (i.e., $2 + 2 = 4$; a triangle has 3 sides that always add up to 180 degrees; greenness is always green and, in all places) because our minds are in touch with the world of Forms. Ideas like truth and

---

[12] Kreeft, *The Platonic Tradition*, 13.

[13] B. Jowett, trans., *Plato's The Republic* (New York: Vintage Books, 1960), 6.511–3.

[14] Kreeft, *The Platonic Tradition*, 14.

[15] Kreeft, *The Platonic Tradition*, 14.

goodness are not produced in our minds; instead, they come to our minds. And in coming to our minds, they function as a judge of our minds, depending on our minds' conformity to them.[16]

But that takes us to the question of what kind of mind knows the Forms. It is an epistemological question in that we need to articulate what kinds of *knowing* there are, which allows us to *see* the metaphysical reality behind the mask of the physical world. Platonic thought observes five kinds of knowing, which all begin with wonder.

1) Ordinary, unreflective knowing; sense perception and common sense.

2) Scientific knowing, in the modern scheme, uses proofs of empirical testing and mathematical measurement. This mode of knowing determines what works and what can be extracted or used from a particular object or thing. The wonder ceases when the objective is attained, like a magician revealing how he does a specific trick. The wonder is gone once the secret is revealed. Science wants to remove the element of wonder because it entails the loss of control, which is too steep a price to pay.

3) Philosophical knowledge of reasons and causes by logical reasoning, such as Plato sought after. Science follows a similar path but wonder ceases when knowledge is attained, but in philosophy, such an end is more challenging to achieve.

4) Wonder within wonder, the contemplation of truths for their own sake, where knowledge in this mode of thought leads to more wonder, like that of a child.

5) Mystical knowing is the end because nothing else can be suggested. "It is an active, actual experience of the ultimate," in the biblical sense, an intimate knowing of another in sexual union; a knowing that is beyond yourself, even out of one's self-conscious. It is our end, "which cannot be put into words," for it "is the whole point of philosophy and, indeed, of human life itself."[17]

Platonism's expanded horizon to metaphysics and knowledge has profound implications for the human ethic and, thus, human existence. The question pertinent to humanity is: "What *ought* I to be and do?" And it's grounded in metaphysics. If we are merely bags of flesh formed

---

[16] Kreeft, *The Platonic Tradition*, 15.

[17] Kreeft, *The Platonic Tradition*, 16, 17.

through random chance processes, which are just nothing more than chemical reactions taking place until they run their course, then all that matters is doing what one can to meet one's temporal needs.

If nature is the final reality, then meaning and purpose end here. But, if one can know the Absolute Good, one can judge relative standards by the Good, including my soul and the community in which one exists. Seeing the Good with our souls and functioning off that objective standard gives humans a foundation of *Ideas* to judge all other things. If not, then someone else must play God—a tyrannical and idolatrous one. But, then again, compared to what standard?

II. Platonism in Christianity

Genesis 1:27 is the essence of Platonic thought: "God created man in his own image." *Image* is fundamental to Platonic Ideas because created reality is the image of the eternal, spiritual reality. These Ideas for Plato are the eternal archetypes. And *things* are the representations of *the* Ideas that Christians (beginning with Augustine) locate in the Mind of God. Three differences exist between Plato and the Bible. 1) Plato taught that there are abstract, eternal essences; the Bible teaches that there is an eternal, single, *personal* triune essence, the I AM, the subject who necessarily exists, not the object, as Plato's Ideas are. 2) In Scripture, man is a subject who *alone* is made in God's image. 3) For mankind, the heart, not specifically the mind, is the location of the faculty of loving and choosing.[18] Scripture has examples of *Platonizing*, such as Jesus, in John 4:34, when he says that his food is to do the will of his Father. Here Jesus is using matter to image spirit. Paul does the same "Platonic reversal" when he refers to earthly fathers as images of God the Father and his fatherhood over Christ, after which earthly families are named (Ep 3:14). The human representation of things are metaphors or images to demonstrate *the* true spiritual reality. Again, Paul refers to Christ as the *image* of the invisible God (Col 1:15), the Word made flesh is the physical image of an immaterial Divine being.

The *Logos* is the culminating principle, from where all wisdom comes and points creatures back toward. John identifies Christ as the *Logos*. *Logos* has many meanings, but in John, the *Logos* is the Eternal truth born of woman. In Jesus being attributed as the *Logos*, the idea of

---

[18] Kreeft, *The Platonic Tradition*, 50–1.

Logos is expanded beyond an abstract understanding or definition of *reason, logic,* or Mind. The *Logos* is, in fact, personal. *Logos* has always been the destination for Greek philosophers. So, while it has many meanings, "they can be brought under three headings: metaphysical, psychological, and linguistic."[19] 1) *Logos* means, first of all, realness, essence, form, unity, and principle. 2) It also means wisdom, understanding, knowledge, reason, or logic. 3) And it also means word, words, language, revelation, or explanation. In these three categories, "*Logos* #3 is a mind's externalization of *Logos* #2 as *Logos* #2 is a mind's internalization of *Logos* #1."[20] For example, #3 communicates (reveals/ explains *externally*) #2, wisdom and knowledge, which is the mind's internalization of #1, *form, essence, truth,* and *universal principles.*

The history of philosophy reflects a denial of these three things, in that Premodern philosophy (ancient and medieval) centered on metaphysics, which ended in Nominalism (William of Ockham)—the denial of #1, i.e., intelligible universals. Modern philosophy, as originated with Descartes and Bacon, centered on epistemology, which resulted in the empirical skepticism of Hume and Kant, who claimed that objective reality, what things are in themselves, could never be known—the denial of #2, i.e., the mind's internalization of objective truths. Contemporary philosophy, focused on the philosophy of language, thus manifested in Deconstructionism, which is the denial of #3—that words can communicate objective truths.[21]

Logos, in biblical thought, contains all three meanings (essence, thought, and language), in that the *Logos* was made flesh, God Incarnate, in his Divine essence, created all things by his Word, by *speaking* the world into existence. God gave material reality to his divine Ideas. Human words copy the ideas of things; God's Ideas come first, from which he creates *things* that are copies of his Ideas. I will jump ahead here, but Justin, the early church apologist, saw that Plato was an unconscious observer of the pre-incarnate Christ. He understood that the *Logos* was the Chief Designer, the Principle, and the Truth, but the *Logos* was an impersonal and abstract concept. From Justin's point of view, Platonism found its fulfillment in Christ, *the Logos*, the Mind of

---

[19] Kreeft, *The Platonic Tradition,* 52.

[20] Kreeft, *The Platonic Tradition,* 53.

[21] Kreeft, *The Platonic Tradition,* 53.

God. Thus, from then on, *Logos* in philosophy had a radical paradigm shift: the *Logos* became flesh.

Augustine's adaption of Platonism allowed him to unlock a vision of God that left him in awe and wonder. Aquinas accepts the basic tenets of Plato's Ideas but differs on their independent substantiality. Aquinas writes, they exist in three places: 'before things, in things, and after things'; before things as divine Ideas, in things as Aristotelian forms, and after things as human concepts."[22] All Ideas exist in God's mind; every created thing is known by God, the universal and particular before he creates it; God put the external form into 'things,' and we abstracted them from matter to bring them into our immaterial intellects. This last aspect is the doctrine of abstraction (from Aristotle) added to the doctrine of illumination (from Augustine) to explain how eternal Forms get into our minds. Our "active intellect, which abstracts the form from the matter, is our participation in, and the effect of, God's intellect."[23] Thus, "matter reveals spirit . . . the universe is a kind of appetizer for the Incarnation."[24]

Platonism has a hermeneutical structure, which Aquinas and the medieval church adopted. Because of the Platonic understanding of symbols and images and shadows functioning as masks for the eternal, immaterial, and spiritual reality, God then wrote two books. One book of nature and the other Holy Scripture. Everything earthly was an image of something of the Creator (Ro 1:19–20). The Scriptures, along with the book of nature, were full of signs, which provided a philosophical foundation for the medieval fourfold method of exegesis, which fostered a literal and symbolic interpretation of Scripture.[25] 1) The OT pointed to the Messianic fulfillment in the NT, with figures along the way functioning as symbols or signposts of Christ and other later revealed and fulfilled realities (i.e., Moses as Christ; Exodus symbolizes salvation; the promised land symbolizes heaven, etc.). 2) Persons and events in the narrative symbolize aspects of ourselves and our current lives (e.g., Peter's confession of Christ, then his denial of him.). 3) Events symbolize future, heavenly events; e.g., Jesus heals physical blindness,

---

[22] Kreeft, *The Platonic Tradition*, 60.

[23] Kreeft, *The Platonic Tradition*, 61.

[24] Kreeft, *The Platonic Tradition*, 62.

[25] Kreeft, *The Platonic Tradition*, 62.

which "symbolizes the healing of our mental and spiritual blindness in the Beatific Vision in heaven."[26]

The philosophical foundation for this method of interpretation is due to the Platonic understanding that words have meaning. Events have meaning, which God carries out, and thus "events can rightly be seen as words, as *signs* and not just things." The modern schematic of Deconstructionism says that words *do not* have objective meaning. It denies that words are signs, reducing them to things that are either the cause or effect of power. A Deconstructionist mindset reduces the world around us because if humans depend on words for meaning and truth, then the contemporary scheme shackles people to their caves because they can never justify their assumptions. They cannot follow the path of wonder if words cannot articulate and lead the way to the bigger world.[27] One of Aquinas' most important contributions, which was a crucial distinction added to Platonism, is the doctrine of analogy. Again, the Platonic *Ideas* are the basis of physical reality, with the physical reality pointing back to the eternal reality. Symbolic and literal understanding cannot hold together if we do not have the means of talking about them. For Aquinas, reality itself was analogical. The doctrine of analogy is more than words, language, thought, or concepts; instead, analogies are first of all in being.[28] For example, the word *good* has different connotations when used as an attribution for God, man, a dog, food, etc. This means that the form of *goodness* is not univocal (literally, "the same voice"), with only one universal meaning that must be the same when applied to anything. Goodness, instead, has an analogical predication, which means it is partly the same and different when used in various contexts of reality (e.g., a *good* weapon kills; *good* medicine heals).

The essential element of existence is *being*. This fundamental principle is the separation between God and creatures. And it is analogical. According to Aquinas, God *is* being; humans *have* being. God's essence and existence are necessary; creatures must be given essence and existence. God gives existence to a thing's essence by creating it. We can conceive of a strange creature and its essence, but only its existence actualizes its essence. God is pure existence and essence. Aquinas' distinction between existence and essence is a crucial addition

---

to Plato's theory of Forms (or Ideas). And it came from the biblical revelation of creation, *ex nihilo*.[29] Creation from nothing is not a Platonic concept but a Judeo-Christian doctrine. For Aquinas, God knows all essences, for they all exist in his mind, and then he chooses to give existence to an essence. In Plato, all essences eternal. Aquinas and Plato agree that all possible Forms are in the Mind of God. Aquinas did not subtract anything from Plato; instead, he made an addition based on the biblical doctrine of creation.

Before moving on to our study, we have one more character to familiarize ourselves with from the Jewish tradition, particularly the influence of Greek conceptions of God with that of Judaism. And that is Philo of Alexandria.[30] He is a fascinating figure because it seems scholars either love him or hate him, in that some credit him with radically altering the OT view of God, thus plunging the Judeo-Christian faith into pagan philosophy.[31] Philo's view of the God of the Pentateuch is that of one who is intimate and provident, unlike the gods espoused in Neoplatonism. A tenet of Greek philosophy is the view that the universe

---

[29] Kreeft, *The Platonic Tradition*, 64.

[30] Philo of Alexandria (c. 25 BC–c. AD 40) was a *Hellenistic Jewish philosopher whose thought presents the first major confrontation of biblical faith with Greek thought.* Son of a prominent Alexandrian family, Philo was educated both in the Jewish faith and in Greek philosophy and culture. "Philo Judaeus," in Walter A. Elwell and Barry J. Beitzel. *Baker Encyclopedia of the Bible* (Grand Rapids, MI: Baker Book House, 1988), 2:1684.

[31] Stead, *Antiquity*, 120. Interestingly enough, Martin Hengel, in his *Judaism and Hellenism*, identifies evidence of assimilation between Greek and Jewish concepts of God, writings which express a widespread attitude that Greeks and Jews believe in the same God but appropriate with diffident names. Judaism appears to be a true philosophy of ethical monotheism, with which "clear-sighted Greeks" also agreed. For the Greeks, Zeus and Dis were references to the one true God. Hengel refers to an astonishing statement by Jewish military officer and historian Josephus (37-c. 100), who, commenting on Moses, says that he "represented God as unbegotten, and immutable, through all eternity, superior to all mortal conceptions . . . and though known to us by his power, yet unknown to us as to his essence. I do not now explain how these notions of God are the sentiments of the wisest among the Grecians, and how they were taught them upon the principles that he afforded them. However, they testified, with great assurance, that these notions are just, and agreeable to the nature of God, and to his majesty; for Pythagoras, and Anaxagoras, and Plato, and the Stoic philosophers that succeeded them, and almost all the rest, are of the same sentiments, and had the same notions of the nature of God." *Against Apion* 2.167–8. Flavius Josephus, *The Works of Josephus: Complete and Unabridged, New Updated Edition*, trans. William Whiston (Hendrickson Pub, 1980), 804. From this, Hengel concludes: "The God of the philosophers is fundamentally the God of Israel" (266).

is eternal, but Philo does not believe as such because it runs contra to the Old Testament's teaching of God's providence over his creation. In his commentary on Genesis, Philo reflects on God's good creation, in which God determined to bring about "a corporeal world," which is "perceptible to the external senses," based on his "archetypal idea [of creation] conceived in his intellect."[32]

God as the Cause of all things is indescribable. In fact, "the living God," writes Philo, "is so completely indescribable, that even those powers which minister unto him do not announce his proper name to us."[33] God's revealing of himself to Moses as "I Am Who I Am" in Exodus 3:14 conveys his holiness and wholly otherness as Creator. And because of God's incomprehensibility, the light of God is imperceptible to the physical senses (but the eye of the soul can receive the impression of his appearance),[34] and, therefore, cannot be named.[35] Philo understands that we can only know *that* God exists; however, we can *know* God through his relationality, in that he gives us a name upon which we are to call, so that man can "be brought into relation with it"[36] connecting his personal nature to the one who sovereignly creates.[37]

III. Conclusion

The brief survey on Greek Philosophy, particularly Platonism, purposed to identify some key concepts that function, and still do function, in the framework of the early Christian doctrine of God. We cannot escape the use of philosophy; instead, we need to subject it to the documents of the

---

[32] *On the Creation*, 1.15–16. C. D. Yonge, trans., *The Works of Philo: Complete and Unabridged, New Updated Edition* (Peabody, Mass: Hendrickson Publishers, 1993).

[33] *On the Change of Names*, Yonge, *The Works of Philo*, 2.14.

[34] *On the Change of Names*, 1.3, 6. *The Works of Philo*.

[35] Weinandy, *Does God Suffer?* (Notre Dame, IN: University of Notre Dame, 2000), 77, points out Philo's commitment to the Hebrew text in that his designation of God as "He Who Is" purposed "to intensify the biblical truth that God is the one who truly is, the 'living' God." By naming God [as such], he more clearly designates him as the Creator of all that exists, thus he cannot be placed among anything else in existence.

[36] *On the Change of Names*, 1.13. G. H. Whitaker F. H. Colson, *Philo of Alexandria, Works (Loeb Classical Library in 12 Volumes)*.

[37] David T. Runia, *Philo of Alexandria and the Timaeus of Plato*, Philosophia Antiqua (Leiden: Brill, 1986), 436–7, quoted in Janet Martin Soskice, "Athens and Jerusalem, Alexandria and Edessa: Is There a Metaphysics of Scripture?," *International Journal of Systematic Theology* 8, no. 2 (April 2006): 157.

Faith. And this is where Christians parted ways from pagans. Unlike a pagan description of reality that was disconnected from an objective source of knowledge, "Christians felt the need to develop a single set of words to describe a God who could not be imagined, but of whom they had direct knowledge, thanks to his self-revelation in the Bible and in Jesus Christ."[38]

Second-century philosophy found increasing favor with Christianity because while it posited that God was impassable, ungenerated, invisible, immutable, incomprehensible, and immeasurable, the Christian Scriptures, the revelation of God, transcended philosophy because knowledge of the Father (i.e., positive ascriptions) could only come through the prophets who were led by the Spirit. Thus, Christian theology is the divine doctrine, not of human origin.

---

[38] Gerald Bray, *God Has Spoken: A History of Christian Theology*, 1st ed. (Wheaton, IL: Crossway, 2014).

2

THE APOSTOLIC–ANTE-NICENE ERA

The early church continued in the tradition of the NT in its conceptual understanding of God. However, in the first generation, those following the apostolic age, we find reflections of philosophical theology in such figures as Clement of Rome, Ignatius, Justin, Athenagoras, Irenaeus, Clement of Alexandria, and Tertullian. In their writings, we find similar attributions as found in the NT, such as: "God," "Lord," "Father," "Most High," "Majesty," "Almighty," "Master," and "the Holy One." But we also find other designations used for God: "The Great Demiurge," (*1 Clem.* 20.11 & *Diogn.* 8.7.) "God of the Powers," (*Herm. Vis.* 1.3.4) and "All Creating God" (*Diogn.* 7.2).

However, the fundamental ideas on God are almost exclusively derived from Scripture. The negative adjectives "invisible" (Col 1:15), "eternal" (Ro 16:26), and "imperishable" (1Co 15:50) the apostle Paul uses to speak of God. Therefore, though some scholars do not want to admit it, elements of Hellenism were present before the New Testament writings.[1] As we will see, following the NT era, philosophical constructs

---

[1] However, that is not to imply Christianity was Hellenized; rather, we just see an appropriation of philosophical categories prior to the rise of the Christian faith, beginning with the Septuagint, the Greek version of the Hebrew Old Testament. See, Gavrilyuk, *The Suffering of the Impassible God*, 37–46. Instead, the inverse is what we do see: "the Christianization of Hellenism," observed in the appropriation of Greek philosophical concepts. Robert Louis Wilken, *The Spirit of Early Christian Thought:*

began to form in Christian theology, thus producing a type of language, albeit *foreign* to Scripture, yet necessary to formulate a divine grammar.

I. THE APOSTOLIC FATHERS & THE EARLY SECOND CENTURY

The transition into the second century posed significant challenges for the church and the competing philosophy and cultural milieu: How do Jerusalem and Athens align? And how do the Bible and philosophy align? How can these competing views become compatible? Should they mingle together? A new body of doctrine becomes the guiding revelation for the second-century Christians. Still, much work is to be done considering the church's identity being that of Christ because of its affirmation that there is only one God who is the Father of Jesus Christ who is *also* God of God. While philosophers argued for the sake of arguing, early Christians were in a hostile environment and had much more at stake: the health of the church and their eternal lives.

The Christian religion did not appear to reflect the surrounding philosophy that it quickly developed. Because of its uncompromised commitment to the Bible, it had greater organization and coherency as a religion compared to the pagan religions it rubbed shoulders with. However, Christian doctrine developed through an incorporation of Platonic ideas, providing a substance metaphysic that aided the Faith in constructing its doctrine of God. Christianity thus became a philosophy.[2] But, unlike the Philosophers, who cared about logic for its own sake, Christian philosophers were first and foremost *Christians*. They used the tools of philosophy for consistency and coherency in expositing what the Scripture teaches about God, as the church encountered "Christian" heretical opposition that promoted aberrant views of God and Christ. Christians committed to the authority of Scripture used what aligned with their convictions, as derived from the Scriptures, making Christian philosophy, in fact, Christian *theology*.

Early Christian fathers primarily adopted aspects of contemporary philosophy to address the skeptics of their time, using it as a tool for evangelism, the handmaiden of theology. The abstract terms of philosophy, such as impassibility, immutability, incomprehensibility, omnipotence, omniscience, omnipresence, and so on, provided a manner

---

Seeking the Face of God (Yale University Press, 2005), xvi.
[2] Stead, *Antiquity*, 79.

of speaking intelligibly (i.e., a divine grammar) about how God could become a man yet as man be also God. The Gentile philosophers viewed reality as the *to on*, "that which is" a supreme impersonal being. To defend the God of the Bible, the church fathers established that God is transcendent yet personal, not "that which is," but rather, "*he who is*" (*ho on*), an infinitely greater and better view of ultimate reality—the Supreme Being of the cosmos, made flesh in the Lord Jesus Christ.[3]

Gnosticism was a pervading threat to the early church. Differences between Christian and Gnostic teaching did not stem from variances in language; instead, it was a worldview issue. The early Christians saw God as the transcendent Creator; Gnostics saw God as a distant, unattached negation of the world.[4] It was an unhistorical, syncretistic way of thinking, using philosophical concepts and schemes with often outlandish interpretations.[5] They claimed a higher way, negligent of faith, reason, and knowledge.

Valentinus, a Gnostic, though the closest to orthodox Christianity, proposed an emanation theory that suggested that God's being is "developing out of a primal mysterious unity into a series of powers or 'aeons,' collectively called 'the *pleroma*' or 'fullness' (of the Godhead),"[6] from which God arrived at an incomplete conception of himself. This process then repeats itself, becoming a series of powers that are other beings he has imparted himself to, which have moved away from the initial unity, thus diluting perfection and making allowances for sin.[7]

The early Christian response to the question of its God as the starting point in physics, logic, and ethics (these were the critical points of coherency in Stoicism)[8] was that God is the *monarchia*, the sole ruler of all, which kept them aligned with the OT doctrine of God.[9] Greek thought understood history in cycles; the OT and NT Scriptures teach

---

[3] Bray, *God Has Spoken*, 986.

[4] Richard M. Grant, *The Early Christian Doctrine of God*, Richard lectures (Charlottesville: University Press of Virginia, 1966), 16.

[5] Gerhard May, *Creatio Ex Nihilo: The Doctrine of "Creation out of Nothing" in Early Christian Thought* (London; New York: T&T Clark, 2004), 119.

[6] Stead, *Antiquity*, 70.

[7] Stead, *Antiquity*, 70–1.

[8] Stead, *Antiquity*, 45.

[9] Jaroslav Pelikan, *The Christian Tradition: A History of the Development of Doctrine, Vol. 1: The Emergence of the Catholic Tradition* (Chicago, IL: University of Chicago Press, 1975), 37.

that there is one timeline governed by God, with a beginning and an end. He is the Alpha and the Omega, the beginning and the end. The first understandings of Christ were that he was either subordinate to the Father or eclipsed the Father. Both concepts were insufficient, but at some level, made sense of the biblical account, and thus we have the emergence of a nascent Christian theology.[10]

God as Creator is one of the chief designations used about the God of the Bible. When the apostolic fathers speak of him as Creator, the foundation to the doctrine of *creatio ex nihilo* is assumed, in the sense that God "made out of what did not exist (μὴ ὄντος) everything that is" (*Herm. Man.* 1.1; *Herm. Sim.* 1.1.6). The apostolic fathers were committed to monotheism, by which they confessed that "God is the true and only God" (*Diogn.* 3.2). Therefore, holding to the divine transcendence and absolute monarchy of God was of primary importance. Emphasis on these aspects, along with the unrestricted sovereignty of God, arose due to the challenge and threat of polytheistic and pantheistic teachings. This following statement from the *Shepherd of Hermas* encapsulates the foundation of the second-century Christian doctrine of God: "God is one, who created all things and set them in order, and made out of what did not exist (μὴ ὄντος) everything that is, and who contains all but is himself alone uncontained" (*Herm. Man.* 1.1; *Herm. Sim.* 1.1.6). When reading the apostolic fathers, we do not find a well-developed metaphysical framework. However, we will see a divine grammar take shape as we progress. I offer a sampling from notable figures, with more attention to the greater contributors in developing and refining a divine grammar and the doctrine of God.

This study will not get too "wrapped up" in the historical details. The aim is to trace out the development of divine grammar. With that said, such a study *is* historical. Therefore, some attention to church history is necessary because the context has a catalytical import to formulating such language within the theological culture, which we find expressed and codified in the historic church Councils.[11]

---

[10] Osborn, *The Emergence of Christian Theology*, 37.
[11] Lewis Ayres, *Nicaea and Its Legacy: An Approach to Fourth-Century Trinitarian Theology* (Oxford University Press, 2006), 274.

Ignatius of Antioch

Ignatius of Antioch (died C. 107) was the apostolic father closest in thought to the New Testament writers. While enroute to Rome to face martyrdom, he wrote many letters to churches in cities he passed through, encouraging them to remain united in the Faith. Ignatius' letters outside the New Testament documents were an extremely important witnesses to the development of church structure and theological reflection.[12]

Ignatius faced opposition from Christian Docetists who taught that Christ only "seemed to suffer." They assert that Christ did not suffer because the *true* God is eternal and cannot die. To maintain the paradoxical tension between Christ's humanity and his deity, Ignatius established a *via media* in the Christian doctrine of God to express and maintain the incarnation. He states that Christ is eternal, invisible, and impassible, yet he is human, visible, and suffered and died on the cross.[13] As Richard Grant points out: "... in the church before Ignatius' time such language (1) had been currently used in regard to God the Father and (2) had next been applied to Christ as God."[14] In one particular phrase, Ignatius conflates the language, showing the ontological oneness of God and Christ, when he writes, "There is one only physician, of flesh and of spirit, generate [**BEGOTTEN**] (*gennētos*) and ingenerate [**UNBEGOTTEN**] (*agennētos*), God in man, true Life in death, Son of Mary and Son of God, first passible (*pathētos*) and then impassible (*apathēs*), Jesus Christ our Lord" (*ad. Eph.* 7.2; *AF*²). Ignatius' language, however, brought about challenges for the Nicenes, in that his reference of *agennētos* (unbegotten in his Godhead) was not characteristic of the Son but of the Father.[15]

His expression above "is as close as Ignatius gets to a 'two-nature' Christology."[16] On the one hand, he aimed to emphasize that Christ's

---

[12] John Behr, *Formation of Christian Theology: The Way to Nicaea*, First., vol. 1 (Crestwood, NY: St. Vladimirs Seminary Press, 2001), 81.

[13] Behr observes that "Ignatius emphatically describes Christ as God, using the articular 'God' (ὁ θεὸς) in a quite dramatic fashion." Behr, *Formation of Christian Theology*, 1:84.

[14] Grant, *The Early Christian Doctrine of God*, 15.

[15] Aloys Grillmeier, *Christ in Christian Tradition: From the Apostolic Age to Chalcedon*, 2 Revised edition. (Westminster John Knox Press, 1988), 88.

[16] Behr, *Formation of Christian Theology*, 1:91.

human existence came through human generation; thus, it was real and not docetic (i.e., having the appearance of physicality). On the other hand, he was divine, preexistent, and ingenerate, existing *not* through birth but having no beginning.[17] Very distinctly, Ignatius writes, "There is one God who manifested himself through Jesus Christ his Son, who is his Word that proceeded from silence" (*Mag.* 8.2). The one Lord Christ "was passible (παθητός), subject to all things that belong to created being, such as change and death, nevertheless *through* his death he manifested true life and impassibility."[18]

In his letter to the Romans, Ignatius expresses one of the central aspects of the Christian confession, in that Christ's passion was not the suffering and death of a mere man; but rather, it was the passion of God:

> It is better for me to die on behalf of Jesus Christ, than to reign over all the ends of the earth. "For what shall a man be profited, if he gain the whole world, but lose his own soul?" Him I seek, who died for us: Him I desire, who rose again for our sake. This is the gain which is laid up for me. Pardon me, brethren: do not hinder me from living, do not wish to keep me in a state of death; and while I desire to belong to God, do not ye give me over to the world. Suffer me to obtain pure light: when I have gone thither, I shall indeed be a man of God. Permit me to be an imitator of the passion of my God. (*Rom.* 6)

The incarnation was not just a story; it had ethical, theological, and metaphysical implications. But the problem of one God was a severe obstacle in that for the Christian story to make sense, as a coherent body of *true*, revealed teaching, the story of salvation, the story of creation to recreation, with Christ as the center, the claim of one God, one God as Father and Son, and one God as first principle needed to be reconciled and a precise grammar to do so. This was the first task in properly ordering the structure of Christian theology.[19]

Clement of Rome

Clement (died c. 100) was a presbyter and bishop in Rome. Origen claimed that he is the Clement mentioned in Philippians 4:3, but it is

---

[17] G. L. Prestige, *God in Patristic Thought*, Reprint. (Eugene, OR: Wipf and Stock Publishers, 2008), 38.

[18] Behr, *Formation of Christian Theology: The Way to Nicaea*, 1:91.

[19] Osborn, *The Emergence of Christian Theology*, 3.

more probable that he is the writer "Clement" listed in the *Shepherd of Hermas*, a Christian writing from the mid-second century. In the few documents from Clement, we see that he does not have a speculative or a developed metaphysical doctrine of God; instead, he emphasizes the shared titles/names of "Master" and "Creator" between God and Christ and stays close to scriptural appellations, consistently expressing sovereign lordship over the universe.

Clement gives the title of "Master of the universe" (*ho despotēs tōn hapantōn*) to the Lord Jesus (*1 Clem.* 8.2). And it is a common title that we see often of Christ, but he uses it elsewhere speaking of God in general as the "all seeing God and Master" (*1 Clem.* 55.6; 64.1). Interestingly, reference to the incarnation is scant, with the only explicit statement in *2 Clem.* 9.5. He writes, Christ ". . . became flesh (even though he was originally spirit [*prōton pneuma*])." But a Trinitarian formula is intrinsic to his monotheism when he writes, "Have we not one God and one Christ and one Spirit of grace that was shed upon us?" (*1 Clem.* 46.6). While Clement speaks of God as "the Father and Maker of the whole world," (*1 Clem* 19.2), he also attributes *creator* status to Christ, calling him "the great Creator and Master of the universe," who providentially guides all things, seasons, oceans, seas, winds, and all living things (*1 Clem.* 20.11). Encouraging his listeners to trust in God's promises and to remain faithful, he also wants them to have a proper fear of him, and he reminds them of God's power as *the* Creator, who "by his majestic word he established the universe, and by a word he can destroy it" (*1 Clem.* 27.4). Clement's warning implicitly expresses his understanding that God's creates *ex nihilo*. And a few paragraphs later, he expounds further, offering an explicit statement that affirms *ex nihilo*. He writes,

> For the Creator and Master of the universe himself rejoices in his works. For by his infinitely great might he established the heavens, and in his incomprehensible wisdom he set them in order. Likewise, he separated the earth from the water surrounding it, and set it firmly on the sure foundation of his own will; and the living creatures which walk upon it he called into existence by his own decree. (*1 Clem.* 33.2–3)

In what is the oldest, complete Christian sermon that has survived,[20] which is referred to as *Second Clement*, speaking of the grace of God in

---

[20] Noted by Holmes, *AF*[1], 102.

having compassion and mercy, he writes, "We had no hope of salvation except that which comes from him, and even though he had seen in us much deception and destruction. For he called us when we did not exist [*ouk ontas*], and out of nothing [*ek mē ontos*] he willed us into being" (2 *Clem*. 1.8).

Clement's speculative doctrine of creation is based on the implications of biblical passages about God as transcendent from the universe. As we will see throughout this study, the doctrine of *creatio ex nihilo* is a normative assumption derived *from the text*. Creation is a product of God's will; he decrees that something exists, and he wills it into being. In Clement of Rome, we do not see explicit essence–language deployed, seeking to articulate a divine grammar for God. Instead, the names of God hold firm in his thinking, but we do see the emergence of the doctrine of *creatio ex nihilo*.

II. THE ANTE-NICENE FATHERS

Justin Martyr

The early Christian apologist of the Faith, Justin Martyr, was born of pagan parents in Samaria. Around AD 130, Justin converted from pagan philosophy to Christianity. He was still a philosopher but taught Christianity, the true philosophy. His appearance marks a distinct shift in the audience of Christian writings to that of pagans. In Justin, we see a greater level of sophistication in his theology than in Ignatius.

In his writings, Justin records a *dialogue* he has with a Graeco-Samaritan named Trypho, in which Justin gives an account of his pilgrimage through Stoic, Peripatetic,[21] and Pythagorean instruction. Platonism was his last stop before converting to Christianity. The ideas and concepts he derived from Platonism (i.e., that of incorporeal objects and transcendent Ideas), Justin says, gave "wings to his mind." But he still couldn't *fly*. Justin's retelling of his Christian conversion begins with an encoutner he has with "an old man" who asks him to define God. Justin offers a customary philosophical response: "That which is uniformly and consistently always the same and provides the cause of existence for all other beings." The old man was a Christian and agreed with him,

---

[21] It is synonymous with Aristotelianism. The word's primary use is to describe a teacher who works in different schools.

reflecting the common Christian philosophical theology of this time. However, knowing *this* God is of greater importance for the Christian.[22]

The elderly man's inquiry into Justin's comprehension of God disrupted Justin's Platonism, as a Platonic perspective is incapable of establishing a connection between a created being and the Divine Essence. Justin turned to divine revelation in the Old Testament, which led him to the Faith. Platonic philosophy does not lead one to the Christian Faith; instead, it stimulates one's thinking of the beyond in a conceptual framework. *Revelation* was the key to true knowledge of God. However, two central concepts on the nature and being of God shared between the two views are 1) that God is immutable, uncreated, eternal, and imperishable. And 2) he is the ultimate cause of all that exists; he is the ground of being. "God alone is unbegotten and incorruptible ... but all other things after him are created and corruptible" (*Dial.* 5). God is the creator of all things and "is superior to the things that are to be changed" (1 *Apol.* 20). While the old man criticized Justin's religious knowledge of God, he was on familiar ground when it came to the nature and being of God. Justin rejects literal interpretations of biblical metaphors that depict God having arms, hands, feet, and a soul, "like a composite being" (*Dial.* 114). God does not "come down" or "go up" for anything, either when the Bible says God went up from Abraham (Ge 18:22), or when God came down to look at the tower of Babel (Ge 11:5), or when God shut Noah into the Ark (Ge 7:6). Because, as Justin writes,

> ... the ineffable Father and Lord of all neither has come to any place, nor walks, nor sleeps, nor rises up, but remains in His own place, wherever that is, quick to behold and quick to hear, having neither eyes nor ears, but being of indescribable might; and He sees all things, and knows all things, and none of us escapes His observation; and He is not moved or confined to a spot in the whole world, for He existed before the world was made. (*Dial.* 127)

To respond to those who claim that Justin was dependent on Plato for his doctrine of creation, in the following excerpt we see that Plato is dependent on Moses. In the ancient world, the older source was expected to be considered authoritative over the newer one.[23] Justin

---

[22] Grant, *The Early Christian Doctrine of God*, 18–9.
[23] Craig A. Carter, *Contemplating God with the Great Tradition: Recovering Trinitarian Classical Theism* (Grand Rapids, MI: Baker Academic, 2021), 247.

follows the same approach. He shows a cohesive acceptance in Plato and Moses in that we agree with Moses, as we should, that God created *ex nihilo*, and with Plato, that God shaped what was formless into form, as Genesis 1:2 posits. The key to understanding *creatio ex nihilo* is that the doctrine asserts matter does not exist eternally alongside God.[24] Justin writes,

> And that you may learn that it was from our teachers—we mean the account given through the prophets—that Plato borrowed his statement that God, having altered matter which was shapeless, made the world, hear the very words spoken through Moses, who, as above shown, was the first prophet, and of greater antiquity than the Greek writers; and through whom the Spirit of prophecy, signifying how and from what materials God at first formed the world, spake thus: "In the beginning God created the heaven and the earth. And the earth was invisible and unfurnished, and darkness was upon the face of the deep; and the Spirit of God moved over the waters. And God said, Let there be light; and it was so." So that both Plato and they who agree with him, and we ourselves, have learned, and you also can be convinced, that by the word of God the whole world was made out of the substance spoken of before by Moses. And that which the poets call Erebus, we know was spoken of formerly by Moses. (Justin, *1 Apol.* 59)

Lastly, Justin affirmed the sovereignty of God, in a sense making it something that defines or gives the credentials of true divinity, when he writes: "Whence we become more assured of all things He taught us, since whatever He beforehand foretold should come to pass, is seen in fact coming to pass; and this is the work of God, to tell of a thing before it happens, and as it was foretold so to show it happening" (*1 Apol.* 12).

Theophilus of Antioch

Little is known about him, but he was the first to apply the term *triad* when speaking of the Godhead. A bishop of Antioch (died c. AD 188), he proffers a strict transcendental monotheism, stating that God's form is "ineffable and inexpressible" (*Autol.* 1.3). Theophilus offers a litany of appellations regarding the nature of God; to note a few: God is incomparable in power, unfathomable in greatness, and unrivaled in

---

[24] Carter, *Contemplating God with the Great Tradition*, 248.

wisdom. God does not have a beginning because he was never brought into existence, thus he is immutable (*Autol.* 1.4).

Teaching against the Platonic concept of the coeternity of God and matter, Theophilus writes, "If God is uncreated and matter uncreated, God is no longer according to the Platonists, the Creator of all things" (*Autol.* 1.3). Theophilus was showing the inconsistency in the Platonic claim that God is the creator of all things, yet matter was eternal. But God is uncreated, thus unalterable. If matter were like God, then matter would be uncreated and unalterable. God's power is supreme in that he did not create out of existent materials (for "what great thing is that?" Theophilus says), rather, he manifests it by making whatever he pleases "out of things that are not" (*Autol.* 1.3). And because God is uncreated, he is not needy, like the created; "he stands in need of nothing" (*Autol.* 2.10).

God's act of creating was through "His own Word internal within His own bowels, [having] begat Him, emitting Him along with His own wisdom before all things." The Word, the "governing principle," (*arche*) being the Spirit of God, power of the highest, made the heavens and the earth to make himself known through his works (*Autol.* 2.10). And when Genesis 1:1–2 says, "In the beginning, God created the heavens and the earth, and the earth being without form and void, and darkness was upon the face of the deep; and the Spirit of God moved upon the water," this "sacred Scripture," Theophilus writes, "teaches at the outset, to show that matter, from which God made and fashioned the world, was in some manner created, being produced by God" (*Autol.* 2.10). God first created the matter used in the forming of the earth. In Theophilus, we have a great example of philosophy being synthesized with Scripture, with the sacred Scripture having primacy in doctrinal formulations.

Irenaeus

Irenaeus (c. 120–202), Bishop of Lyons in southern France, was one of the most important Christian writers of the second century. Irenaeus grew up in Asia Minor under the preaching of the apostolic father Polycarp and moved to southern France, becoming "elder" (presbyter) in Lyons. We will examine his profound and standard work against Gnosticism, *Against Heresies*. He opens book 2 of *Against Heresies* with the confession of the one Creator God, "who made heaven and earth, and all the things that are therein." There is no one above him, nothing before or after him, nor is he influenced by anyone or thing, but created all things by his own free will. For Irenaeus, God is "the only Lord, and only Creator, the only Father, alone containing all things, and Himself commanding all things into existence" (*Adv. Haer.* 2.1.1). Irenaeus, though recognizing that God is incomprehensible and is known only through Christ, adopts the Platonic framework that God is the source of all good things. Man can be devout and religious, speaking of God as the source of all that is good, with the same view of God being inscribed in the biblical text.

Irenaeus speaks of the folly of those who "endow God with human affections and passions" (*Adv. Haer.* 2.13.3). He shows that their folly is due to not knowing the truth as taught in Scripture. He writes, "*If they had known the Scriptures*, and been taught by the truth, they would have known, beyond doubt, that God is not as men are; and that His thoughts are not like the thoughts of men. For the Father of all is at a vast distance from those affections and passions which operate among men" (*Adv. Haer.* 2.13.3).[25] Irenaeus was one of the first to express the idea of God's transcendence when he wrote, "We possess eternal duration from His [*hyperochē*] transcendence, not from our own nature" (*Adv. Haer.* 5.2.3). And then Irenaeus articulates the classical expression of the simplicity of God, with the implications from the previous statement, that affections and passions (i.e., emotions) are not proper to him. He writes:

> He is a simple, uncompounded Being, without diverse members, and altogether like, and equal to Himself, since He is wholly understanding, and wholly spirit, and wholly thought, and wholly intelligence, and wholly reason, and wholly hearing, and wholly seeing, and wholly light, and the whole source of all that is good— even as the religious and pious are wont to speak concerning God. (*Adv. Haer.* 2.13.3)

Later in book 2, Irenaeus responds to pagan claims that God (i.e., *demiurge*) has an "animal" nature. His response is a beautiful expression of the complete uniqueness of God apart from all created things. And he

---

[25] Emphasis added. In *Adv. Haer.* 5.7.1 Irenaeus distinguishes man's compositeness as being made flesh and the soul, which is simple and not composite.

ties his description of God into the Scriptures as the Lord of all in his triune operations. He writes:

> He (the Creator) made all things freely, and by His own power, and arranged and finished them, and His will is the substance of all things, then He is discovered to be the one only God who created all things, who alone is Omnipotent, and who is the only Father founding and forming all things, visible and invisible, such as may be perceived by our senses and such as cannot, heavenly and earthly, "by the word of His power;" (He 1:3) and He has fitted and arranged all things by His wisdom, while He contains all things, but He Himself can be contained by no one: He is the Former, He the Builder, He the Discoverer, He the Creator, He the Lord of all; and there is no one besides Him, or above Him, neither has He any mother, as they falsely ascribe to Him; nor is there a second God, as Marcion has imagined; nor is there a Pleroma of thirty Æons, which has been shown a vain supposition; nor is there any such being as Bythus or Proarche; nor are there a series of heavens; nor is there a virginal light, nor an unnameable Æon, nor, in fact, any one of those things which are madly dreamt of by these, and by all the heretics. But there is one only God, the Creator—He who is above every Principality, and Power, and Dominion, and Virtue: He is Father, He is God, He the Founder, He the Maker, He the Creator, who made those things by Himself, that is, through His Word and His Wisdom—heaven and earth, and the seas, and all things that are in them: He is just; He is good; He it is who formed man, who planted paradise, who made the world, who gave rise to the flood, who saved Noah; He is the God of Abraham, and the God of Isaac, and the God of Jacob, the God of the living: He it is whom the law proclaims, whom the prophets preach, whom Christ reveals, whom the apostles make known to us, and in whom the Church believes. He is the Father of our Lord Jesus Christ: through His Word, who is His Son, through Him He is revealed and manifested to all to whom He *is* revealed; for those [only] know Him to whom the Son has revealed Him. But the Son, eternally co-existing with the Father, from of old, yea, from the beginning, always reveals the Father to Angels, Archangels, Powers, Virtues, and all to whom He wills that God should be revealed. (*Adv. Haer.* 2.30.9)

In utilizing philosophy as a handmaiden to theology, Irenaeus develops a scripturally coherent understanding of the Divine essence.

Clement of Alexandria

Clement of Alexandria (c. 150–c. 215) was the head of the Catechetical School of Alexandria (c. 190) and the teacher of Origen. Concerned that Christianity is not seen as unsophisticated, Clement sought to reconcile his faith with the best of Greek philosophy. He believed that the kernels of truth found in Plato and Greek Philosophy were preparatory for the Gentiles in leading them to Christ, just as the Law was a guide or guardian for the Hebrews.[26] Clement's esoteric exegesis and speculative theology emphasized a higher knowledge, which was obtained only through the Logos.

In his *Exhortation to the Heathen* (*Protr.*), Clement contrasts the truth of Scripture and the Christian Faith to that of paganism, intending to win pagans to Christ. The pagan gods, Clement writes, "are the images of demons; but God made the heavens, and what is in heaven" (*Protr.* 4). Pagan worship is directed toward God's works, not God himself. The sun, moon, and stars were made to measure time, but pagans "absurdly imagine" these things as gods. His word established these things, "and all their host by the breath of his mouth" (Ps 33:6). Clement understands that the work of creation is brought into being *ex nihilo*, writing: "How great is the power of God! His bare volition was the creation of the universe. For God alone made it because He alone is truly God. By the bare exercise of volition, He creates; His mere willing was followed by the springing into being of what He willed" (*Protr.* 4). However, *ex nihilo* does not entail being coming from *non*-being; instead, God created through Godself. There were no preexistent materials from which God created. The Philosophers sometimes assert truthful things of divine inspiration, but they fall short of seeing the divine being behind all of it. Clement writes, "They confess that God is one, indestructible, unbegotten, and that somewhere above in the tracts of heaven, in His own peculiar appropriate eminence, whence He surveys all things, He has an existence true and eternal" (*Protr.* 6).

Clement cites various poets and philosophers giving testimony to what they see as true and wise, but ultimately unable to reach the proper height and origin of knowledge and salvation. While the heathens orate in beautiful diction, wordiness, and seduction, "the divine Scriptures and

---

[26] Nathan P. Feldmeth, *Pocket Dictionary of Church History*, (IVP Academic, 2008), 41.

institutions of wisdom form the short road to salvation" (*Protr.* 8). Clement begins his exposition of Scripture highlighting the transcendence of God, his wholly otherness from the pagan gods. He cites the prophet Jeremiah, who, unlike the heathen poets, is gifted with the wisdom from the Holy Spirit, says, "Am I a God at hand," he says, "and not a God afar off? Shall a man do ought in secret, and I not see him? Do I not fill heaven and earth? Saith the Lord" (Je 23:23). And then he strings together various passages from the prophet Isaiah, with a few more from Jeremiah, who says:

> Who shall measure heaven with a span, and the whole earth with his hand?" [Isa 40:12] Behold God's greatness, and be filled with amazement. Let us worship Him of whom the prophet says, "Before Thy face the hills shall melt, as wax melts before the fire!" [Isa 64:1,2] This, says he, is the God "whose throne is heaven, and His footstool the earth; and if He open heaven, quaking will seize thee" [Isa 66:1]. Will you hear, too, what this prophet says of idols? "And they shall be made a spectacle of in the face of the sun, and their carcasses shall be meat for the fowls of heaven and the wild beasts of the earth; and they shall putrefy before the sun and the moon, which they have loved and served: and their city shall be burned down" [Je 8:2; 30:20; 4:6] (*Protr.* 9).

Clement's purpose in citing these prophets is to manifest the unique distinction of God's being and wisdom from idols (pagan gods), as the prophets did. He offers a litany of passages to further strengthen his point, such as Exodus 3:11, Isaiah 46:9, Proverbs 8:22, 6:11, Jeremiah 10:12, and Romans 1:21, 23, 25 (*Protr.* 9). The pagan gods are an "image of an image," which means the pagan gods are mere idols "senselessly" fashioned after the image of sinful, evil, and corrupted man. But the true image of God, Clement writes,

> is His Word, the genuine Son of Mind, the Divine Word, the archetypal light of light; and the image of the Word is the true man, the mind which is in man, who is therefore said to have been made 'in the image and likeness of God,' [Ge 1:26] assimilated to the Divine Word in the affections of the soul, and therefore rational; but effigies sculptured in human form, the earthly image of that part of man which is visible and earth-born, are but a perishable impress of humanity, manifestly wide of the truth. (*Protr.* 10)

Clement emphasizes the notion of providence in the activity of God, which shows he is living and able to exercise divine power, in contrast to "fire," "water," "shooting stars, and comets, which are produced by atmospheric changes" (*Protr.* 10). This living and powerful God, the only true God, manifested his "unsurpassable benevolence," accomplishing a great work in so brief of space, through the Lord, who was despised but became the expiator of sin. The Lord of the universe, the Son of God, was made equal to mankind in assuming humanity and fashioning himself in the flesh, in which he then "enacted the drama of human salvation" (*Protr.* 10).

In bringing his book to a close, Clement concludes with the graciousness of God in the power of the gospel, exhorting the heathens to leave their errors and turn to Christ in obedience. God is gracious, needing nothing, and wills to bestow upon creatures the "enjoyment of immortality," in which he confers upon them both "the Word and the knowledge of God, my complete self." Clement urges the Greeks to see that the Father is their Creator, expressing his desire to restore them "according to the original model," which "is symphony, this is the harmony of the Father, this is the Son, this is Christ, this is the Word of God, the arm of the Lord, the power of the universe, the will of the Father" (*Protr.* 12).

Clement's following treatise that we will take up in our study is *The Instructor* (*Paedagogus*), a manual of Christian ethics. Clement writes that this work aims "to improve the soul, not to teach, and to train it up to a virtuous, not to an intellectual life." This work, therefore, is medicinal, in that "those who are diseased in soul require a *paedagogue* to cure our maladies." Christ's teaching is to first exhort, then train, and finally teach. Therefore, this work is the last phase of instruction according to that model, with Christ the Word as *the* Instructor (*Paed.* 1.1).[27] Due to the scope of this work, we find little in the form of speculative doctrine or theology proper. Nevertheless, we will extract a few remarks that pertain to Clement's doctrine of God.

Clement writes that the *Instructor*, the Son of the Father, is "God in the form of man," and is "devoid of passion."[28] God and the Word "both

---

[27] *Exhortation to the Heathens* was the exhortative and training sections in this model of teaching.

[28] Clement notes in God's dealings with instructing man, God "condescends to emotion on man's account" (*Paed.* 1.8).

are one," and "God is one, and beyond the one and above the Monad itself" (*Paed.* 1.8). He took on the form of man to redeem him because mankind is "his workmanship." Clement notes a distinction between mankind and the rest of creation in how God created both; man, he framed by himself, his own hand, and breathed "into him what as peculiar to himself." Whereas the rest of creation, God "made by the word of command alone" (*Paed.* 1.3). Clement remarks that "God is good on His own account" and "alone is wise, from whom comes wisdom" (*Paed.* 1.9, 10), in what seems to be an understanding of God's simple being, from which his attributes originate, not which he received. In these few statements, we see critical elements of a classical doctrine of divine simplicity emerge.

The Stromata

Clement's *Stromata*, or Miscellanies, is a varied work of theology, unsystematic in its expression, with a critical topic on philosophy's role in the development of theology in response to an outgrowth of Alexandrian Gnostics. In *The Stromata*, we come across more of Clement's speculative notions on the doctrine of God and a brief treatment of anthropomorphic language. Because his intentional audience is non-Christian Greeks, he deploys philosophy as a preparatory discipline to the Christian faith.[29] As God is the cause of all good things, with the Old and New Testaments as school masters to reveal Christ to the Jews, Clement writes, "Perhaps philosophy too was a direct gift of God to the Greeks before the Lord extended his appeal to the Greeks. For philosophy was to the Greek world what the Law was to the Hebrews, a tutor escorting them to Christ" (Ga 3:24) (*Stra.* 1.5.28).[30]

One of the challenges that accompanied the Hellenic mind was its gross misunderstanding of the ontological nature of Deity. The Greek gods were merely projections of man, exhibiting *passions* that swayed them to act in unrighteous anger, wickedness, and perversion. They had creaturely forms, thus they spoke and acted in a creaturely manner, albeit

---

[29] Henny Fiskå Hägg, *Clement of Alexandria and the Beginnings of Christian Apophaticism*, Oxford early Christian studies (Oxford: Oxford University Press, 2006), 69.

[30] English translation cited is from Clement of Alexandria, *Stromateis, Books 1–3 (The Fathers of the Church, Volume 85)* (CUA Press, 2010). Citations from *Books 4–7* are from, *ANF.*

much more powerful than humans. But the God of the Bible is *impassible*. He is not a creature; he is uncreated, thus not like Greek pagan gods, who, while considered 'gods', were still contained within and circumscribed by the created realm. Therefore, Clement must explain to his audience how we are to understand passages that ascribe human affections or passions to God. Clement says:

> It seems that we continually think of the Scriptures in worldly terms in such respects, making analogies from our own passions, wrongly accepting our understanding of the will of God (who is impassible) by the analogy of the stirrings within us. If we, who have a capacity for hearing, were to imagine a similar condition in the Almighty, we should be committing a godless error. It is not possible to speak of the divine in its actual nature. But even though we are fettered to flesh, it is possible for us to hear the Lord, accommodating himself to human weakness for our salvation, in the words of the prophets. (*Stra.* 2.16.72)

We must not confuse creature and Creator. Clement observes the vast distinction between God and creatures when he states that "it is not possible to speak of the divine," his incomprehensible sublimity and glory "in its actual nature." If we think we can describe him as he is, the all-powerful One, we would be in great error. Therefore, because of our weak and "fettered" flesh, with Clement implying that even our creaturely mode of listening to the prophets' declarations is part of that weakened condition, God accommodated himself to us to reveal Christ. When a sinner obeys, repents, and believes upon the Lord for salvation with great joy, the Lord "has set his own seal on our joy." God "receives joy without having experienced outward change because the person of his purpose has found joy in repentance" (*Stra.* 2.16.73).

A few sentences later, Clement addresses the Gnostic thought of emanation, whereby creation is an emanation, a spontaneous outflow of the divine nature. His point was to emphasize the distinction between God and man, in that God is uncreated, thus he does not have a natural relation to creatures. Clement writes, "It makes no difference whether we were formed from nothingness or from matter, since the former has no existence at all, and the latter is totally distinct from God—unless anyone is going to have the impertinence to say that we are a part of him and of the same substance as God" (*Stra.* 2.16.74). Clement's statement is an implicit reference to the doctrine of *creatio ex nihilo*. His ontological doctrine of God affirms a *total distinctness* from creatures, which, for Clement, provides the backdrop to display God's rich mercy and unsurpassing grace in that he shows his goodness to creatures who are, "by nature 'alienated' from him , . . hav[ing] nothing to do with him (in our essential being or nature)" (*Stra.* 2.16.75).

At the end of book 4 of Clement's *Stromata*, we find a few interesting statements on God, the Son, and the Spirit. Clement tends to extend his liberties when venturing into speculative theology. While not unorthodox, it makes his style unique. In chapter 25 of book 4, Clement explains that man's perfection comes through God's knowledge and love. He writes that God, in his essence, cannot be a "subject for demonstration." However, Christ, the Son "is wisdom, and knowledge, and truth . . . and he is susceptible of demonstration and of description." The collective powers of the Spirit become one and "terminate in the same point—that is, in the Son." But the Spirit cannot be declared regarding his powers. Clement writes:

> And the Son is neither simply one thing as one thing, nor many things as parts, but one thing as all things; whence also He is all things. For He is the circle of all powers rolled and united into one unity. Wherefore the Word is called the Alpha and the Omega, of whom alone the end becomes beginning, and ends again at the original beginning without any break. Wherefore also to believe in Him, and by Him, is to become a unit, being indissolubly united in Him; and to disbelieve is to be separated, disjoined, divided. (*Stra.* 4.25)

He concludes this chapter by emphasizing God's eternal nature, being "without beginning," who "is being" . . . "the first principle of the department of action," . . . "of reasoning," and "of judgment" (*Stra.* 4.25).

In books 5–7, we piece together doctrinal statements representative of the classical doctrines of God. In an almost confession-like manner, Clement articulates the doctrine of divine simplicity, which he grounds in the uniqueness and unity of God. He starts with passages from the prologue of John's Gospel, referring to "the only-begotten God" as the one revealing the Father, who comes from the "invisible and ineffable bosom of God." A few sentences later, he writes:

> how can that be expressed which is neither genus, nor difference, nor species, nor individual, nor number; nay more, is neither an event, nor

that to which an event happens? No one can rightly express Him wholly. For on account of His greatness, He is ranked as the All and is the Father of the universe. *Nor are any parts to be predicated of Him.* For the One is indivisible; wherefore also it is infinite, not considered with reference to inscrutability, but with reference to its being without dimensions, and not having a limit. And therefore, it is without form and name. (*Stra.* 5.12, emphasis added)

For Clement, "nothing is antecedent to the Unbegotten." The unbegotten, the Logos made Flesh as our Lord Christ, Clement writes, "is the cause of all good things, as the first efficient cause of motion" (*Stra.* 7.2). That which does exist would not exist at all, "had God not willed it." God foresees all things, possessing "from eternity the idea of each thing individually . . . taking in the whole in one view. . . . [And] in one glance, He views all things together, and each thing by itself" (*Stra.* 6.27).

Clement's philosophical framework understands that God does not have a physical body, even though Scripture uses terms denoting God standing, sitting on his throne, using his right hand and right arm, or moving. While Scripture designates these terms to God, "[t]he First Cause is not then in space, but above both space, and time, and name, and conception" (*Stra.* 5.11). Likewise, the Son of God, having the same essence as the Father, Clement writes: "is never displaced; not being divided, not severed, not passing from place to place; being always everywhere, and being contained nowhere; complete mind; the complete paternal light; all eyes, seeing all things, hearing all things, knowing all things, by His power scrutinizing the powers" (*Stra.* 7.2).

Clement concludes with what becomes the embodiment of christological doctrine in the Great Tradition: He "is the power of God . . . a power incapable of being apprehended by sensation . . . as being the Father's most ancient Word before the production of all things, and his Wisdom" (*Stra.* 7.2). And it is this God "who gave himself in sacrifice for us . . . from that which needs nothing to that which needs nothing which is impassible form that which is impassible" (*Stra.* 7.3).

Tertullian

Next to Augustine, Tertullian (c. 160–225) "is the most important and original ecclesiastical author in Latin."[31] Tertullian's writings were penetrating and direct; most were heretical refutations of Gnostic teachings, especially Marcion, the most formidable heretic of the early church. Precise language in defining the essence and being of God was of the upmost importance. This is evident in the fundamental effect Tertullian's ideas had on later expositions by Athanasius and Augustine and other church fathers, and the Councils of Nicaea (325) and Chalcedon (451) and their lasting formularies. It is said, Tertullian's use of the Latin *trinitas* was the first application of the term *trinity* to Deity.[32] The Chief principle of Christian theology for Tertullian is that "'God is not, if He is not one;' because we more properly believe that that has not existence which is not as it ought to be." But, to ask what God is, will reveal that "he is not otherwise than one" (*Adv. Marc.* 1.3). Here, Tertullian offers this definition of God:

> God is the great Supreme, existing in eternity, unbegotten, unmade, without beginning, without end. For such a condition as this must needs be ascribed to that eternity which makes God to be the great Supreme, because for such a purpose as this is this very attribute in God; and so on as to the other qualities: so that God is the great Supreme in form and in reason, and in might and in power. (*Adv. Marc.* 1.3)

Tertullian understood that God revealed himself "first from *nature*, and afterwards authenticated by *instruction*." God reveals himself by his works (Ro 1:19–20), and God reveals himself "through his revealed announcements" (*Adv. Marc.* 1.18).[33] The bulk of Tertullian's writings were polemical and apologetic. Marcion blamed God for man's fall, and Tertullian responded, starting his defense with God as Creator, whose attributes of goodness, foreknowledge, and power cannot be questioned. His creation testifies to God's attributes in that it shows his goodness

---

[31] Quoting A. Grillmeier, *Christ in Christian Tradition*, 140, in, Joseph M. Hallman, "The Mutability of God: Tertullian to Lactantius," *Theological Studies* 42, no. 3 (September 1981): 374.

[32] "Tertullian," by K.J. Bryer in *Who's Who in Christian History* (Wheaton, IL: Tyndale House, 1992).

[33] For example, Hebrews 1:1–3.

and his power because his creation "springs out of nothing" (*Adv. Marc.* 2.5). Tertullian defends God's foreknowledge of the fall yet shows God is free of sin, in that because of God's foreknowledge, he "proclaimed a caution against it [the Fall] under the penalty of death" (*Adv. Marc.* 2.5). A few chapters later, he affirms that nothing can happen against the will of God, writing:

> For, while holding this earnestness and truth of the good God, which are indeed capable of proof from the rational creation, you will not wonder at the fact that God did not interfere to prevent the occurrence of what He wished not to happen, in order that He might keep from harm what He wished. (*Adv. Marc.* 2.7)[34]

Tertullian points the blame back to man, stating that God "constituted him free, master of his own will and power." He states that God would not have imposed a law on man "had it not [been] in his power to render that obedience which is due to law." God "sets before man good and evil," which man will either be obedient or resistant to God's calling, threatening and/or exhorting from sin. With that said, Tertullian writes, "God, however, did foreknow that man would make a bad use of his created constitution" (*Adv. Marc.* 2.7).[35]

Threatening, calling, and exhorting aside, Tertullian affirms that God has unilateral power within the wills of men to fulfill his purposes. However, for heretics like Marcion (to whom Tertullian is responding), such power implicates God as the author of evil. In the classic example of the hardening of Pharaoh's heart (Ex 7–14), Tertullian makes no

---

[34] Interestingly, Augustine has a similar saying: "In sinning, they did what God did not will in order that God through their evil will might do what He willed." Quoted in John Calvin, *Concerning the Eternal Predestination of God*, 1st edition (Louisville, KY: Westminster John Knox Press, 1997), 123. Calvin's citation of Augustine is not an exact quote but seems to be a conflation of a few similar statements from *Aug., Enchir.*, 101, 102.

[35] Regarding foreknowledge and man's fall, see 2.7. And here we see Tertullian's view of man's will, which does not fall in line with a Reformed view (or even a classical Arminian view). Tertullian held that man's freedom of will was a gift to be enjoyed, which was the common view held among the early church fathers. However, the nature of the will was not a pressing topic of debate, so though they assumed a libertarian view of man (an anachronistic use of the phrase), there wasn't a serious discussion on the matter until the time of Augustine and Pelagius. But Tertullian does not dismiss the foreknowledge of God, keeping the tension between man's liberty and divine sovereignty.

qualms about it: "*God* hardens the heart of Pharaoh" (*Adv. Marc.* 2.14). But God's act of hardening, writes Tertullian, is not a *sinful* evil, which belongs only to the devil; instead, it is a *penal* evil, God's act of divine justice against disobedience. In making this distinction, Tertullian balances the antinomy required for consistency in interpretation. Such careful handling of Scripture does justice to texts, such as Isaiah 45:7 ("I create evil"), whereby a surface reading *seems* to implicate God as the author of evil in the manner Marcion and other heretics have assumed. Tertullian affirms the truth of God's involvement behind evil but grounds it in God's holy and righteous will, which removes any implication of God as the author of evil that puts his holiness and goodness in question. Therefore, following Tertullian's distinction of evils, God's authorship of *penal* evil, in the case of Pharaoh, resulting in God's hardening of his heart, is because "[h]e deserved . . . to be influenced to his destruction [because] he had already denied God . . , having long been guilty before God of Gentile idolatry, worshiping the crocodile in preference of the living God" (*Adv. Marc.* 2.14).

Tertullian's doctrine of God carries the proper distinction between God and man, in that God is alone good by nature, whereas man, who exists by creation, "is not disposed to good, but by creation, not having it [goodness] as his own attribute to be good." God bestowed goodness on man; therefore, because he is not intrinsically good as God is, he has the liberty to do good or evil (*Adv. Marc.* 2.6). Though Tertullian does not articulate a doctrine of divine simplicity, his argument of God's intrinsic goodness belonging to Godself *alone* seems to establish this logical understanding intuitive of divinity.[36]

In his treatise against Hermogenes, God's uniqueness, and his qualities of divinity, Tertullian writes, "By his sole possession of them, [God] is One" (*Adv. Herm.* 1.4). "Whatever belongs to God belongs to himself alone"; whatever creatures have come from God; "we receive it; it doesn't come from ourselves" (*Adv. Herm.* 1.5). And this view of divinity, as Tertullian sees expressed in Scripture, leads him to the doctrine of *creatio ex nihilo*, stating that before all things came to be, when God created, "there was present with him no power, no material, no nature which belonged to any other than himself" (*Adv. Herm.* 1.17).

---

[36] It is important to understand that divine simplicity is not merely an attribute of God, as many have mistakenly assumed; rather, simplicity is the *divinity* of God.

Using Romans 11:36 to frame his argument, Tertullian intends to demonstrate the absurdity of denying God's work of creation from nothing. He writes:

> This rule is required by the nature of the One-only God, who is One-only in no other way than as the sole God; and in no other way sole, than as having nothing else (co-existent) with Him. So also He will be first, because all things are after Him; and all things are after Him, because all things are by Him; and all things are by Him, because they are of nothing: so that reason coincides with the Scripture, which says: "Who hath known the mind of the Lord? or who hath been His counsellor? or with whom took He counsel? or who hath shown to Him the way of wisdom and knowledge? Who hath first given to Him, and it shall be recompensed to him again?" Surely none! (*Adv. Herm.* 1.17).

While he defended *ex nihilo*, Tertullian's specific aim was against Hermogenes' opinion that matter is eternal (*Adv. Herm.* 1.3), which is grounds for heresy because it places creation at the ontological rank of the Creator.[37] While Hermogenes doesn't "acknowledge any other Christ as Lord," writes Tertullian, "he takes from Him everything which is God, since he will not have it that He made all things of nothing" (*Adv. Herm.* 1.1). In one of Tertullian's arguments, he connects the phrase, "In the beginning," (Ge 1:1; Jn 1:1) with Proverbs 8:22. This chapter in Proverbs (specifically vv. 22–30) is about wisdom, which the author personifies. The NT refers to Christ as "the power of God and the wisdom of God" (1Co 1:24), whom John calls the *Logos*, the Word, in John 1:1. And it is Christ, the Wisdom and Power of God who created all things from nothing (Jn 1:3).[38]

---

[37] The problem in holding to the view that matter is eternal is that God, by definition, is uncreated. He, alone, is *the* necessary being. If matter is eternal, then it too is uncreated, and it must be part of God or *is* God, thus making it *the* necessary 'being' as well. But matter is physical and is mutable. God is spirit and perfectly immutable. And Scripture makes it clear that God spoke the world into existence (Ge 1; Ps 33:6, 9; 147:15, 18; 148:5). Tertullian's argument can be schematized in the following way: 1.1. God=supreme; 2. Supreme=unique; 3. Therefore God is unique (one). 2.1. unique=that to which nothing is equal; 2. God is unique; 3. Therefore nothing is equal to God. 3.1. Matter, if it is eternal, is equal to God; 2. Nothing is equal to God (=1.3); 3. Therefore matter is not eternal. Cited from J. H. Waszink, *ACW* 24, 32, (110) in Hallman, "the Mutability," 374.

[38] See *Adv. Herm.*, 1.29 for a wonderful treatment on the formation of the earth.

Proverbs 8:22 states, "The Lord acquired me at the beginning of his creation, before his works of long ago." Heretics, however, use this passage to advocate that Christ, who is Wisdom personified, is a created being because it states he was "acquired" by the Lord. Tertullian begins by observing that *in the beginning* only means the initial one. It does not refer to substance but rather inception (*Adv. Herm.* 1.1). In connecting it to Proverbs 8:22, Tertullian makes the argument:

> For since all things were made by the Wisdom of God, it follows that, when God made both the heaven and the earth *in principio*—that is to say, in the beginning—He made them in His Wisdom. If, indeed, beginning had a *material* signification, the Scripture would not have informed us that God made so and so *in principio*, at the beginning, but rather *ex principio*, of the beginning; for He would not have created *in*, but *of*, matter. When Wisdom, however, was referred to, it was quite right to say, in the beginning. (*Adv. Herm.* 1.20)

A few chapters earlier, Tertullian writes, "Indeed, as soon as He perceived it to be necessary for His creation of the world, He immediately creates it, and generates it in himself" (*Adv. Herm.* 1.18). The *acquiring* of Wisdom was not that God at some point was without wisdom and then acquired it (How could God be without his wisdom and be God?); instead, it was "in fact the beginning of his ways: this meditation and arrangement being the primal operation of Wisdom, opening as it does the way to the works by the act of meditation and thought" (*Adv. Herm.* 1.20). God's creating was done *in Wisdom*.

Tertullian holds that God is immutable yet *mutable*. Responding to the heathen philosophers, he writes, "Come now, do you allow that the Divine Being not only has nothing servile in His course, but exists in unimpaired integrity, and ought not to be diminished, or suspended, or destroyed? Well, then, all His blessedness would disappear, if He were ever subject to change" (*Ad. Nat.* 2.6). Because immutability is a property of eternity, it is impossible, writes Tertullian, "for God either to become less or cease to exist" (*Ad. Nat.* 2.6). And God, being eternal, the *magnum summum*, means not only can he not become less, he also

---

Tertullian makes an interesting argument to defend the plurality in God, in which he points out that the language of Genesis 1:3, "Let there be . . .", it is clear that he who commands and he who creates (executes) are different, "for indeed, he would not be issuing a command if he were all the while doing the work himself, while ordering it to be done by the second." *Adv. Prax.*, 12.

cannot become more.[39] God's eternality means that God is not of antiquity nor in novelty but rather "in its own true nature. Eternity has no time. It is itself all time. It acts; it cannot then suffer" (*Adv. Marc.* 1.8).

Tertullian, however, expressed a mutability in God, which flows from himself being eternally good and just, as he judges human sinfulness, having the feelings of a judge, such as offense and anger.[40] Therefore, I think it is safe to assume Tertullian was expressing what we call *relational* or *communicable* attributes to his creation. In raising an adversary (mankind), it became necessary for God to express anger and offense, displayed temporally because his goodness demands that he punish injustice. It would be unbecoming—"unworthy"—"of the Divine Being as not to execute retribution on what He has disliked and forbidden" (*Adv. Marc.* 1.26). Marcion's god, Tertullian argues, cannot feel and cannot punish; therefore, he cannot be God. In God's attributes of goodness and justice, his severity is good because it is just (*Adv. Marc.* 2.16).[41]

While Tertullian intimates that God has emotions, he is careful to claim that we must understand them not in the manner as man has them. Man's emotions, his passions, are due to his corrupt condition. God and man have different natures, with God, being divine, is incorruptible, thus he does not have what is proper to creatures. So, in the Scripture's attribution of human features (i.e., eyes, hands, and feet) and sensations to God, these must not be compared with human beings, *univocally* speaking. Instead, they are supremely attributed to God. Tertullian writes:

> These sensations in the human being are rendered just as corrupt by the corruptibility of man's substance, as in God they are rendered incorruptible by the incorruption of the divine essence. Do you really believe the Creator to be God? By all means, is your reply. How then do you suppose that in God there is anything human, and not that all is divine? Him whom you do not deny to be God, you confess to be not human; because, when you confess Him to be God, you have, in fact, already determined that He is undoubtedly diverse from every

---

[39] Hallman, "The Mutability of God," 375.

[40] Hallman, "The Mutability of God," 379.

[41] In *Adv. Marc.* 2.14, Tertullian explains that goodness and justice are both attributes advanced together, in that goodness conceives all things while justice arranged all things. The fear of judgment; therefore, contributes to good and not evil.

sort of human condition. Furthermore, although you allow, with others, that man was inbreathed by God into a living soul, not God by man, it is yet palpably absurd of you to be placing human characteristics in God rather than divine ones in man, and clothing God in the likeness of man, instead of man in the image of God. And this, therefore, is to be deemed the likeness of God in man, that the human soul has the same emotions and sensations as God, although they are not of the same kind; differing as they do both in their conditions and their issues according to their nature. (*Adv. Marc.* 2.16)

Therefore, God, in his incorruptible nature is pleased, and though he gets angered, he does not get irritated, nor can he be tempted (Ja 1:13); he will be moved but not subverted (*Adv. Marc.* 2.16). So, while Tertullian does not define a theory of analogy, he understands that God's feelings are analogous to our own. God's feelings move him in a manner fit to his own and man's feelings affect him in a way equally his own (*Adv. Marc.* 2.16). The texts that speak of God repenting or relenting, as in Jonah (3:9–10; 4:2), Marcion uses to discredit Tertullian's God as a good judge, for a good judge does not return on his decrees. Again, Tertullian, referencing texts such as First Samuel 15:29, shows the lack of consistency in Marcion's understanding of the Creator-creature distinction (though these terms are not used in his writings) (*Adv. Marc.* 2.24). Tertullian takes Marcion through an introductory theology proper lesson, whereby he says that no one would bear Marcion's views of God if he denied his foreknowledge, which is a denial of his divinity; it is a proper attribute of it. So then, what kind of nonsense is Marcion implying here? Using the clearer passages (1Sa 15:29) to interpret the obscure ones (Jn 3:10), Tertullian hinges his argument on the essence and nature of God:

God will never repent of an act of justice. And it now remains that we should understand what God's repentance means. For although man repents most frequently on the recollection of a sin, and occasionally even from the unpleasantness of some good action, this is never the case with God. For, inasmuch as God neither commits sin nor condemns a good action, in so far is there no room in Him for repentance of either a good or an evil deed. (*Adv. Marc.* 2.24)

Divine repentance cannot be seen in human categories because repentance is proper only of the creature, not God. Of *what* and *to whom* does God "repent"? Tertullian uses the words of Scripture to state his case ("he is not a man that he should repent"). What is the meaning, then, of God repenting? He writes, "For it will have no other meaning than a simple change of a prior purpose; and this is admissible without any blame even in a man, much more in God, whose every purpose is faultless" (*Adv. Marc.* 2.24).[42]

Divine Economy—The Evolution of the Trinity

A fundamental teaching or *Rule* that functions as an interpretive framework the early church fathers developed is that of *economy* (Gk. *oikonomia*), which refers to the arrangement or order of the works of God.[43] But, as we will see later, another interpretative framework utilized in exegesis is that of the ECONOMY (OIKONOMIA) and theology (*theologia*) distinction. In this mode, *oikonomia* is the theological discourse that pertains to God's divine acts in time, following the redemptive biblical narrative. *Theologia* is speculative theological discourse about the essence of God, the mystery of the internal RELATIONS of the blessed Trinity.

Interpreters of Scripture can derail Christian teaching by confusing the two when doing theology. The error one generally makes is using *oikonomia* to develop or articulate a *theologia*, which happens by assuming that the revelation of God *in time* is the lens through which we are to understand the essence of God who is *not in time*. If one's approach is not ordered rightly, for example, then one will struggle to manage the tension between the divine and human aspects of Christ, resulting in an inconsistent, heretical Christology.

Tertullian speaks of the divine economy in reference to the Godhead, whereby "this one only God has also a Son, His Word, who proceeded from himself" (*Adv. Prax.* 2). And the Spirit *proceeds* from the Father through the Son (*Adv. Prax.* 4). The economy is the articulation

---

[42] Tertullian concludes, "Now in Greek the word for repentance (μετάνοια) is formed, not from the confession of a sin, but from a change of mind, which in God we have shown to be regulated by the occurrence of varying circumstances." Hallman points out that in Tertullian there are three types of mutability: God changes to become the judge of human sinfulness; God feels various emotions, appropriate to judging and his goodness; and his will changes in accord with changing circumstances of history (381). Does this imply that God is mutable? No. Rather, we see in Tertullian an inconsistency in his theology. Either he did not understand or fully realize the implications of the Platonic philosophical presuppositions in his doctrine of God.

[43] "οἰκονομία," in Bauer, *BDAG*. The Latin equivalent is *dispensatio*.

(by way of revelation) of the unity of God distributed into a Trinity, *ordering* the three PERSONS, yet one substance, of number without division. God is One, and the economy of the one God is Father, Son, and the Spirit, of which all that has appeared in the Father "reappears unchanged, alike in worth, substance, and power in the other Persons of the Trinity."[44] Tertullian's introduction of *persona*, referring to each: the Father, Son, and Spirit, "would become enshrined in the Western tradition."[45]

Tertullian's development of the doctrine of the Trinity provides clarity regarding Jesus, particularly since the church confesses Christ as

---

[44] Prestige, *Patristic Thought*, 101.

[45] Stephen R. Holmes, *The Quest for the Trinity: The Doctrine of God in Scripture, History and Modernity* (Downers Grove, IL: IVP Academic, 2012), 71. Furthermore, the use of *persona* or the Gk. *Prosopon*, functions as an interpretive tool in the early church that articulates the doctrine of the Trinity in a non-speculative manner. Tertullian writes: "But almost all the Psalms which prophesy of the person of Christ, represent the Son as conversing with the Father—that is, *represent* Christ (as speaking) to God. Observe also the Spirit speaking of the Father and the Son, in the character of a third person: "The Lord said unto my Lord, Sit Thou on my right hand, until I make Thine enemies Thy footstool" (*Adv. Prax.*, 11). Using a prosopological reading, whereby the historical figures in the text (e.g., David in Ps 110:1; cf. Ac 4:25, Luke writes, "You said through the Holy Spirit, by the mouth of our father David . . .") are actually God, the Spirit, and/or Christ speaking to God in the *prosopon*, or character of David, for example. See Bates, *The Birth of the Trinity*; also, Carter, *Interpreting Scripture*. The Messianic and prophetic passages, such as Psalm 2:7; 22, and Psalm 110, where David writes, "and my Lord says to my Lord," is actually Christ speaking, through David, to the Father, which is then fulfilled in the created world when Christ arrives. David is the character, through whom the Spirit spoke. So, "the Psalms do not merely speak of Christ; rather, in the Psalms Christ actually speaks" (205). In looking back to the OT utterances of the triune God, the prophets took on the *prosopa* (Greek for persons, characters, or masks) in the grand theodrama, making a person-centered exegesis, which contributed greatly to the development of the Trinity, in the emphasis of "person" language and one-God "substance" language to express the three-in-one mystery (Nicaean orthodoxy). The key point is that a prosopological reading of the text reveals to us a divine dialogue (Trinitarian discourse) taking place through the prophets by the Divine Spirit, who is not chronologically constrained, which is then literally fulfilled in Christ. The Logos was inspiring David so that the Psalms become Christ's own speech. Carter writes: "The difference between prosopological exegesis and typological exegesis is that in typological exegesis we may see Christ opaquely in the OT text, but in prosopological exegesis we actually hear Christ speak clearly in the text" (208–9). Holy Scripture manifests the living presence of God, as the author and the main character.

God of God. He shows the distinction of persons (*personas*) in the Godhead (i.e., *una substantia*), which we see throughout Scripture, where we have ascriptions to each of the persons (e.g., Jn 1:1–18; 16:7–15; Mt 3:16–7; 28:19; 2Co 13:13) and also the fulfillment of key Messianic texts in the Old Covenant (1Co 15:24–8; Ps 8:6; 110:1). However, Tertullian at times does use *persons* and *beings* interchangeably,[46] which will become a problem later, with the sophisticated development of the doctrine of divine simplicity, the backbone of Trinitarian theology.

Critics of the teaching of the Trinity in Scripture questioned Tertullian's beliefs by citing passages such as Isaiah 44:24, which mentions God stretching "out the heavens by myself; who alone spread out the earth." In response, Tertullian argues the point, already noted, that Christ is the Wisdom and Power of God (1Co 1:24; 2:11), also referring to Psalm 33:6, "by the Word of the Lord were the heavens made." When was God without his Wisdom and Power? How did God create? In considering the debate, it seems that we have two equally valid viewpoints in opposition. Tertullian, however, reconciles the alleged contradiction, writing that the point of "alone" is to distinguish monotheism from idols. God *alone*, and not other gods (who do not exist), created the universe. God as Creator is the chief identifying mark of the only true God. God, having created alone, stretched out the heavens alone—*with his Son*. The Son, also, has the distinct designation as Creator (Jn 1:1–3; Col 1:15–6; He 1:2).

However, Scripture states that there is only one, true God (Dt 6:4). Tertullian retaining both *equally valid* claims in Scripture, expresses that the Father and the Son are two, "not by severance of their substance;" instead, "from the dispensation [economy] wherein we declare the Son to be undivided and inseparable from the Father—distinct in degree, not in state" (*Adv. Prax.* 19). The identity of Christ as God manifests in the works he does, which only God can do. Exegeting John 10:30, 32, 34–8, showing the inseparability of the divine works, Tertullian writes,

> It must therefore be by the works that the Father is in the Son, and the Son in the Father; and so it is by the works that we understand that the Father is one with the Son. All along did He therefore strenuously

---

[46] In *Adv. Prax.*, 4, he writes, "the Father and the Son are two *separate persons* . . . [and] He who subjected (all things), and He to whom they were subjected must necessarily be two different Beings." Emphasis added. See also, *Adv. Prax.*, 22.

aim at this conclusion, that while they were of one power and essence, they should still be believed to be Two; for otherwise, unless they were believed to be Two, the Son could not possibly be believed to have any existence at all. (*Adv. Prax.* 22)

The Son, who is indivisible from the Father, being everywhere with him, was revealed according to the divine economy, whereby, at the right time, the Son would be regarded on earth as he is in heaven (*Adv. Prax.* 23).

Tertullian delves into a fascinating discussion about the evolution of the Son proceeding from the Father, the outworking of the *economy*, as illustrated by the operation of human thought and consciousness. He refers to the Word as Reason, and God having *reason* in himself, before the beginning of all things, had not yet *spoken*. God, silently by Reason, planned in himself what he would utter through his Word. And, likewise, this "voice of reason" we have in our heads, silently within us meeting us with a word at every moment of our thoughts. "Whatever we think, there is a word; whatever we conceive, there is reason" (*Adv. Prax.* 5). "This word," Tertullian writes, "in a certain sense, is a second *person* within you, through which in thinking you utter speech, and through which also, (by reciprocity of process) in uttering speech you generate thought" (*Adv. Prax.* 5). This second person utters speech in our mind and externally when we decide to speak out. So then how much more supreme is this in God since we are made in his likeness and image? And by this, Tertullian established "a fixed principle," "that even before the creation of the universe God was not alone, since he had within himself both Reason and, inherent in Reason, His Word, which He made second to Himself by agitating it within Himself" (*Adv. Prax.* 5). When God decided to create, he spoke *his mind!* Through Reason and Wisdom,[47] God creates what has already been made in his mind and intelligence (*Adv. Prax.* 6.).

The revelation of God in Christ, the image of God (2Co 4:4; He 1:3), Tertullian argues that the Father is always invisible and the Son visible.[48] Following the pattern of thought we observed in the previous paragraph, Tertullian writes, "The Father acts by mind and thought; while the Son, who is in the Father's mind and thought, give effect and

---

[47] For Tertullian, Wisdom is the Holy Spirit.
[48] Scriptures supportive of his claim are Ex 33:20; Dt 5:26; Jg 13:22; Jn 1:18; 1Ti 6:16; 1Jn 1:1–2.

form to what he sees" (Jn 5:19, Jesus only does what he sees the Father doing.)(*Adv. Prax.* 15). Thus, all things were made by the Son, and without him was not anything made (Jn 1:3). To dispel the Gnostic heresy that the Son and Spirit are emanations from the Father, Tertullian uses an illustration from nature to demonstrate the unity and sameness that each person of the Godhead share. His intention is vital to understanding Trinitarian monotheism: "Everything which proceeds from something else must needs be second to that which it proceeds, without being on that account separated" (*Adv. Prax.* 8). To illustrate this important point, Tertullian alludes to a tree and its root, a fountain and a river, and the sun and its rays. He writes:

> Following, therefore, the form of these analogies, I confess that I call God and His Word—the Father and His Son—*two*. For the root and the tree are distinctly two things, but correlatively joined; the fountain and the river are also two forms, but indivisible; so likewise the sun and the ray are two forms, but coherent ones. (*Adv. Prax.* 8)

While those illustrations are instructive for the Father and the Son, what about the Spirit? In response, Tertullian speaks of a tree, its root, and its *fruit*. How perfectly fitting is this illustration! Each is distinct, yet "nothing is alien from that original source whence it derives its own properties" (*Adv. Prax.* 8). While all illustrations break down,[49] Scripture teaches us that creation reveals a Creator. So, we should see the stamp of God on things all around us. While God is Spirit, thus invisible, he has given us things in his creation that provide a glimpse of his glory (Ro 1:19–20).

From Tertullian, we get a *"rule of faith"* understanding of the divine economy, in that there is distinction but not diversity (i.e., separation) (*Adv. Prax.* 11). The order of the triune God, Father of the Son, and the Son in the Holy Spirit, Tertullian writes, "produces three coherent Persons, *who are yet distinct* One from Another. These Three are one *essence*, not one *person*, as it is said, 'I and my Father are One,' in respect

---

[49] As Gerald Bray notes, "The trouble with them [e.g., the root, shoot, and fruit illustrations] was that although a source, a river, and a canal contain the same substance (water), they do not interact in a personal way. Given that personal interaction within the Godhead was the only way the gospel could be understood, this was a fatal weakness, and so images drawn from nature, sometimes referred to as 'vestiges of the Trinity' (*vestigial Trinitatis*) eventually disappeared from serious theological discourse." *God Has Spoken*, 987.

of unity of substance, not singularity of number" (*Adv. Prax.* 25, emphasis added). But again, we see a lack of precision in Tertullian's expression of the economy, writing that "the Father is the entire substance [*de substantia patris*], but the Son a derivation and portion of the whole," which Tertullian argues from the Son's own words: "My father is greater than I" (Jn 19:28) (*Adv. Prax.* 9). Trinitarian orthodoxy does not hold to the Son as a portion of the whole; instead, "there are three divine *hypostases* [*personas*] that are instantiations of the divine nature: Father, Son, and Holy Spirit."[50]

However, Tertullian's contribution adds greater substance to the church's confession that Christ is Lord, the Logos who is God. We have language to speak about the three without fragmenting Christian monotheism. The divine life still needs to be explored so that we have a grammar to communicate that which is ineffable.

Hypostatic Union

When God takes on flesh, we are faced with the mystery of how this could be. Does the Son change into a human? If God became man by way of change, then he would no longer be God. How do the two natures unite in one without losing one or the other? God cannot go from uncreated divinity to created humanity. Tertullian works through this dilemma of how the Word became (clothing himself in) flesh, first dispelling the idea of transfiguration. God could not have become man through transfiguration because it is "the destruction of that which previously existed" (*Adv. Prax.* 27). That which is transformed ceases to be what it once was and begins to be what is not. We hold that God is "unchangeable, and incapable of form, as being eternal." So, if Jesus is a compounded substance, that of flesh and Spirit, we lose the two distinct natures, having neither but "a kind of mixture , . . a third substance" (*Adv. Prax.* 27).

Because Scripture speaks of the Son of God as Son by the "Spirit of holiness," and the Son of David, "according to the flesh" (Ro 1:3–4), Tertullian writes, "We see plainly the twofold state, which is not confounded, but conjoined in One Person—Jesus, God and Man" (*Adv. Prax.* 27). So then, what does that mean in regards to how we are to speak of the natures (theologically called the *communicatio idiomatum*)

---

[50] Holmes, *Quest for the Trinity*, 200.

of each together in the one person, yet distinct and preserved? What we have in Christ is a union of the two, whereby the Divinity does all things suitable to itself (e.g., miracles, wonders, mighty deeds) and the flesh "exhibited the affections, which belong to it" (e.g., hunger, thirst, temptation, and death). Therefore, "in one *Person* they no doubt are well able to be coexistent" . . . in that the apostle calls him the "Mediator between God and Men," thus affirming the Son's "participation of both substances" (*Adv. Prax.* 27).

With that said, Tertullian expresses the importance of avoiding "blasphemy against God," being careful to denote that when we speak of "God" dying, we affirm that God did not die after the divine nature; instead, he died after the human nature (*Adv. Prax.* 29). However, heretics emerge to challenge this orthodox concept. In this discussion, they assert that in the Son's suffering, the Father is a "fellow-sufferer" (*Adv. Prax.* 29). The invisible Father, who is the eternal Spirit, cannot suffer. The charge, however, is that the Father should suffer with his Son because they are united as one. He responds by referring to the distinction of persons in the Godhead, that the "Father is separate from the Son, though not from him as God." To illustrate his point on how the Son and Father can be one, yet only the Son suffers, Tertullian refers once again to an analogy from nature, writing:

> For even if a river be soiled with mire and mud, although it flows from the fountain identical in nature with it, and is not separated from the fountain, yet the injury which affects the stream reaches not to the fountain; and although it is the water of the fountain which suffers down the stream, still, since it is not affected at the fountain, but only in the river, the fountain suffers nothing, but only the river which issues from the fountain. (*Adv. Prax.* 29)

In the Son's suffering, his cry to the Father was a "voice of flesh and soul" from the humanity of Jesus. Tertullian says, "It was uttered so as to prove the impassibility of God, who 'forsook' His Son, so far as He handed him over, His human substance to the suffering of death" (*Adv. Prax.* 29). And while he forsook him, not sparing him, but in delivering him up, in the end, he received him back, as we reread Jesus' cry, not of dereliction, but this time of reception, he says: "Father, into your hands I entrust my spirit." And he breathed his last (Lk 23:46).

Hippolytus

Hippolytus (c. 160–236), while he was an important theologian in the third century, was not considered an original-thinking theologian like Tertullian or Origen. However, that does not mean his writings were not insightful or profound; instead, he compiled from the giants before him while applying his own style; fueled by a passion for the gospel of Christ, he held the line—the *rule of faith*—to maintain and continue orthodoxy. He was not a prolific theologian in the area of theology proper. However, he does offer some divine grammatical morsels in the context of refuting heresy.

In his treatise against the heretic Noetus, Hippolytus critiques the arbitrary handling of Scripture. He specifically points out that Noetus and his associates rely solely on one class of passages to form their arguments refuting the deity of Christ. Hippolytus identified the same error made by the heretic Theodotus, who selected passages that focused on the humanity of Christ to demonstrate that he was only a man (*Contra Noetum.*, 3). To address Noetus, Hippolytus exposits various texts from the New Testament, emphasizing the logical implications of such passages that declare that no one can see God, but Christ, the Logos, who *is* with him, comes from him, and has made him known (Jn 1:1, 18). Hippolytus also refers to passages that speak of Christ's lordship and enthronement, ruling over all creation in that the Father has subjected it to him (1Co 15:25–8), the universe he made for himself (Col 1:15–6). He has the power to judge (Jn 5:22), to raise the dead and give life (5:21), and to forgive sins (1Jn 1:9). Many other passages attest to this truth of Christ's unity and deity with the Father.

Hippolytus' next move is to expound the divine economy, the "three-fold manifestation" of the one God (*Contra Noetum.*, 8). He begins with the affirmation that "there is one God in whom we must believe, but unoriginated, impassible, immortal, doing all things as He wills, in the way He wills, and when He wills" (*Contra Noetum.*, 8). His foundation is the foundation of all the ancient fathers, grounded in the *rule of faith*, set out in the earliest creeds of the church. In his words, we see monotheism asserted, the uncreated, eternal, and immutable essence and being of God and his sovereign, omnipotent power to do what he wants. And it is this truth that Hippolytus condemns Noetus for not knowing. And it is the Holy Scriptures that declare these things, which those who seek to "be skilled in the wisdom of this world," "mastering the dogmas of the philosophers," will be unable to learn unless they go to the "oracles of God" (*Contra Noetum.*, 9).

God has given truths in Scripture to us to be discerned. Hippolytus expounds further, beginning with God—subsisting alone with nothing but himself, who then determined to create the world. God had creation in his mind, and then by uttering his word, the Word brings creation into existence. God was alone, but he was a plurality, with his wisdom, power, and counsel with and in him, for "he was the All." Through reason, wisdom, and power, the one God was pleased to speak into existence what he conceived in his mind. Hippolytus, most pointedly emphasizing the sovereign power of God, writes, "When He wills, He does; and when He thinks, He executes; and when He speaks, He manifests; when He fashions, He contrives in wisdom. For all things that are made He forms by reason and wisdom—creating them in reason and arranging them in wisdom." That is why he is the "Author, and fellow-Counselor, and Framer of all things." The Word whom God begat, who was invisible, only visible to God alone, becomes visible *by utterance*—Light of Light—to the "world in order that the world might see him in his manifestation and be capable of being saved" (*Contra Noetum.*, 10).

In explaining the economy, Hippolytus asserts that there are *not* two Gods. Referring to familiar illustrations of water from a fountain and rays from the sun, he writes, "There is but one power, which is from the All, which is the Father, from whom comes this Power and Word." The Word is the mind, Reason, which he has spoken into the world, manifesting as the Son of God. Because he is from the All, not as an emanation or 'spark' of the All, all things are by him, and he alone is of the Father, and thus fully of the All (*Contra Noetum.*, 11). As the One cause of all things, Hippolytus refers back to the Law and Prophets, which he gave to his people through the Holy Spirit, who spoke through them "so that they might declare the Father's counsel and will."

Interestingly, Hippolytus adopts a prosopological reading of the text, whereby Christ acts in the Prophets to speak of himself to the audience and the Father. Hippolytus writes, "Acting then in these (prophets), the Word spoke of himself. For already he became His own herald and showed that the Word would be manifested among men.

And for this reason, he cried: 'I was sought by those who did not ask; I was found by those who did not seek me' [Is 65:1] (*Contra Noetum.*, 12)." As noted earlier, this tactic of interpretation represents Nicene Trinitarian theology. Again, seeing the ontological nature of the biblical text, i.e., the living Word of God, we can cogently and coherently argue for a Trinitarian doctrine within the pages of Scripture without needing to lean heavily on philosophy.

Origen

Origen (c.185–254) was an Alexandrian theologian born in a Christian family. He was trained in both secular and religious literature. His range of learning was vast, and he is considered one of the greatest of early Christian thinkers, whose work is still very influential and controversial today. In his *De Principiis*, Origen begins discussing whether God has a body since Scripture speaks of God as light and a consuming fire (*De Princ.*, 1.1.1).[51] God is a consuming fire (Dt 4:24; He 12:29); however, we are not to understand such designations literally. God does not consume "bodily matter, wood, hay or stubble." He consumes "evil thoughts," "wicked actions," and the "desires for sin" in those whom the Father and the Son make their abode (*De Princ.*, 1.1.2). The Spirit is not a being that can be "divided into bodily parts" or be "partaken by each one of the saints." The Spirit is an "intellectual being and subsists[52] and exists distinctly" (*De Princ.*, 1.1.3).[53] As an intellectual being, God is worshipped in spirit and truth, contrasted against material places of worship, thus distinguishing "God from bodies" and "from shadows or an image" (*De Princ.*, 1.1.4).

Origen brings philosophical language into his theology, specifically *negative* or *apophatic* ascriptions of God (i.e., classical designations), expressing that he is "incomprehensible and immeasurable" (*De Princ.*, 1.1.5). God is "many degrees far better than what we perceive him to be." To explain, Origen illustrates a creature's ability to see a spark compared

---

[51] English citations of Origen's work *De Principiis* are from John Behr, trans., *Origen* (New York: Oxford University Press, 2020).

[52] That which *subsists* or has *subsistence* refers to a being whose essence naturally requires it to exist in itself; it exists essentially by its own identity and is completely self-sufficient for its own existence. See, "Glossary."

[53] In the preface, Origen seems to be unsure of the nature of the Spirit, whether it is deity or creature, "born or not-born." *De Princ.*, Preface, 4.

to the sun's brightness. When speaking of the differences between God and man by degree, his intention, using the spark and the sun analogy, is to demonstrate the difference between God as having an "intellectual nature" and a creature having a "bodily nature." A creature can behold a spark of light, but it cannot behold the sun's glory. God is an intellectual, bodiless being; "the human intellect is not able to grasp or see" (*De Princ.*, 1.1.5). However, God has revealed himself in a manner that creatures can behold, as the sun's rays can be seen as they beam through a window. The brightness of the rays that we can see reflects the glory of their source, which we cannot see. Origen writes, "Because our own intellect is not able to behold God as he is, it understands the father of the universe from the beauty of his works and the comeliness of his creatures" (*De Princ.*, 1.1.6).

At this point, Origen defines God as "a simple intellectual being (*natura*), accepting in himself no addition whatever; so that he cannot be believed to have in himself a more or a less, but is, in all things, *monas* [unity], or, if I may say, *henas* [oneness] (*De Princ.*, 1.1.6). The "first principle of all things" is that God is simple. God cannot be "composite and diverse," for he "necessarily exists free from all bodily admixture." God is Spirit (i.e., an intellectual being) and, therefore, does not need space, a sphere, or a body to move. Human beings are both body and soul, where the soul grows with the body, is limited by it, and can be hindered by its weaknesses. Arguing from Matthew 11:27[54] that God is an intellectual being, thus invisible, God's invisible nature does not mean he "eludes or escapes the gaze of frailer creatures; but because by nature it is impossible for him to be seen" (*De Princ.*, 1.1.8). Origen says it is only proper for bodied creatures to be seen, whereas being seen "cannot be predicated either of the Father or the Son" because, as Scripture tells us, "No one *knows* the Son except the Father, and no one *knows* the Father except the Son and anyone to whom the Son desires to reveal him" (*De Princ.*, 1.1.8).[55] The Son's revealing of himself and the Father is not a physical seeing as bodies are seen; instead, it is a spiritual revealing phenomenon of participating in divinity through the eyes of the heart.

---

[54] In 1.1.9, Origen responds to an objection regarding his understanding of the way creatures *see* (cannot see) God drawn from Matthew 5:8. Origen says that the text further supports his view in that *heart* in Scripture is the intellect of a person.
[55] Mt 11:27.

Having come to the end of his discussion regarding the nature of God, Origen moves on to explore the divine nature of Christ and his human nature, which "in the last times he took on account of the economy" (*De Princ.*, 1.2.1). As observed in Tertullian, Origen follows the typical pattern of beginning with Christ as the begotten Wisdom/Word of God.[56] Dismissing the idea of God being without his Wisdom, even though we speak of the Son, "who was indeed born of him, and derives from him what he is," nevertheless, we speak of what is beyond the limits of what we can understand. But when God decided to manifest his wisdom—to utter his Word, as observed in creation, we are to understand when Solomon says, "she was created the beginning of the ways of God,' that Wisdom is 'containing within herself the beginning and the reasons and the species of the entire creation'" (*De Princ.*, 1.2.2).

Origen further interprets this view of the Word as Wisdom, representing the commencement of God's ways. This interpretation rejects the notion of the Word/Wisdom being created at a specific point in time, as it is foolish to think that God was ever devoid of wisdom. Rather, the Word discloses all that is to come to exist from the Wisdom of God—his mind, containing all the secrets and mysteries of God, thereby, "she is called the Word, because she is, as it were, the interpreter of the secrets of the intellect" (*De Princ.*, 1.2.3). In the Word's disclosing the secrets and mysteries of God, he is also, as Scripture tells us, *the truth* and *the life* (Jn 14:6). Arguing from what is rational, Origen remarks that which is living can only come from that which is *life*, and for such things to *truly* exist, the source of all that is must also be true, having been derived from the truth. "How could rational beings exist, unless the Word or Reason preceded them?" (*De Princ.*, 1.2.4).[57]

---

[56] I say "normal pattern" because the common starting point of Christology and explication of the Triunity of God in much of the church fathers was with the identity of Christ as the Logos (Jn 1:1) and the Wisdom and Power of God (1Co 1:24). And making the connection between the OT, with the "Let there be . . ." divine fiat passages in Gen 1 and God's act of speaking the world into existence in Ps 33: 6 and 9, to the Logos, through whom all things were created (Jn 1:3; Col 1:15–6; He 1:3), the analogy of the intellectual reality of God as mind, thought, and utterance functioned as a helpful approach in explaining the divine economy.

[57] Interestingly, (in 1.3.6, 7, 8.) in Origen's understanding of the Trinity as it relates to creation and creatures, he says that "all rational beings are partakers of the Word of God, that is, Reason, and in this way, as it were, bear certain seeds, implanted within them, of Wisdom and Justice, which is Christ." The Spirit, however, is the work of grace

Origen's purpose is to intricately explore and vividly explain the divine economy of God. Thus far, he has skillfully highlighted aspects that we can readily grasp. Now, he ventures deeper into the profound nature of God, aiming to understand how the Son is the offspring of the Father, yet shares a timeless existence with him. However, as he humbly and honorably observes, "It is abominable and unlawful" to equate the generation of the Son from the Father as the same kind of generation found in humans and animals. The Father's generating of the Son is "something exceptional and worthy of God, for which can be found no comparison at all, not merely in things, but even in thought or imagination, such that a human mind could comprehend." So then, how is the Son begotten from the Father? Origen replies that his begetting is "an eternal and everlasting begetting, just as brightness is begotten from light" (De Princ., 1.2.4). Origen then concludes, expressing the distinction that his sonship is by nature, not by adoption in the Spirit. The nature of divinity is timelessly eternal. So, to speak of the eternal from the temporal, we quickly realize that we are without words and concepts to delineate what eternal begetting means. Explanations from nature, simple expressions of complex ideas, must suffice.

That said, while we are confined to human language to confess the things of the divine, we have much room for speculation from that which we deduce from Scripture and creation. In Christ being called the *image of the invisible God*, Origen wants to know *how* or *what* this term means. His reasoning for doing so is so we "might perceive how God is rightly called Father of his Son" (De Princ., 1.2.6). When we think of "images," things that are painted, sculpted, or carved are images of something, whether of something in creation or just of the mind. But the Son is the invisible image of the invisible God, so how is an image without form said to be of that which does not have form? Origen, referencing Genesis 5:3, says it has been written that Adam begot Seth in his own image and form; thus, "the image preserves the unity of nature and substance of a

---

and works in those who are already walking with the Son and the Father. Humanity, without distinction, participates with the Father and the Son, but only those who are holy participate in the Holy Spirit. Origen then points to First Corinthians 12:3, where Paul writes, "No one can say that Jesus is Lord except in the Holy Spirit." So, how does one attain God? First, they are from the Father; second, they are from the Word, as rational beings; third, they become holy by the Spirit, becoming "capable of Christ anew." His soteriology seems to place the Spirit *after* belief.

father and of a son." We see in human begetting that the form and function are preserved in our offspring—i.e., what is proper of humanity. Christ is the image of God; he is the form and function of God—i.e., what is proper of divinity, having been preserved in that image. So, as human children do all that their human fathers do (according to nature), the Son, as the image, likeness, and offspring of God the Father, likewise does all that his Father does (per the divine nature).

Origen needs to shift his exposition in an abstract direction to illustrate where the parallel deviates from the temporal. He writes, "By the fact that the Son does all things like the Father, the image of the Father is formed in the Son, who is assuredly born of him, as an act of his will proceeding from the intellect." The act of his will is the begetting of the Son; God produces his actions by his will, whereby the Son is the **SUBSISTENCE** of what God wills. God is an intellectual being, so for the parallel to suffice, we must use language befitting an unborn, uncreated intellectual being. The Son as the Word is "not perceptible to the senses" since he is Wisdom, without body, and is also the true light who enlightens everyone. Therefore, Origen writes, the Savior "is the *image of the invisible God* and Father" (*De Princ.*, 1.2.6). This relation and revelation is how we come to God. The Son's relation to the Father himself, as Wisdom, Light (the splendor of the glory of God, as God is light) (*De Princ.*, 1.2.7),[58] and Truth, reveals the Father to us, as his image. And this image, which the senses cannot perceive, is the *means* by which we come to a knowledge of God. Origen references Matthew 11:27 again, emphasizing the *knowing* (in contrast to seeing) the Son and the Father, but only by *knowing* through the Son's revealing of the Father to whom he chooses. When the Son reveals the Father, this *knowing of* the Father is understood according to Christ, when he says, "He that has *seen* me, has *seen* the Father also" (*De Princ.*, 1.2.6)[59] Thus, knowing *is* seeing.

Origen warns against those who speak of Christ as an *emanation* of God "to divide the divine nature into parts and divide the God and

---

[58] Based on Hebrews 1:3, where Christ is said to be the *splendor of the glory of God and the express image of his substance*, Origen speaks of Christ as the splendor of the light of God, who proceeds from him, which is how we come to understand and perceive God *as light*.

[59] Jn 14:9, emphasis added.

Father as far as they can." While the specific terminology is not used, we see a developing metaphysical understanding of the doctrine of divine simplicity functioning as a safeguard for the divine economy. Origen is not done with the question of Christ as the express figure of God's substance or subsistence, specifically, how Wisdom might also "be called *the express figure of the substance* of God in *her* revealing God to others" (*De Princ.*, 1.2.8). To explain, Origen offers a helpful illustration from material things, in which he looks to Philippians 2:6–7, where Paul speaks of Christ when in the form of God *emptied himself*, to show that Christ's display is "the fullness of divinity." Suppose there was a statue of such magnitude that it fills the entire world so that no one could see it. Then, another statue is created similar to this one, having the complete countenance of the magnitudinous statue, which is "absolutely indistinguishable" from it but measurable, unlike the immeasurableness of the first statue. Origen writes, in like manner,

> the Son of God emptying himself of equality with the Father [the magnitudinous statue] and showing us the way by which we may know him, becomes the express figure of his substance, so that we, who are unable to look upon the glory of the pure light while it remained in the magnitude of his divinity, may, by his becoming for us *the splendor*. (*De Princ.*, 1.2.8)

So, how does the illustration from statues explain Origen's point? The Son of God confines himself to a small body—the second statue preserves every similarity to the Father, as displayed in the Son's immense power and works, revealing the "invisible greatness of the God and Father in him"—the first statue. Therefore, such is the reason why Christ can say, "The one who has seen me has seen the Father," "I and the Father are one," and "I am in the Father and the Father is in me."[60]

Origen moves on to discuss divine omnipotence being shared by the Father and the Son, by which God is referred to as *Almighty*. God displays his almighty power in the Father's exercise of power over all things through his Word, whereby all things become subject to the Son and the Father in the Son's possession of all things. Origen sees the culmination of this display of God's *almighty* power through Christ in First Corinthians 15:27–8 and Philippians 2:9–11, where the Father has put all things under the subjection of the Son, as demonstrated in

---

[60] Jn 14:9; 10:30; 14:11.

the Son's exaltation. All of creation—things in heaven, on earth, and under the earth—will bow and every tongue will confess that Jesus is Lord, *to the glory of God the Father*—when the Son becomes subject to the Father, "so that God may be all and in all" (*De Princ.*, 1.2.10).

Continuing the theme of divine power, Origen ensures that this power is pure and clear, demonstrating the Wisdom displayed in this act of power. The power displayed in Wisdom is contrary to the power and wisdom of created things. Origen intends to emphasize further that the power of God in subjugating creation is righteous and pure. It is evident that he is striving to eliminate any suggestion of tyrannical rulership in Christ's lordship. To buttress his point, Origen speaks of the Son of God, using language and concepts of immutability and divine simplicity, as "unalterable and unchangeable, and every good quality is in him essentially, such that it can never be changed or altered."[61] Concluding his exploration of Christ, Origen reiterates the notion of the divine economy, writing, "the primal goodness is recognized in the God and Father from whom both the Son, being begotten, and the Holy Spirit, proceeding, without a doubt draw into themselves the nature of that goodness, which exists in the source, from whom the Son is born and the Spirit proceeds" (*De Princ.*, 1.2.13).

Impassibility

Origen's interpretation of Numbers 23:19 in the Greek LXX meant that God is impassible. However, Origen's claim that God both rejoices and grieves seems to mark a boundary within his philosophical-theological framework. Language about God having emotions must be reserved for instructing simple believers. *Anthropomorphism* functions as a means of ascribing human qualities or traits to God so that God can relate to mankind. Origen saw this language as instructional, not truly stating something real. But, to some, this language seems to have theological

---

[61] In his treatment of the Holy Spirit, as manifested in God's providential powers, we see another nascent notion of divine simplicity when Origen writes that these unique providential powers "are in God, more, which *are* God." *De Princ.*, 1.4.3. (Emphasis added). In his treatise against Celsus, Origen remarks, "Whereas the doctrine of the Jews and Christians, which preserves the immutability and unalterableness of the divine nature, is stigmatized as impious, because it does not partake of the profanity of those whose notions of God are marked by impiety, but because it says in the supplication addressed to the Divinity, 'Thou art the same,' it being, moreover, an article of faith that God has said, 'I change not.'" *Cont. Cels.*, 1.21.

significance.[62] Origen, following Ignatius, spoke of the suffering Christ. Tatian[63] and Clement called Christ "the God who suffered."[64] However, they were speaking of the paradox of the incarnation, the divine-human person of Christ, not the nature of God as God.

In his commentary on Matthew, Origen speaks of this paradox as a distinguishing mark of deity manifested in Christ when he writes, "As a lover of men He who was impassible suffered the emotion of pity, and not only had pity but healed their sick, who had sicknesses diverse and of every kind arising from their wickedness" (*Comm. Matt.* 10.23.). His comment seems to imply that impassibility is an intrinsic aspect of God, who, astonishingly in the person of Jesus, can "suffer the emotion of pity." But later in life, Origen, apparently having changed his mind on impassibility, expresses in a homily on Ezekiel but referring to Deuteronomy 1:31 that God endures our ways "just as the Son of God bears our emotions. The Father himself is not impassible."[65] Important to consider is the understanding of *emotions* in an ancient context compared to our modern notions of the word. *Emotion* is a modern term that has been anachronistically forced into the ancient context, causing much confusion in modern theology's reception and interpretation of the early church writers.

Origen and others semantically extended our knowledge of God through the revelation of God in Christ, way beyond the negative concepts provided in philosophical theology. Philosophical theology offers the contours of the transcendence of God. Still, it lacks precision as a framework for revelation in that God's self-revelation of himself in Christ provides a knowledge of God not solely located *via negativa*.[66]

---

[62] Grant, *The Early Christian Doctrine of God*, 28–31.

[63] Originally from Assyria (upper Mesopotamia), Tatian (died c. 180) acquired extensive Greek learning. He became a Christian in Rome following a long period of travel. For several years, Tatian was an adherent of Justin and his teaching. But after Justin's death, he retreated into the Encratite sect and lived mostly thereafter in the empire's far eastern provinces. The Encratite doctrines were heavily Gnostic in character. The sect believed that matter is evil and maintained varied ascetic practices, including prohibition of marriage. Comfort, Douglas, and Mitchell, *Who's Who*.

[64] *Orat.* 13; *Protr.* 106, 4; *Paed.* 2, 38, 1.

[65] *Ezech. Hom.* 6.6 quoted from Grant, *The Early Christian Doctrine of God*, 30.

[66] A philosophical approach to theology that asserts that no finite concepts or attributes can adequately describe God, but only negative terms—origin Latin, literally 'negative path.'

God must have some positive, thus, personal concern for mankind. However, to speak of passions in God was to make God sub-human, so affirming that God has passions seemed only to denigrate him.[67]

While the relationship between philosophy and theology has proved difficult, the early church fathers began with the Christian Faith and utilized the philosophical framework and language of their era, leading to profound insights. The only form of philosophy they outright rejected was Epicureanism because it was materialistic. To quote Robert M. Grant in full (and conclude our discussion of Origen):

> In relation to the doctrine of God, then, what the early Christian theologians show us is that by continuing along some of the lines marked out in the New Testament and by making more explicit use of philosophical ideas they tried to work out some of the implications of the basic self-revelation of God—in terms adequate for their own times. They began with faith (which they interpreted philosophically too) and used philosophy as a language of interpretation. Because they continued to recognize that God could not be contained in the philosophical terminology, they remained open to fresh insights and new ways of explanation.[68]

Novatian

Novation (c. 210–280) was a highly educated priest, theologian, and writer who led the Roman clergy during the vacancy between popes Fabian and Cornelius in 250–51. In *On the Trinity*, Novatian's theology advances beyond Tertullian's earlier thought in maintaining the eternal Sonship of Christ (*cf.* Christology). Novatian clearly explains biblical anthropomorphisms in terms of God's accommodation of human language. He uses the doctrine of Trinitarian circumincession and anticipates what later theology came to call the 'hypostatic union' of the two natures of Christ in one person and the 'communication of idioms' between the natures.[69]

As noted, Novatian's work on the Trinity was a further advancement than others before him (esp., Tertullian). Not much is stated as to why he wrote the treatise; however, it seems that he aimed to

---

[67] Grant, *The Early Christian Doctrine of God*, 31–2.
[68] Grant, *The Early Christian Doctrine of God*, 33–4.
[69] D.F. Kelly, "Novatian," in Sinclair B. Ferguson and J.I. Packer, *New Dictionary of Theology*, (Downers Grove, IL: InterVarsity Press, 2000), 472.

articulate the Trinity following the *rule of faith*—the Creed. He provides a crucial section where delves into anthropomorphic language. This is vital because theology can go astray when a theologian loses his grounding and allows figurative and idiomatic language to shape his interpretive decisions about God. Scripture is an accommodation of God to man, whereby he communicates to mankind in language based upon what man sees in creation (Ro 1:19–20). To be consistent in how we speak about God regarding his essence and acts, we must not take figurative language about God, particularly about God having hands, arms, feet, eyes, ears, face, etc., literally. To do so would be to express a view that contradicts what the Bible teaches about God's nature and essence, which is beyond comprehension.

Novatian divides his treatise into thirty-one chapters. We are not going to cover all of them. We are more concerned with chapters two through nine, where he devotes his attention to the essence and attributes of God as triune. In chapter two, he begins with God as above all things, containing all things, immense, eternal, transcending man's mind, inexplicable in all discourse, and loftier than all sublimity. Theology should start with God—always. Novatian discusses God's unboundedness in time and space, writing:

> For we read that He contains all things, and therefore that there could have been nothing beyond Himself. Because, since He has not any beginning, so consequently He is not conscious of an ending; unless perchance—and far from us be the thought—He at some time began to be, and is not above all things, but as He began to be after something else, He would be beneath that which was before Himself, and would so be found to be of less power, in that He is designated as subsequent even in time itself. For this reason, therefore, He is always unbounded, because nothing is greater than He; always eternal, because nothing is more ancient than He. (*The Trinity*, 2)

God is always "unbounded," "has no time," "does not come to an end," and is "debtor to no one" (*The Trinity*, 2). Novatian considers God's majesty, which man's mind cannot conceive, lacking the eloquence to approach and speak of it. God cannot be declared because to declare him (*as he is*) would be to contain him. Novatian sees that all human discourse about God encompasses and contains him; thus, whatever is thought and spoken about God is less than He. He writes, "We can in some degree be conscious of Him in silence, but we cannot in discourse unfold Him as He is." Novatian stresses the unbounded glory of God because God is uncreated being. We cannot even fathom what uncreated, omnipresent, omnipotent, omniscient, eternal, and necessary being is. And when we acknowledge that before we embark on theological discourse, we situate ourselves in the proper place to engage in discourse. We begin our talk about God by recognizing we cannot truly talk about God. So then, when we talk about God, *what* are we speaking about? After all, Scripture is God's Word to us about himself, so we must be able to use his words to express something about him.

Novatian reminds us that the words given to us allow us to comprehend something about the essence of God as revealed, not as he is. He writes, "For should you call Him *Light*, you would be speaking of His creature rather than of Himself—you would not declare Him; or should you call Him *Strength*, you would rather be speaking of and bringing out His power than speaking of Himself; or should you call Him *Majesty*, you would rather be describing His honor than Himself" (*The Trinity*, 2). But he then asks how we can say or think about what is greater than all words and thoughts. How can we grasp God? Interestingly, *one grasps God when one grasps that one cannot grasp him*. Novatian concludes, "For He is above all that can be said. For He is a certain Mind generating and filling all things, which, without any beginning or end of time, controls, by the highest and most perfect reason, the naturally linked causes of things, so as to result in benefit to all" (*The Trinity*, 2).

In chapter 3, Novatian describes how a creature can *learn* and *know* God. If God is, as Novatian writes, "above all that can be said," then what can we say about him? Novatian answers:

> And since by the gaze of our eyes, we cannot see Him, we rightly learn of Him from the greatness, and the power, and the majesty of His works. "For the invisible things of Him," says the Apostle Paul, "from the creation of the world, are clearly seen, being understood by those things which are made, even His eternal power and Godhead;" so that the human mind, learning hidden things from those that are manifest, from the greatness of the works which it should behold, might with the eyes of the mind consider the greatness of the Architect. (*The Trinity*, 3)

He cites Paul's words in Romans 1:19–20. God has revealed himself through creation, so by what we *see* with our eyes—his glorious works, we can understand (*know*) who God is—his eternal power and divine nature. But does that mean mankind can know God through purely natural theology or general revelation? Novatian does not clarify. Now, mankind has rejected the truth about God, which Paul says was plainly revealed (Ro 1:19–20). God's evidence of his existence, eternal nature, and divine power are clearly known, but man has rejected it. In that sense, mankind *naturally* knows enough about God to the point that its rejection of him is a willful rejection of the truth about God; therefore, all of mankind is under condemnation. But, with that said, we have yet to see if Novatian delineates the general knowledge of God and the unique knowledge of God through Christ.

In chapter 4, Novatian discusses God apophatically; he explains what God is not, thus leading us to speak of God's perfections. God is *immutable*, which means he is always good and the same; he is *infinite*, having no beginning or end; he is incorruptible and immortal. These negative ascriptions of God, saying what God is not, tell us much about him. Novatian, regarding God's immutability, writes,

> Thus there is never in Him any accession or increase of any part or honor, lest anything should appear to have ever been wanting to His perfection, nor is any loss sustained in Him, lest a degree of mortality should appear to have been suffered by Him. But what He is, He always is; and who He is, He is always Himself; and what character He has, He always has. (*The Trinity*, 4)

Novatian explicitly discusses God's immutability, and he grounds this perfection in God himself. In doing so, we get a hint of the doctrine of divine simplicity (more to come in chapter 5). Novatian writes, "For whatever it be in Him which constitutes Divinity, must necessarily exist always, maintaining itself by its own powers, so that He should always be God. And thus, He says, "I am that I am" (Ex 3:14). God can only be God by what God is in himself. All that is in God is God. Nothing can be God except God—completely. He cannot *have* an attribute or quality; otherwise, it would be something ('parts') he acquired from another source. Novatian continues this theme of negative ascriptions of God, demonstrating their necessary existence in God if he is to be perfect and beyond all comprehension.

In chapter 5, Novatian argues that we cannot ascribe any human vices to God though Scripture uses them (i.e., anger, indignation, and hatred) of him. And this is what we call *anthropomorphic* language or human-like language. We can only understand anger and wrath from a creaturely perspective, which can corrupt man. But God cannot be corrupted. Novatian refers to them as "passions," which "are rightly said to be in men , . . but not rightly . . . in God" (*The Trinity*, 5). And how is man corruptible by these, but God is not? Novatian writes, "These things, forsooth, have their force which they may exercise, but only where a material capable of impression precedes them, not where a substance that cannot be impressed precedes them. For that, God is angry, arises from no vice in Him." Novatian is saying that such vices corrupt man because man can be impressed or acted on because he is material; thus, passions are proper to what can be impressed or acted upon. God cannot be impressed by passions because they do not properly belong to his Divine Substance, and God cannot be acted upon by anything other than God's perfect, holy self, which is impassible. When God is said to be angry or have hatred, such notions in God do not arise out of vice as they do in man; instead, Novatian writes,

> He is [angry] for our advantage for He is merciful even then when He threatens, because by these threats men are recalled to rectitude. For fear is necessary for those who want the motive to a virtuous life, that they who have forsaken reason may at least be moved by terror. And thus all those, either angers of God or hatreds, or whatever they are of this kind, being displayed for our medicine,—as the case teaches,— have arisen of wisdom, not from vice, nor do they originate from frailty; wherefore also they cannot avail for the corruption of God. (*The Trinity*, 5)

Scripture uses words that help us understand in some sense what God thinks about sin and wickedness; however, God's display of anger and hatred at humanity, resulting in various acts of judgment and curses, as Novatian stated, flow from wisdom and holiness. Because God cannot be "impressed" as creatures can, which is proper for finite, fallen sinners, God responds through God's perfections, which are always derived from himself. So, since God is holy, he only acts in holiness, and nothing can "impress" upon him that will corrupt him in a manner that does not act in accordance with his perfect holiness.

In the conclusion of chapter 5, Novatian provides a further explication of divine simplicity, which serves as the foundation for God's perfections and also demonstrates why man is imperfect and corruptible. Basically stated, man can be corrupted because he has body parts; God is not constructed or associated with bodily parts. Now, this does not imply that body parts are evil or wicked in themselves, as God's creation. Novatian writes:

> He is simple and without any corporeal commixture, being wholly of that essence, which, whatever it be,—He alone knows,—constitutes His being, since He is called Spirit. And thus those things which in men are faulty and corrupting, since they arise from the corruptibility of the body, and matter itself, in God cannot exert the force of corruptibility, since, as we have said, they have come, not of vice, but of reason. (*The Trinity*, 5)

Many in contemporary theology hold to some version of divine simplicity by merely affirming that God does not have body parts. But simplicity is more than confirming that God does not have body parts; it affirms his divinity. His simplicity is the constitution of his divinity, just as compositeness is the human constitution. We see the logic in Novatian's thought, understanding that God's being is Spirit. Does a Spirit have parts? As a spiritual being or referred to as an intellectual being or a being of reason, he must be simple—not composite—if he is to be omnipresent, omniscient, omnipotent, and all the other appellations of deity ascribed to him. Just think, can God be everywhere present all at once if he has a body? Thus, he must be simple, i.e., not composed of parts that make up what he is. To be everywhere, God must be a simple being.

Toward the end of his treatise, Novatian considers some objections to the hypostatic union, precisely the argument that if Scripture tells us that Christ died, then it must be accepted that Scripture is likewise telling us that God died. Novatian responds, expressing that the Scripture is clear on the matter, but his objectors do not understand what they are reading. Therefore, Novatian, demonstrating the folly of their ways, shows the absurdity of accepting what Scripture does not say, namely that Christ is not *only* God; rather, he is man *and* God.

He writes, "If Scripture were to set forth that Christ is God only, with no association of human weakness mingled with his nature," . . . then their arguments might work (*The Trinity*, 25). If Christ is pure deity or deity only, and the Scripture tells us Christ died, then we could conclude that God died. But that is impossible, writes Novatian, because Scripture tells us that our Lord is man *and* God. You can see up to this point the consistency in his argumentation without even really making an argument; instead, he is just taking all of Scripture into consideration—the *rule of faith*—ensuring a balanced approach as it pertains to passages that speak to the humanity and deity of Christ.

Novatian now explains what is proper to both natures. Beginning with the deity, he writes, "Who cannot understand that the divinity is impassible, although the human weakness is liable to suffering?" He makes the critical distinction between the divine and human nature— impassibility. God cannot suffer; man does suffer. Again, Novatian repeats the point that should be so easily understood: that the Word took on flesh, manifesting himself in the person of Jesus Christ, and that when he died, it was not that God died but that which died in him was man. To support his argument, he goes to Jesus' words in Matthew 10:28, where he talks about having no fear in man, who can only kill the body, whereas God destroys both body and soul. So, he says in the same manner Jesus' flesh died on the cross, not his soul.

I appreciate Novatian's direct reference to Scripture instead of engaging in metaphysical speculation. He argues that his objectors have made fallacious errors by overlooking what Scripture teaches about Christ being fully man. Novatian's response emphasizes the importance of balancing interpretations of Scripture. Giving too much weight to texts about Christ's deity or humanity can lead to heresy, so precision is crucial.

In chapter 29, Novatian offers a systematic exposition of the person and work of the Spirit, in which we see his hiddenness. Yet, he is observed everywhere, present and active, in that he is weaved in throughout Scripture, manifesting himself in the divine economy. The Spirit writes Novatian,

> is not new in the Gospel, nor yet even newly given. . . . He is therefore one and the same Spirit who was in the prophets and apostles, except that in the former He was occasional, in the latter always. But in the

former not as being always in them, in the latter as abiding always in them; and in the former distributed with reserve, in the latter all poured out; in the former given sparingly, in the latter liberally bestowed; not yet manifested before the Lord's resurrection, but conferred after the resurrection. (*The Trinity*, 29)

He is the Spirit of truth, sent to declare all things to the disciples, strengthening their hearts and minds, and has given gifts to the children of God. Novatian writes that the Spirit . . .

> placed prophets in the Church, instructs teachers, directs tongues, gives powers and healings, does wonderful works, offers discrimination of spirits, affords powers of government, suggests counsels, and orders and arranges whatever other gifts there are of *charismata*; and thus make the Lord's Church everywhere, and in all, perfected and completed. (*The Trinity*, 29)

Since the eternal Spirit dwells in Christ, the Spirit's outpouring onto the church is how we can say the fullness of Christ has been displayed and manifested in the church. The Spirit is "working in us for eternity," training our bodies to "advance in immortality" by restraining "insatiable desires, controls immoderate lusts, quenches unlawful fires, conquers reckless impulses, repels drunkenness, checks avarice, drives away luxurious revelings, links love, binds together affections, keeps down sects, orders the rule of truth, overcomes heretics, turns out the wicked, guards the Gospel" (*The Trinity*, 29).

Concluding our examination of Novatian's doctrine of the Trinity, we will focus on his final argument, which delves into the *ad intra* relations, specifically Jesus' begottenness from the Father in relation to origination in time. He begins with a doxological statement of God the Father, as the founder of all of creation, having no beginning because he is invisible, infinite, immortal, and eternal—the one God (*The Trinity*, 31). But when speaking of the Son of God, Novatian must explain how we understand Christ as begotten of the Father yet having no beginning as he is God of God, the exact image of the Father. While the Son is born of the Father, "he is always in the Father," unless there was a time when the Father was not the Father, having preceded the Son. But that is not the case.

Novatian, however, considers that in some sense, there is a beginning in the Son (not a temporal one), whereby the Father willed that the Son be, and the Son proceeded from the Father. His beginning is something that has always been in the Father, but as the Creator of all things, in that, the Son "is before all things, but after the Father, since all things were made by him, and he proceeded from him of whose will all things were made" (*The Trinity*, 31). The language used may seem unusual because, as Novations continues discussing the Son's begottenness from the Father and being before all things, he emphasizes that the Son does not have a beginning separate from the Father. The Son is fully God, sharing in the full blessedness of the Father. He addresses the objection that if the Son is born from the Father, this would imply a second person taking away from the Father the characteristic of being the one God. To show that the Son's begottenness does not entail the separation of being in God, as in two beginnings, two fathers, two invisibilities, and thus two Gods, Novatian writes,

> whatever He is, He is not of Himself, because He is not unborn; but He is of the Father, because He is begotten, whether as being the Word, whether as being the Power, or as being the Wisdom, or as being the Light, or as being the Son; and whatever of these He is, in that He is not from any other source, as we have already said before, than from the Father, owing His ORIGIN to His Father, He could not make a disagreement in the divinity by the number of two Gods, since He gathered His beginning by being born of Him who is one God. (*The Trinity*, 31, emphasis added)

Scripture clearly shows the full divinity of the Son with the Father. Abiding by what Scripture says about the Father and the Son (and the Spirit), we can know that they are both God of all and the one and only true God.

The demonstration of deity and unity in the Godhead, Novatian writes, comes through how the Father and the Son manifest what belongs to divinity (i.e., majesty and Lordship). Though not expressly referencing it, what follows is Novatian's exposition of First Corinthians 15:24–28. The divinity of God is declared by the Son, who Novatian says is also "an Angel," not in a creaturely constitution, but as the Messenger who has come "to announce the Great Counsel of God," thus declaring the Father's divinity. And in the revelation of his Son, the Father subjects all things to the Son, in which the Father gives and directs majesty and Lordship to his Son. And then this is reciprocated, whereby the Son demonstrates his unity of divinity with the Father, in that "the Son refers all that he has received to the Father, remitting again to the Father the whole authority of his divinity" (*The Trinity*, 31).

Novatian refers to this reciprocation of divinity as the Son's "communion of substance to the Father." However, he does not metaphysically tease out "communion of substance," as his use of "substance" seems to be a metaphysical statement. The demonstration of returning and reflecting majesty and divinity appeals to the unity of the Father and the Son "so that reasonably God the Father is God of all, and the source also of His Son Himself whom He begot as Lord. Moreover, the Son is God of all else, because God the Father put before all Him whom He begot" (*The Trinity*, 31).

Council of Nicaea
325

We have observed up to this junction a metaphysical grammar taking shape, which will become further refined in the later writers. It is important at this point to take note of the controversy in the formulation of a divine grammar. Clarity was lacking and imprecision led to tumultuous christological and Trinitarian debates, which came to a head in the Arian conflict. This had political implications as well, as peace and unity were fracturing, and Emperor Constantine saw himself as the protector of the church. He sent an edict dated May 23rd, 325 calling the whole church to a Council in Nicaea. It was the first of its kind. Every bishop from every part of the Roman Empire needed to be present. The Council met from May to the end of July 325.[1]

The Council of Nicaea (325 AD) was significant because it led to a remarkable unity and consensus among the church fathers, who concluded that non-biblical nomenclature was necessary to preserve biblical teaching.[2] Adoptionists denied that the Son is God of God; the Sabellians saw the Son as the same *person* (**HYPOSTASIS**) as the Father. The Arians believed Christ was a creature God made. Therefore, the church was forced to address these views and see if these assertions

---

[1] Hanson, *The Search for the Christian Doctrine of God*, 152.
[2] Hanson, *The Search for the Christian Doctrine of God*, 162.

correspond with scriptural truth.[3] Arianism was the crux of the debate. The Council declared the Son to be the Wisdom and Power of God in *ousia* and *hypostasis*, indicating he was a concrete being (aka., *enhypostasis*), having his subsistence in the person of Christ and "not an impersonal influence or attribute of God."[4]

The Apostles' Creed crystalized a scriptural formula in "sublime simplicity" and "liturgical solemnity" for the catholic Faith. However, unanswerable questions surfaced in the theological trenches, resulting in a massive search for the *Christian* doctrine of God, thus the need for an ecumenical council in 325. Nicaea produced a creedal statement employing the technical term *homoousios*[5] as definitive to the theological stance in the Nicene Creed. However, forging the term that all could agree upon was a virulent yet delicate matter. In philosophical and theological discourse, it was already a conditioned yet ambivalent term. Second-century Gnostics used it alongside notions of emanation to indicate "same ontological status" or of "similar kind." Others used the term to describe the act of semi-divine beings being made from pre-existing substances.[6] Obviously, a torrential debate ensued. But when the debating ended (though temporarily), the fathers reached a consensus on *ousias* language (also *gennētos*) deployed in the Creed. When reading the section of the Creed stating,

> And in one Lord Jesus Christ, the only Son of God, **begotten from the Father** before all ages, God from God, Light from Light, true **God from true God, begotten, not made;** of the same essence as the Father—

St. Athanasius' definition expresses the conciliar understanding:

> That the Son is not only like to the Father, but that, as his image, he is the same as the Father; that he is of the Father; and that the resemblance of the Son to the Father, and his immutability, are

---

[3] Leo D. Davis, *The First Seven Ecumenical Councils* (Liturgical Press, 1990), 71.

[4] Prestige, *God in Patristic Thought*, 201.

[5] This chapter will not dive into the deep waters of the historical details behind the term nor the arguments among the parties involved. I defer readers to Hanson, *The Search for the Christian Doctrine of God*; J. N. D. Kelly, *Early Christian Creeds*, 3rd ed. (A&C Black, 2006); Ayres, *Nicaea and Its Legacy*; Khaled Anatolios, *Retrieving Nicaea: The Development and Meaning of Trinitarian Doctrine* (Grand Rapids, MI: Baker Academic, 2011).

[6] Ayres, *Nicaea and Its Legacy*, 93.

different from ours: for in us they are something acquired and arise from our fulfilling the divine commands. Moreover, they wished to indicate by this that his generation is different from that of human nature; that the Son is not only like to the Father, but inseparable from the substance of the Father, that he and the Father are one and the same, as the Son himself said: "The Logos is always in the Father, and, the Father always in the Logos," as the sun and its splendor are inseparable.[7]

From this expression, the Council declared 1) the Son is *out of* the Father's *ousia (ek tes ousias tou Patros)*. 2) The Son is *of the same essence* (**CONSUBSTANTIAL**) *homoousios* with the Father. 3) And as the same essence as the Father—*ousia* or *hypostasis*, the Son is *begotten, not made*.[8] The Son comes from the Father as light comes from light. Through this term, the Council was, in effect, announcing judgment—*anathema* to those who affirmed otherwise, most notably the Arians.[9] However, as Gerald Bray notes, embarrassingly, "By 381, it was no longer possible to accept the Nicene anathema in the form in which it had originally been expressed, because more people were coming to realize that the Son was indeed a different *hypostasis* from the Father, but that they also shared the same *ousia*."[10]

These key statements are the conciliar expressions of orthodoxy enshrined in all creeds[11] and confessions to follow, setting apart scriptural truth from heresy. The Scriptures assert that the Word of God is God *of* God, being consubstantial (i.e., of the same substance) with the Father, though not a "part" of him. All christological and Trinitarian doctrine rests on this scriptural foundation. The church fathers' deployment of

---

[7] Athanasius, *De Decret. Syn. Nic.*, c. xix. et seq.

[8] Bray, *God Has Spoken*, 308, notes the terms *ousia* and *hypostasis* were still regarded as synonyms for the divine being, but later *hypostasis* was used to speak of the persons in the Trinity and *ousia* the oneness of the three.

[9] Frances M. Young and Andrew Teal, *From Nicaea to Chalcedon: A Guide to the Literature and Its Background*, 2nd ed., (Baker Academic, 2010), 43, notes the well-known historical fact of Constantine's intervention at the Council, leading a majority to condemn Arius and accept the Nicene Creed.

[10] Bray, *God Has Spoken*, 308.

[11] Ayers notes, The creed "was not used directly for catechetical purposes or in worship: the theology for which the creed was a cipher rather came to shape the interpretation and presentation of local baptismal creeds—at times by the insertion into existing creeds of phraseology from Nicaea." *Nicaea and Its Legacy*, 256.

homoousias and *hypostasis* set dogmatic formulation in motion. However, the Nicene Creed did not serve as a universal standard of faith; instead, it was the starting point of a terminological evolution (one could even say revolution), which continued until the century's end.[12] Another Council would need to be called to make the final decision about the technical meanings of *ousia* and *hypostasis*.

Nicene Creed

We believe in one God, the Father almighty, maker of heaven and earth, of all things visible and invisible.

And in one Lord Jesus Christ, the only Son of God, begotten from the Father before all ages, God from God, Light from Light, true God from true God, begotten, not made; of the same essence as the Father.

Through him all things were made. For us and for our salvation he came down from heaven; he became incarnate by the Holy Spirit and the virgin Mary and was made human. He was crucified for us under Pontius Pilate; he suffered and was buried. The third day he rose again, according to the Scriptures. He ascended to heaven and is seated at the right hand of the Father. He will come again with glory to judge the living and the dead. His kingdom will never end.

And we believe in the Holy Spirit, the Lord, the giver of life. He proceeds from the Father and the Son, and with the Father and the Son is worshiped and glorified. He spoke through the prophets. We believe in one holy catholic and apostolic church. We affirm one baptism for the forgiveness of sins. We look forward to the resurrection of the dead, and to life in the world to come. Amen.[13]

---

[12] Ayres, *Nicaea and Its Legacy*, 86.
[13] "Nicene Creed | Christian Reformed Church," accessed May 13, 2024, https://www. crcna.org/welcome/beliefs/creeds/nicene-creed.

3

THE NICENE ERA

In the Nicene Era, we are going to look at two key thinkers—Athanasius and Cyril of Jerusalem—heavily devoted to Nicene orthodoxy, as manifested in the Nicene Creed. The Creed was the first of its kind: *A biblical creed utilizing non-biblical terms to establish biblical doctrine.* The Nicene Creed marks the beginning of Christian dogma.

Athanasius

There is much to be said about Athanasius, Bishop of Alexandria (c. 295–373), and his contributions to the Christian Faith, most notably in his utter relentless wherewithal in defending the deity of Christ at the Council of Nicaea in 325. No one did more to ensure the triumph of Nicene orthodoxy during the Arian controversy. In his work, *On the Incarnation*, he demonstrates the necessity of the incarnation for redemption, tackles challenges from Jews and Gentiles, and offers a concise and compelling treatment of the Word's assumption of human flesh. Our exposition of Athanasius will be from his *Contra Gentes* (*Against the Heathen*).

In his *Contra Gentes*, Athanasius establishes Christian theism against the pantheistic philosophies of the heathens. Pantheism asserts that all creation is identical with God. The Christian God is distinct from his creation, and in Athanasius' defense, he argues in the same classical vein as those before him, beginning with apophatic statements of God's "invisible nature and incomprehensibility," who is "unmade," aseity and simplicity, and a few sections later, demonstrating his sovereign power as Creator, who gives being to all things, which he "made out of nothing" and sustains all things by his being and "gives movement to all" (C. Gent., 35, 38).

In chapter 28, Athanasius challenges the pagan notion that God is the cosmic organism. The reason is that it would entail parts in God. He argues that God "stands in need of nothing, but is self-sufficient and self-contained, and that in Him all things have their being" (C. Gent., 28). He aims to refute their error of creation worship, whereby the heathens worship a sun god and a moon god, among others. However, they combine all 'gods' together as one body, calling the whole as God. Athanasius shows the absurdity of such belief by contrasting the God of the Bible with their god of parts. He writes,

> For if the combination of the parts makes up the whole, and the whole is combined out of the parts, then the whole consists of the parts, and each of them is a portion of the whole. But this is very far removed from the conception of God. For God is a whole and not a number of parts, and does not consist of diverse elements, but is Himself the Maker of the system of the universe. For see what impiety they utter against the Deity when they say this. For if He consists of parts, certainly it will follow that He is unlike Himself, and made up of unlike parts. For if He is sun, He is not moon, and if He is moon, He is not earth, and if He is earth, He cannot be sea: and so on, taking the parts one by one, one may discover the absurdity of this theory of theirs. (C. Gent., 28)

His refutation is sound, especially when he says, "for if he consists of parts, certainly it will follow that he is unlike himself, and made up of unlike parts." Athanasius retains the uniqueness and simplicity of God (though not expressly calling it that) in that for God to be who he is in his essence, he must be who he is through himself, not by parts, because he would then be "unlike himself." God must be pure in himself as the "Maker" of all that exists. Athanasius began his argument by pointing out God's aseity.

At the end of chapter 28, he makes another claim as to why God cannot be made up of parts: because that which has parts (i.e., all material beings) "are destined to be divided again, in accordance with the natural tendency of the parts to separation" (C. *Gent.*, 28). So, Athanasius understands that having parts is proper for that which is created, not for that which is uncreated. Why is that? Because material beings are composite beings, having parts constitutes who/what they are. The parts make up what they are, which, Athanasius interestingly sees, will be divided again at some point (C. *Gent.*, 28). To have parts is to be a material being, and all material beings will be divided again.

In chapter 41, he expounds further on the notion of composition but directs his attention to the Word, who, having no composition, is fully present to creation as its Creator but also its sustainer. Using a play-on-words approach, he says as Christ is the *Word*, "he is not after the likeness of human words, composed of syllables." The Word is one syllable. Humans are "composed of parts and made out of nothing," being composite and divisible. It is interesting to notice the adjectival phrases in his statement, which seem to be opposed to each other: composed of parts *yet* made out of nothing. But that is easy to clear up. We must remember that to say God creates out of nothing means that God creates out of nothing *apart from himself* (Ro 11:36).

Athanasius makes another simple/composite contrast. He says, "God possesses true existence and is not composite, wherefore His Word also has true Existence and is not composite" (C. *Gent.*, 41). For Athanasius, non-compositeness is *true existence*. Only God and his Word have *true existence* because God has life in himself, *aseity*. He *is* being; creatures are given being or have their being imparted to them. Only God can have true existence because he *is* his existence. And that is what later formulations of simplicity arrive at (cf. Aquinas, *ST*, 1.3.3), in that God is a necessary, uncreated Being. Therefore, his existence is necessary. He cannot give himself existence or himself being, and he cannot be given essence and existence from some prior supreme being; therefore, the logic of simplicity entails that God is his own essence and is his own existence; his essence and existence are the same.[1] That is what *true existence* is. That which *has* being (essence) and *has* existence, i.e., creatures, are composite beings.

---

[1] Aquinas writes, "God is not only His own essence , . . but also His own existence." *ST*, 1.3.4.

Following his assertion of the non-compositeness (i.e., the simplicity) of the Word as "the one and only begotten God, who proceeds in his goodness from the Father as from a good fountain," Athanasius expresses the "truly wonderful" act by the Word in uniting himself to his creation (C. Gent., 41.1). God's eternal Word, Athanasius writes, has given "substantial existence to Creation," having its "being out of nothing." The creation is by nature weak and mortal, "subject to dissolution," but in "desiring all to exist, as objects of his loving-kindness," so that it does not fall out of existence, the Word "guides and settles the whole Creation." Athanasius makes the distinction between the Creator and the creature in that the creation coming into existence from nothing is, *by nature*, weak, mortal, and composite. He is making the contrast between that which *is* being and that which *has* being is intended to demonstrate the Word's astounding love for a creation, which is "at risk of dropping out of existence." The Word sustains Creation by way of participation. Athanasius writes, "for it partakes of the Word Who derives true existence from the Father." While Athanasius is insinuating that the Word is given his being, we must take note of the distinction he maintains in that the Word "derives true existence," whereas Creation has existence by participation. A few paragraphs ago, we defined what Athanasius meant by *true existence*, which is to have existence in itself and from itself as only God has, which the Word, though said to be from the Father, is "Himself also God." Athanasius grounds his understanding of the Word in Colossians 1:15–16, where the Word is the manifestation of the invisible God, the express image of the Divine nature.

In chapter 42, Athanasius expounds further the *function* of the Word in providence and conservation of his creation, which extends from the general to the particular,[2] in that "there is nothing that is and takes place but has been made and stands by Him and through Him" (C. Gent., 42.2). To explain what he means, Athanasius gives an analogy of a musician fine-tuning his lyre so that a perfect sound manifests when played, with all the notes in unison. He writes,

> so also the Wisdom of God, handling the Universe as a lyre, and adjusting things in the air to things on the earth, and things in the heaven to things in the air, and combining parts into wholes and

---

[2] He is referring to all that is in the oceans and their movement, and the dry ground and all the plant life that clothes it.

moving them all by His beck and will, produces well and fittingly, as the result, the unity of the universe and of its order, Himself remaining unmoved with the Father while He moves all things by His organising action, as seems good for each to His own Father. (*C. Gent.*, 42.3)

The Word is unmoved, as what is proper to Deity. Athanasius remarks about what is surprising to him about the Word, *the Godhead*. That is how the Word's act of providence and conservation is done "by one and the same act of will," moving all things simultaneously. In a "single nod," the Godhead moves everything according to each thing's purpose that he has given it. And this movement by the one who is unmoved produces "a marvelous and truly divine harmony" (*C. Gent.*, 42.4).

What does he mean by this one act of will that all things move? Athanasius offers a few illustrations to express what he means. To give one, which I think is most fitting to support his argument, he explains the nature of the soul, "in that at one time moves our several senses according to the proper function of each, so that when someone object is present all alike are put in motion, and the eye sees, the ear hears, the hand touches, the smell takes in odor, and the palate tastes,—and often the other parts of the body act too, as for instance if the feet walk" (*C. Gent.*, 43.2). Our soul moves every aspect of our body all at once, where our bodies—all the parts, minuscule and large—harmoniously function as one. And in like manner, Athanasius writes, "we must conceive of the whole of Creation, even though the example be inadequate, yet with an enlarged idea. For with the single impulse of a nod as it were of the Word of God, all things simultaneously fall into order, and each discharge their proper functions, and a single order is made up by them all together" (*C. Gent.*, 43.4).

However, as he notes, all illustrations fall short in that we cannot see all the inner workings, the interlocking nexus of the cosmos, the invisible things, and beings, where in some ineffable mystery, he moves all things and sustains all things through his providential care and governance. As omnipresent and omnipotent Spirit, his being is fully present to all creatures, "allotting to each their proper functions," where they move in one way according to the manner the Word moves. Athanasius concludes, saying that the Word demonstrates his Kingship in orchestrating the movement of Creation for "the glory and knowledge of his own Father, so that almost by the very works that he brings to pass he teaches us and says, 'By thy greatness and beauty of the creature proportionably the maker of them is seen'" (*C. Gent.*, 44.4).[3]

To buttress his theology of creation and providence, Athanasius looks to Genesis 1, where we see the divine fiat, the command of creation—Let there be! And he says that Scripture declares that the Word of the Lord created the heavens and the earth by the breath of his mouth" (Ps 33:6). He spoke, and they were made. But Athanasius asks, "To whom was God speaking?" (*C. Gent.*, 46.5).[4] Again, Athanasius holds that God created out of nothing, which does not mean God created material from non-material, but rather, "all things were made in Him and through him." So, then, if God is speaking, who is he speaking to, since nothing exists? Athanasius writes, "If He were commanding and addressing the things He was creating, the utterance would be redundant, for they were not yet in being, but were about to be made" (*C. Gent.*, 46.5). But he does not give a command; rather, God says, "Let us make man." From this, we understand that God is speaking about creation to His Word. With whom else can God speak? Who else can understand God's language but himself? Was not Wisdom with God before the foundations were laid? As we read in Proverbs 8:27, "I was there when he established the heavens, when he laid out the horizon on the surface of the ocean." How can God have wisdom if he were a monadic deity? And if God only had wisdom when he brought creation into existence, then God's wisdom is contingent on creation; it might be said that creation was then necessary to exist for God to show his wisdom.

But being present with God, Athanasius writes, "As His Wisdom and His Word, looking at the Father He fashioned the Universe, and organised it and gave it order; and, as He is the power of the Father, He gave all things strength to be, as the Saviour says: 'What things soever I see the Father doing, I also do in like manner'" (Jn 5:19). And His holy disciples teach that all things were made "through Him and unto Him;" (Col 1:16) (*C. Gent.*, 46.7). We see that Athanasius is following the tradition of those before him, whereby the reference to Christ as the Wisdom of God and the Power of God functions as axiomatic for

---

[3] His closing reference is to Wisdom 8:5.

[4] It is in the imperative mood.

attributing the full deity between the Father and the Son.[5] This sharing of the Divine essence is not by participation as the Word is united to his creation; but rather, Athanasius writes, "by being His very Wisdom, very Word, and very own Power of the Father, very Light, very Truth, very Righteousness, very Virtue, and in truth His express Image, and Brightness, and Resemblance. And to sum all up, He is the wholly perfect Fruit of the Father, and is alone the Son, and unchanging Image of the Father" (*C. Gent.*, 46.8).

In concluding his treatise, Athanasius, utilizing a divine grammar, has rigorously advanced a robust doctrine of God from Scripture and directs the *Gentiles* to the One who can restore their corrupt nature, the Lord Jesus Christ. They should be left to conclude that the Word, Wisdom, Power, and Creator are also their Savior. It is through him that the Father orders worship and praise, as Christ "holds together all things." It is in him where one finds "the prize of life everlasting." And it is also in him where many will find judgment and damnation and death everlasting (*C. Gent.*, 47.4).

Cyril of Jerusalem

Cyril (c. 310–386) was another key defender of Nicene orthodoxy in the Arian controversy. Some, however, label Cyril as an Arian because he avoids the phrase: "of the essence (*ousias*) of the Father" and "of one essence (*homoousion*) with the Father." But when reading his lectures, the overabundance of scriptural support for his understanding of the Triunity of God is refreshing and representative of Nicene orthodoxy. Passage-by-passage, Cyril shows the Divine essence of the Son with the Father, whereby he is the Creator, Sustainer, the Wisdom, the Power, and the fullness of God, but also the Son of David according to the flesh, born of woman.

We are going to work through what is titled "Lecture #11," where Cyril explains the Son of God as begotten of the Father from before all ages and by whom all things were made (*Hier., Cat. Lect.* 11, 64). First, Cyril addresses how Christ is the Son. The Son is the Son by nature, without beginning; he was not made a Son through adoption, being

---

[5] It is quite interesting that the fathers do not instinctually refer to the more obvious texts like John 1:1–3 and Romans 9:5 to substantiate the claim of Christ sharing the Divine essence of the Father.

brought from bondage into a higher state, but he is "eternally begotten by an inscrutable in incomprehensible generation" (*Hier., Cat. Lect.* 11, 65). He does not speculate on the generation, avoiding the use of the typical metaphysical language we often see. He stays close to the lines of Scripture to support his doctrine of the deity of Christ, the eternal Son of God. Beginning with Matthew 1:1, in which we see the genealogy of Christ according to the flesh, Cyril notes that Christ "is the son of David *at the end of the ages*, but the son of God *before all ages*, without beginning" (*Hier., Cat. Lect.* 11, 65). Cyril refers to the divine economy, which manifests God's Word and Spirit from eternity past into creation according to his plan of redemption. This teaching method about Christ is crucial for rectifying a mistaken perception of Jesus as only a human, whom God the Father adopted as his Son, thereby making him Lord and King. To show this distinction, Cyril navigates through various christological passages, making the proper designations that speak of Christ according to his human person and according to the Divine person. As mentioned, this mistake occurs when interpreters place excessive reliance on a specific set of passages, resulting in an unbalanced perspective of Christ. Here, Cyril is addressing those who give undue importance to the passages in Scripture that focus on the humanity of Christ.

Cyril works carefully through christological texts, explaining how Christ is both the Son of David and the Son of God, his humanity, and his divinity. But we must not divide the natures of Christ, seeing them separately. We must see the Son as the person—*hypostatization*—of Jesus Christ. It is the concrete person of Jesus Christ in the incarnation who is fully man and fully divine, so when Scripture shows him doing human acts, it is the person of Jesus acting properly to his humanity. When we see him doing divine acts, it is the person of Christ acting properly to his divinity. Balance and a proper understanding of the incarnation are paramount to formulating a coherent Christology and Trinitarian theology.

Cyril writes that Christ as the Son of David is "subject to time, and to handling, and to genealogical descent: but as Son, according to the Godhead, he is subject neither to time, nor to place, nor to genealogical descent" (*Hier., Cat. Lect.* 11, 65). Cyril references Isaiah 53:8, the most often cited passage by the church fathers, as a direct reference to the generation of the Son from the Father. In the CSB,[6] this passage says: "He was taken away because of oppression and judgment, and who considered his fate? For he was cut off from the land of the living; he was struck because of my people's rebellion." The KJV reflects the generation reading: "He was taken from prison and from judgment: *And who shall declare his generation?* For he was cut off out of the land of the living: For the transgression of my people was he stricken" (emphasis added). It is quite interesting that the early church fathers used this passage (not from the KJV) to speak of the generation of the Son from the Father. This reading is in Augustine, Athanasius, Chrysostom, Hippolytus, Alexander of Alexandria, and Leo the Great.

Citing Isaiah 53:8, together with John 4:24, which says "God is Spirit," Cyril says that "He who is a Spirit has spiritually begotten, as being incorporeal, an inscrutable and incomprehensible generation" (*Hier., Cat. Lect.* 11, 65). A classic passage that often leads to confusion, causing many to mistakenly believe that God the Father adopts Jesus, is the New Testament use of Psalm 2:7 in Jesus' baptism. It reads, "The Lord said unto me you are my Son, today I have begotten you." Cyril explains that the words "You are my Son" refer to the eternal generation of the Son, whereas when it says "Today . . ." refers to Christ's birth in time as the Messiah. Jesus is the Son of God by nature, not by adoption, which is what begotten of the Father means. We beget humans; therefore, by nature, what we beget is human. God, who is Divine essence by nature, in begetting the Son, the Son's nature, likewise, is the Divine essence (*Hier., Cat. Lect.* 11, 66). Cyril continues making scriptural arguments, showing that the Son is God the Father's eternally begotten Son. Cyril does not want to elaborate further than what Scripture teaches. He understands that the subject is quite heavy to discern. He writes:

> But not even the Holy Ghost himself has spoken in the Scriptures concerning the generation of the Son from the Father. Why then do you busy yourself about things which not even the Holy Ghost has written in the Scriptures? Why do you, who know not the things which are written, busy yourself about the things which are not written? There are many questions in the Divine Scriptures; what is

[6] *Christian Standard Bible*, 2020 Text Edition. (Nashville, TN: Holman Bible Publishers, 2017).

written we comprehend not, why do we busy ourselves about what is not written? It is sufficient for us to know that God has begotten One Only Son. (*Hier., Cat. Lect.* 11, 67)

We will end with this set of Scripture proofs that Cyril gives to support his point. These proof texts concisely and sufficiently demonstrate that Christ is the only begotten of the Father. He writes, "For *as the Father has life in himself, so also he has given to the Son life in himself* [Jn 5:26]; and *that all men should honor the Son, even as they honor the Father* [Jn 5:23]; and *just as the Father raises the dead and gives life to them, so the Son also gives life to whom he wants* [Jn 5:21]." The Son is *Very God*, in that the Father is in him (Jn 14:11). In these three passages, John demonstrates the Son's divine nature as being that of the Father by attributing the same divine activity (*energeia*) to him that the Father has, along with the command to honor him just as we honor the Father.

COUNCIL OF CONSTANTINOPLE
381

It was clear that while Nicaea gave metaphysical shape to scriptural statements about God and Christ, confusion loomed as *hypostasis* and *ousia* carried synonymous connotations. Athanasius, a stalwart in the advancement of divine grammar, *still* did not have a word to express the subsistence as persons of Father and Son.[1] The lack of clarity led to instability and factions, with the Arian bishops gaining the upper hand ecclesiastically and politically.

A new emperor, Constantias, took the throne and lent more support to Semi-Arian positions, which saw the Son as *like* the Father. Athanasius continued to produce tracts and treatises defending the Nicene position, but the opposition dominated. Creedal statements surfaced that ignored Nicaea. Goths, Germans, and the Greek East swung Arian. The sudden, abrupt turn from Nicene theology, the exile of key figures from the Council of Nicaea, and surrounding countries becoming Arian was as if "The whole world groaned and was astonished to find itself Arian."[2]

The Trinitarian controversies continued. *Homoousios* was still a muddied term, lending support to various parties in the church to

---

[1] Davis, *The First Seven*, 91.

[2] Jerome, *Dialogus adversus Luciferianos*, 19, cited in Edward Rochie Hardy, *Christology of the Later Fathers* (Westminster John Knox Press, 1954), 22.

explain it. The three stand-out groups were the *Homoeousians*, who believed the Son's *ousia* was *like* the Father's, but not identical to it. The *Homoeans*, who believed the Son acted like the Father but was of a different *ousia*. And the Nicene *Homoousians*, who rejected the *homoean* view because it demoted the Son to a lesser being, and thought it better to use the terms *hypostasis* and *ousia* to indicate the distinction between the Son and the Father, rather than using the terms synonymously.[3]

A new generation of thinkers emerged: the Cappadocians. Exiled Nicaean bishops united with the Cappadocians to attack the Arians full-out, asserting the full divinity of the Son and the Spirit with the Father. In the Cappadocians, we see terminological changes in the utilization of *hypostasis* and *ousia*. *Ousia* is used to speak of the essence of the Godhead, and *hypostasis* is used to indicate the subsistences of the Father, Son, and Spirit.[4] So, we see Trinitarian expressions articulated as "One *ousia* and three *hypostaseis*."

However, the term *hypostasis*, while corresponding etymologically, did *not* correspond in meaning to the Latin substance (*substantia*). With that said, more precision was necessary, in that one could say three *substances* in one *essence*, which contrasts universal-universal instead of particular-universal. Not only did the term have correspondence challenges, but it also had conceptual issues. The divine grammar needed a term to indicate *real* distinctions in the Godhead, denoting the divine reality, not just a creaturely perception of it.[5] Lacking this distinction makes way for **MODALISM**, in that *hypostasis* carries temporal connotations, whereas *ousia* denotes an eternal conception: God is eternally one essence, "but in time and space he could be revealed to us as one *hypostasis* or another."[6] While this was a problem needing further refinement, the good news is Nicene theology became the dominant force heading into the Council of Constantinople in 381. The coequality of the Trinity was recognized as the creed of the empire.[7] Arianism was brought to its end.

---

[3] Bray, *God Has Spoken*, 308–9.
[4] Hardy, *Christology of the Later Fathers*, 23.
[5] Bray, *God Has Spoken*, 317.
[6] Bray, *God Has Spoken*, 318.
[7] Hardy, *Christology of the Later Fathers*, 24.

4

The Post–Nicene Era

A s we move further into the fourth century, a distinct *pro-Nicene* theology emerges.[1] Lewis Ayres identifies three central principles establishing its framework:

1) a clear version of the person and nature distinction, entailing the principle that whatever is predicated of the divine nature is predicated of the three persons equally and understood to be one (this distinction may or may not be articulated via consistent technical terminology);

2) clear expression that the eternal generation of the Son occurs within the unitary and incomprehensible divine being;

3) clear expression of the doctrine that the persons work inseparably.[2]

The divine grammar developed in the preceding eras reached a level of maturity in the fourth century as the philosophical language—*ousia, physis, natura,* and *essentia* (though not limited to only those terms)—becomes normative in elucidating the language of Scripture.[3] With that said, the fathers understood scriptural imagery of light, power, and glory has having material realities in exegesis.

---

[1] Ayres, *Nicaea and its Legacy*, 236.
[2] Ayres, *Nicaea and its Legacy*, 236.
[3] Ayres, *Nicaea and its Legacy*, 278.

Divine simplicity functions as the fundamental *paradoxical* reality between the transcendence of God in distinction from the created order and "the central point of reference for all analogical practice in Trinitarian terminology."[4] The consequences of divine simplicity entail that the operations of the divine persons are inseparable.[5]

Another key principle in the deployment of a divine grammar is the development of a process of analogy, which functions as a correspondence literary tool, forming a bridge *from the created realm* to the uncreated realm. This bridge enables theologizing of incomprehensible concepts into a pedagogical, creaturely vocabulary, helping the imagination ascend to the heavenly realities through grasping it by our physical senses.

This era is remarkable, advancing and refining Nicene orthodoxy in establishing the Trinitarian and christological foundations for the historic Christian tradition to come. In the last few centuries, modern theology poured a new foundation, which eroded quickly, as it was unable to uphold the cardinal doctrines of the Christian faith—established 1600 years ago on the pillars of a pro-Nicene theology.

Gregory of Nyssa

Gregory (330–c. 395), who became the bishop of Nyssa in 371, was a prominent figure in the Christian faith. He was part of the Cappadocian trio, which played a key role in shaping Trinitarian orthodoxy. Gregory's theological expertise was crucial in combating the Arian and Sabellian heresies. In Gregory's writings, we find "an emergence of a pro-Nicene 'grammar' of divinity through his developed account of divine power."[6] We will be surveying a handful of his treatises and letters, observing the rigors of his theology and precision in his argumentation. A monarchial view of the Trinity will be traced out as this is the *key* to a logically sound Trinity, from which many in contemporary theism have drifted.

His longest dogmatic treatise, *Against Eunomius*, is an erudite work. Gregory leaves no stone unturned as he dismantles Eunomius' claims

---

[4] Ayres, *Nicaea and its Legacy*, 286.

[5] Ayres, *Nicaea and its Legacy*, 279. Ayres writes, "The generation of the Son and the breathing of the Spirit occur *within* the bounds of divine simplicity" (281).

[6] Lewis Ayres, "On Not Three People: The Fundamental Themes of Gregory of Nyssa's Trinitarian Theology as Seen in 'To Ablabius: On Not Three Gods,'" *Modern Theology* 18, no. 4 (October 2002): 446.

and objections, responding to his "abuse of our father in God" (*Ep. ad Petrum 1*). I do not intend to trace out the barrage of counterattacks on Eunomius. One observation in this treatise is that Gregory goes to great lengths responding to Eunomius' misunderstanding of *Ungenerate* and *Generate*, i.e., the Father and the Son. This was another aspect of the embroiled battle of the Arian controversy.

In this treatise, we will dedicate minimal time to expounding Gregory's perspectives on the essence and attributes of God. Elements of exposition will be included as they relate to the subject matter to provide a general understanding of the argument. The central point of contention revolved around whether the Son shares the exact nature of God the Father, given his derivation from the Father. The Arians employed diverse tactics to argue that, although mighty and powerful, the Son did not possess the same essence as the Father. Gregory writes two responses to Eunomius, refuting his claim that because the Son is generated from the ungenerate Father, he is not eternal like the Father. Therefore, there was a time when the Son was not. Gregory goes to the mat with Eunomius. Eunomius is confusing terms and categories. *Ungenerate* and *generate* pertain to the relations between the Father and the Son. Eunomius argues that the Son being generated from the Father, who is ungenerate means that there was a time when the Son did not exist; thus, he was *generated* from the Father. He confuses relations with essence. But Gregory sees through his sophistry and refutes him. Below are some of Gregory's remarks explaining the divine economy. He writes:

> For there, with the Father, unoriginate, ungenerate, always Father, the idea of the Son as coming from Him yet side by side with Him is inseparably joined; and through the Son and yet with Him, before any vague and unsubstantial conception comes in between, the Holy Spirit is found at once in closest union; not subsequent in existence to the Son, as if the Son could be thought of as ever having been without the Spirit; but Himself also owning the same cause of His being, i.e. the God over all, as the Only-begotten Light, and having shone forth in that very Light, being divisible neither by duration nor by an alien nature from the Father or from the Only-begotten. There are no intervals in that pre-temporal world: and difference on the score of being there is none. It is not even possible, comparing the uncreate with the uncreated, to see differences; and the Holy Ghost is uncreate, as we have before shown (*Cont. Eun.* 1.26, 70).

When it comes to the essence of God, Gregory holds to the "True Faith" position, which says the essence of God is "incapable of being grasped by any term, or any idea, or any other device of our apprehension" (*Cont. Eun.* 1.42, 99). And while this designation is accepted by all as proper of the Father, orthodoxy holds that the only name given that fully represents that which is beyond the reach of human utterance is the name above all names (Ph 2:9) of the Only-begotten, Jesus Christ our Lord. The words of John the apostle tell us that all that the Father has is the Son's (Jn 3:35; 16:15). Therefore, the Son is God of God.

We find the substance of Gregory's doctrine of God in his *Answer to Eunomius' Second Book* (*Cont. Eun.* 13), which is much shorter than the first. And then we get into his shorter treatises, explicitly devoted to the Holy Spirit and the Holy Trinity. He also remarks on the errors of taking anthropomorphic language too far. A letter to his brother Peter, where Gregory analyzes the terms *ousia* and *hypostasis*, provides the clearest understanding and use of these terms in the Cappadocian's theology.[7] Lastly, and which I find to be his most substantial contribution to the classical doctrine of the Trinity, is his letter *to Ablabius: On 'Not Three Gods.'*

In this second book, Gregory continues his response to Eunomius regarding the generate/ungenerate debate. He begins with the foundational claim, which Eunomius agrees, that the "Godhead is by nature simple." It "is indivisible and without composition." As to disagreement, Gregory writes, our "orthodox confession teaches us to believe in the Only-begotten God so that all men should honor the Son even as they honor the Father, these men, reject the orthodox terms whereby the greatness of the Son is signified as on a par with the dignity of the Father" (*Cont. Eun.* 13, 252). Divine simplicity is a point of contention because, as Gregory argues, the Son is of the same essence as the Father; thus, he is simple and incomposite. Simplicity is the Divine essence. Elsewhere, Gregory notes, "God has a Logos."[8] And he would be without reason if he did not. However, Logos is not merely an attribute; instead, it has an "independent

---

[7] "Letter 35 *To Peter His Own Brother on the Divine Ousia and Hypostasis* (*Ad Petrum 1*)" in Anna M. Silvas, *Gregory of Nyssa: The Letters: Introduction, Translation and Commentary*, (Brill, 2006).

[8] Gregory employs the common approach of explaining the Logos by analogy, in that humans have a logos, the utterance of speech, which goes out from us but then fades away. The Logos, however, as God's speech is imperishable, always existing, and therefore is the simple subsistence of God (*Cat or., Prol.*, 475).

life, not a participated life, else it would lose its simplicity." Furthermore, the Logos has a will but must be equal to his power because "a mixture of choice and impotence would, again, destroy the simplicity" (*Cat or.*, *Prol.*, 471).

With precision, Gregory continues hammering the point that the Son's essence is simple, just as the Father's; though he is generated, his essence is not generated. Gregory stresses this point strongly because his opponents argue that ungenerate is the same as simple essence; therefore, if the Son is generate, then he could not have the simple essence as the Father. In showing the illogical nature of his opponents' claims, Gregory pins them into a corner, whereby they need to either accept the distinction denoted by the terms *ungenerate* and *generate* as proper to either person, not their nature, or they must side with Sabellius who is the father of modalism.

Later, Gregory engages in an interesting discussion about how the Father and the Son communicate (*Cont. Eun.* 13, 271), intending to show that the Son is ungenerate *as the Father*. I entertain this point to illustrate the high level of rigorous and detailed thinking found in many early church fathers. We speak and utter words which require air for us to speak. So, Gregory asks, what is the "medium" of how the words are exchanged between bodies? Gregory discusses "atmospheric space, differing in its nature from the nature of human bodies." It is fascinating to observe the depth of scientific understanding displayed by the church fathers. Whereas many moderns are guilty of chronological snobbery, thinking that humans did not have a developed scientific knowledge of the world. Gregory's point in asking this question is to look at God, who is immaterial, without a body. What medium is there between the Father and the Son to communicate? He says,

> for we hardly stopped to consider that God is not separable into apprehensive faculties, as we are, whose perceptions separately apprehend their corresponding objects; for example, sight apprehends what may be seen, hearing what may be heard, so that touch does not taste, and hearing has no perception of odors and flavors, but each confines itself to that function to which it was appointed by nature holding itself insensible, as it were, to those with which it has no natural correspondence and incapable of tasting the pleasure enjoyed by its neighbors sense. (*Cont. Eun.* 13, 271)

But with God, it is otherwise. God is "All in all." We have senses, which are used for specific things; we taste, see, and touch, which occur in a created world according to what is proper of creatures. God, Gregory says, is "at once sight, and hearing, and knowledge, and there we stop." For "it is not permitted us to ascribe the more animal perceptions to that refined nature." The point Gregory is getting at is that the Son communicates with the Father, before creation. If the Father and the Son communicate, what "medium exists and must need to exist in order for the Father and the Son to communicate?" The Son and the Father are before creation; voice and speech came to be *in* creation. The answer: there is no medium between the Father and the Son because there is no separation; there is no disconnection; the Father and the Son are inseparable, having a "union and blending of spiritual with spiritual through identity of will" (*Cont. Eun.* 13, 272).

Gregory addresses an objection from the creation account in Genesis. Is this not a case where the Father is speaking to his Son? Gregory notes that the Father and the Son are inseparable and have an identity of will. But in the creation account, the Father shares his will with the Son—by speaking. If they are of one will and share that identity because they are in union, why is the Father speaking to the Son in a manner that seems like he is communicating his will to him, and then he creates?

Gregory emphasizes the importance of maintaining a consistent metaphysical understanding between the created and the uncreated. He reminds us that the medium of Scripture has been given to us in our language and conception of the physical world to help us comprehend the things of God.[9] We believe that God creates by speaking. However,

---

[9] Regarding the place and importance of Scripture in constructing theology, Gregory writes, "we make the Holy Scriptures the rule and the measure of every tenet; we necessarily fix our eyes upon that, and approve that alone which may be made to harmonize with the intention of those writings" (*De an.*, On the Soul and the Resurrection, NPNF, 5:439). And in *Ad Eusth.* 3, On the Holy Trinity, 5:326–27, he writes: "They allege that while we confess three Persons we say that there is one goodness, and one power, and one Godhead. And in this assertion they do not go beyond the truth; for we do say so. But the ground of their complaint is that their custom does not admit this, and Scripture does not support it. What then is our reply? We do not think that it is right to make their prevailing custom the law and rule of sound doctrine. For if custom is to avail for proof of soundness, we too, surely, may advance our prevailing custom; and if they reject this, we are surely not bound to follow

we have no way of understanding the actual act of creating. Revelation 4:11 says that by the will of God, all things exist and were created. Moses records God's demonstration of the power of his will through the medium of human language so that we can comprehend God's act of bringing the world into existence in some manner. Gregory writes,

> The scriptural account of the Creation is the learner's introduction, as it were, to the knowledge of God, representing to our minds the power of the divine being by objects more ready to our comprehension (for sensible apprehension as an aide to intellectual knowledge), on this account, Moses, by saying that God commanded all things to be, signifies to us the inciting power of his will, and by adding, "and it was so," he shows that in the case of God there is no difference between will and performance (*Cont. Eun.* 13, 273).

By his will, he creates. He speaks everything into existence. Nothing is too hard for him. God, by his wisdom, has gifted us with speech to match the capacity of our natures. The Divine nature vastly differs from ours in that nothing is univocal (identical meaning) between us. At this point, Gregory is referring to anthropomorphic language in Scripture, which describes things about God in creaturely terms so that we get to know what God is *like* because we cannot truly understand what God *is*.

Importantly, especially in our modern context, Gregory is emphatically against a univocal reading of passages from Scripture that speak of God having eyes, fingers, feet, or "smells." To do so is to make God an "anthropomorphous deity, after the similitude of what we see among ourselves" (*Cont. Eun.* 13, 274). Rigid anthropomorphic language puts us dangerously close to bringing the Creator *as he is* down to the creature. God does come down to his creatures, but he does so by the Word. We cannot apply such figures of speech to the Divine essence until he manifests himself in human nature. Maintaining this distinction is paramount for upholding a consistent theology that retains a proper Creator-creature distinction.

Towards the end of his Answer to Eunomius, Gregory treats the subject of divine accommodation as it relates to that which is Uncreated and incomprehensible, being able to reveal and relate to creatures. Gregory's words, some of which are most often attributed to Calvin's

---

theirs. Let the inspired Scripture, then, be our umpire, and the vote of truth will surely be given to those whose dogmas are found to agree with the Divine words."

lips, show God's act of grace in accommodating himself to human language. Gregory writes,

> But since that which is by nature finite cannot rise above its prescribed limits, or lay hold of the superior nature of the Most High, on this account He, bringing His power, so full of love for humanity, down to the level of human weakness, so far as it was possible for us to receive it, bestowed on us this helpful gift of grace. For as by Divine dispensation the sun, tempering the intensity of his full beams with the intervening air, pours down light as well as heat on those who receive his rays, being himself unapproachable by reason of the weakness of our nature, so the Divine power, after the manner of the illustration I have used, though exalted far above our nature and inaccessible to all approach, like a tender mother who joins in the inarticulate utterances of her babe, gives to our human nature what it is capable of receiving. (*Cont. Eun.* 13, 292)

Interestingly, Gregory says that in God's act of accommodating himself to man, speaking in his language, he also assumes wrath, pity, and "such-like emotions." Modern theology attempts to describe God as having emotions in the same way that humans do. Classical theology understands that God, as Gregory indicates, accommodates *to* man's emotions "so that through feelings corresponding to our own infantile life might be led as by hand, and lay hold of the Divine nature by means of the words which His foresight has given" (*Cont. Eun.* 13, 292). What does Gregory mean by that? It is without question that God is not subject to any passions, such as pleasure, pity, or anger. But yet we see in Scripture, as Gregory points out, that the Lord takes *pleasure* in his servants; he is *angry* with those who fall away from the righteous path; he shows *mercy* to those who don't deserve mercy. So, what is God's purpose in expressing himself in a manner that is not proper of the Divine nature? Gregory writes, according to God's foresight, these words are for teaching us and helping our infirmity, through the display of his providence,

> by using our own idioms of speech so that such as are inclined to sin may be restrained from committing it by fear of punishment, and that those are overtaken by it may not despair of return by the way every repentance when they see God's mercy, while those who are walking uprightly and strictly may yet more adorn their life with virtue, as knowing that by their own life they rejoice in Him Whose eyes are over the righteous. (*Cont. Eun.* 13, 292)

Gregory maintains consistency in his understanding of the essence of God and that of man. Scripture is the medium of God's accommodation to mankind, so we can somehow know what is unknowable. In Christ, the Word of God makes himself known to man in a mysterious act. He enters his creation, taking on flesh, fully becoming man so that the Divine life can exist as man. This same life, "one and continuous in itself, infinite and eternal, in no wise bounded by any limit to its infinity," has chosen to do the impossible of bounding himself in human flesh. The Divine nature, "simple, uniform, and incomposite" (*Cont. Eun.* 13, 298), took on that which is complex, multi-formed, and composite. We must never rid ourselves of the mystery; instead, we must discern the mystery.

While there is extensive discussion about the Father and the Son, there seems to be relatively little mention of the Spirit. Gregory, however, has a short treatise in defending the deity, CONSUBSTANTIALITY, and coeternality of the Spirit, written against the followers of Macedonius. He was a Semi-Arian who believed that the Spirit was not a person of the Godhead but a divine energy diffused throughout the universe. They see the Spirit as inferior to the Father and the Son, having no share of honor and only having the power needed according to what God has assigned him (*Adv. Mac.* 2, 316). At the onset of his treatise, Gregory, following the form of the "True Faith," as articulated in the Nicene Creed,

> We, for instance, confess that the Holy Spirit is of the same rank as the Father and the Son, so that there is no difference between them in anything, to be thought or named, that devotion can ascribe to a Divine nature. We confess that, save His being contemplated as with peculiar attributes in regard of Person, the Holy Spirit is indeed from God, and of the Christ, according to Scripture, but that, while not to be confounded with the Father in being never originated, nor with the Son in being the Only-begotten, and while to be regarded separately in certain distinctive properties, He has in all else, as I have just said, an exact identity with them. (*Adv. Mac.* 2, 315–6)

Gregory's response to his opponents is amusing because there is no need to generate a new, profound argument to make his case. Instead, he says, "What then shall be our way of arguing?" We shall answer nothing new, nothing of our own invention . . . we shall fall back upon the testimony of Holy Scripture" (*Adv. Mac.* 2, 316). Scripture reveals the divine qualities of the Spirit, which means the Spirit, exactly as the Father and the Son, is also "simple, uniform, and incomposite," having all the perfections of the true Deity. As we often see in many of the fathers, Gregory supports his argument through an analogy from nature, using fire as an example. He writes,

> Fire naturally imparts the sense of heat to those who touch it, with all its component parts; one part of it does not have the heat more intense, the other less intense; but as long as it is fire at all, it exhibits an invariable oneness with itself in an absolutely complete sameness of activity; if in any part it gets cooled at all, in that part it can no longer be called fire; for, with the change of its heat-giving activity into the reverse, its name also is changed. (*Adv. Mac.* 2, 316)

Fire is fire, through and through, not having parts that can be more or less fire, for it is all fire. If it can be cooled, then it can no longer be called fire. Likewise, the Spirit has all the divine perfections, fully and completely. It would need to be changed if it could change to the reverse because it would no longer be Divine. Gregory's point is that Scripture reveals that the Spirit has all the qualities of the Father and the Son; therefore, he must be called Divine as the Father and the Son. If he had any quality that was not proper to the Divine essence, then he could not be worthy of glory and would not be the Spirit. Gregory observes the perfections of the Spirit as of the Father and the Son, as Scripture teaches: the Spirit is "absolutely good, and omnipotent, and wise, and glorious, and eternal. . . . He does not possess these attributes in measure only [as an emanation of God would have]. . . . The Holy Spirit is single and simple in every respect equally, . . is Himself Goodness, and Wisdom, and Power, and Sanctification, and Righteousness, and Everlasting, and Imperishability" (*Adv. Mac.* 2, 316–7).

After his treatise on the Spirit, we encounter a brief discussion on the Trinity, the Godhead, and the Spirit, in response to an opponent's claim (Eustathius) that the Trinity implies three Gods. Gregory clarifies: "We anathematize any man who says that there are three Gods and hold him to be not even a Christian" (*Ad Eusth.*, 326). Gregory briefly explains Eustathius' charge: "We divide the persons and do not employ any of the names which belong to God in the plural." The charge is that he speaks of the three persons but only one Godhead having power instead of speaking of three as having power, goodness, etc.. Scripture, says his opponents, does not support such a doctrine. Immediately replying to this charge, Gregory writes, "Let the inspired Scripture, then, be our umpire, and the vote of truth will surely be given to those whose dogmas are found to agree with the Divine words" (*Ad Eusth.*, 327). Gregory refers to Colossians 2:9 and Romans 1:20, demonstrating that the Scriptures confine us to one God, speaking of Christ having the fullness of deity and the creation indicative of his divine power and Godhead. To speak in plurals of power and deity is to fall into tritheism. His opponents see that the Father is God, and the Son is God, but render the Spirit as having power from the Father and the Son, separate from the Divine nature, thus the Divine glory.

In response, Gregory articulates the Trinity doctrine. The Father, Son, and Spirit are joined as one, with the Spirit included "with the Father and the Son in life-giving power." Having an inseparable association, the appellations of Good, Holy, Wise, Eternal, Righteous, Chief, and Mighty belong to all three. Gregory then grounds his claim with simplicity language, stating, "For all the Divine attributes, whether named or conceived, are of like rank one with another, in that they are not distinguishable in respect of the signification of their subject. . . . But the thing to which all the attributes point is one; and, if you speak of God, you signify the same Whom you understood by the other attributes" (*Ad Eusth.*, 327). From this understanding of the Divine essence, when we see its operations in Scripture, all three, for example, sanctify, give life, light, comfort, and all other graces. Gregory's approach is biblical; Scripture manifests God's identity in his creation and redemptive operations. And since the Scriptures testify that the Father, the Son, and the Spirit operate in a manner that is proper to God alone—and in one motion, in line with Divine Scripture, Gregory affirms that we must conclude that each is fully God, having the "undistinguishable character of their [divine] substance" (*Ad Eusth.*, 329).

On "Not Three Gods" to Ablabius

To Ablabius, though short, is a polemical address whereby Gregory lays out a complex argument in response to the claim that three Divine persons equal three gods. Ablabius (his opponent, to whom the letter is addressed) charges Gregory with teaching that there are "three Gods." It is an objection that many of us might have thought about or had to explain to others, even to the Jehovah's Witness who knocks on your door. Gregory's Trinitarian (Eastern) theology differs from the Western view, most notably in its *monarchial* form,[10] which was consistent with many of the early church fathers. The Eastern view posited that to affirm one God, there must be *one* God. And, as that one God—the Father, which Scripture and the early creeds of the church affirm, is the source from which the Son and the Spirit come.[11] We moderns see such language and think Gregory is drifting away from Trinitarian orthodoxy. However, that is not the case. The Son and the Spirit are of the same nature as the Father. According to Gregory, when the divine persons are referenced *together* in the NT, we see an order in the Godhead: the one God, the Father, and one Lord, Jesus Christ (e.g., 1Co 8:6). For Gregory, what classifies all three to be of the same nature is their power and activity as manifested in creation and Scripture. Gregory develops this argument in this letter to show that we believe in one God, not three Gods.

The crucial issue in the debate concerns the *grammar* of divinity. Lewis Ayres points out that "the fourth-century controversies are, in part, easily misunderstood if they are conceived as concentrating on the question 'is the Son (and the Spirit) divine?'"[12] It was understood that the Father was the *arche*, the Source, from which the Son and the Spirit come. The challenge was accepting that the Son was truly the exact nature of the Father. The Divine essence was understood to be simple

---

[10] This letter, however, is not the broadest treatment of Gregory's *monarchia* Trinitarian theology. Rather, it is an acute summary of his theology which undergirds his response to Ablabius. See his *Catechetical Orations 1–4*.

[11] With the intentions of advancing an ecclesial response against the Arian claim that Christ was a created being, a sixth-century church council in Toledo, Spain added the word *filioque* (*and the Son*) to a creed describing the procession of the Holy Spirit, thereby affirming that the Holy Spirit was sent by the Father *and the Son* (Jn 14:26; 15:26). The Eastern church objected to the addition because it was a speculative move beyond what Scripture teaches about the Spirit. While there were other factors, this controversy initiated the formal Schism of 1054 between the Roman Catholic and Eastern Orthodox churches. The debate pertains to the problem of affirming Jesus as the Source, equal to the Father, in sending the Spirit. Reason being, to be monotheists, there can only be one Source, who is the Father. If Jesus is the Source as the Father is, then we have two Gods. For an accessible summary of the *filioque* controversy, see Robert Letham, *The Holy Trinity: In Scripture, History, Theology, and Worship* (Phillipsburg, N.J: P&R Publishing, 2004), 201–20.

[12] Ayres, "On Not Three People," 449.

and inseparable. Therefore, to affirm "real" distinctions in the Divine essence, where the persons exist as individual *hypostases*, was problematic.[13] As noted, the grammar of divinity needs to be developed. Gregory's approach marks a broad shift in pro-Nicene theology in its discussion of the Son being *homoousias* with the Father, *sharing* the Divine essence, while both the Son and Spirit come from the Father and act in creation.[14]

On the surface, Ablabius' charge seems valid. How is our belief in a triune God consistent with monotheism? Gregory begins his letter by stating Ablabius' argument, which goes like this:

> Peter, James, and John, being in one human nature, are called three men: and there is no absurdity in describing those who are united in nature, if they are more than one, by the plural number of the name derived from their nature. If, then, in the above case, custom admits this, and no one forbids us to speak of those who are two as two, or those who are more than two as three, how is it that in the case of our statements of the mysteries of the Faith, though confessing the Three Persons, and acknowledging no difference of nature between them, we are in some sense at variance with our confession, when we say that the Godhead of the Father and of the Son and of the Holy Ghost is one, and yet forbid men to say "there are three Gods?"? (*Ad Abl.*, 331)

Gregory is very forthright about the difficulty of this issue. We have a language problem. We enumerate the Divine persons but do not admit the plurality, as we would Peter, James, and John. They have the same nature as humans, but we designate them as distinct beings from each other. Thus, we have three men, whereas, when it comes to persons of the Godhead, each having the divine nature, we *do not* have three Gods. Gregory delineates this further. When we speak of men, we say Luke is a man or Stephen is a man, but we do not say Stephen is Luke or Luke is Stephen. There is a separation of persons—beings, though having the shared nature of man, they are considered separate from each other. "Man" is not proper to Luke; it is common to him, as it is to Stephen and any other man who has lived, lives, or will live. The nature of man is

---

[13] In a letter to his brother Peter, Gregory analyzes the terms *ousia* and *hypostasis*, providing the clearest understanding and use of these terms in the Cappadocians' theology. "*Letter 35 To Peter His Own Brother on the Divine Ousia and Hypostasis (Ad Petrum 1)*" in Silvas, *Gregory of Nyssa: The Letters* (Brill, 2006).

[14] Ayres, "On Not Three People," 450, 51.

inseparable, not capable of increase or decrease. Although it appears in a plurality, it is nevertheless complete and not divided with the individuals—Stephen and Luke—who participate in it.

Gregory points out that the challenge lies in the manner in which we speak about people. In the singular, we refer to groups (people, army, or mob). Though understood to be a plurality, "man" is still considered one, even though the one nature of "man" is exhibited as a plurality. As it pertains to God, we must confess that God is One according to Scripture (Dt 6:4), though the name "Godhead" extends through the Holy Trinity. The disparity lies in that we know it is improper, "in the case of human nature . . . to extend the name of the nature *by the mark of plurality*" (*Ad Abl.*, 332; emphasis added). Even though an army is composed of a plurality, human nature is only one; it is not multiplied. Thus, with God, it is improper for us to associate the name Godhead with the divine nature because, as Scripture teaches us, the divine nature is "unnameable and unspeakable." So, whatever name we use to speak of the divine nature, such names cannot signify the nature itself. What does Gregory mean by that? Gregory writes:

> For we say, it may be, that the Deity is incorruptible, or powerful, or whatever else we are accustomed to say of Him. But in each of these terms we find a peculiar sense, fit to be understood or asserted of the Divine nature, yet not expressing that which that nature is in its essence. For the subject, whatever it may be, is incorruptible: but our conception of incorruptibility is this,—that that which is, is not resolved into decay: so, when we say that He is incorruptible, we declare what *His nature does not suffer*, but we do not express *what that is* which does not suffer corruption (*Ad Abl.*, 332–3; emphasis added).

We do not perceive divinity directly. Instead, we do so by process of what Gregory calls *epinoia* (this concept will be fleshed out further when we get to Basil of Caesarea), or the process of abstracting conceptions or reflecting on the things about God, based upon what he has revealed to us in creation and Scripture—which provides us a guiding grammar to speak *analogously*, though truthfully, about God. However, we understand that we cannot know God in the truest sense. Somehow, we can "touch" God; however, he always remains unknown.[15] Gregory says this process of *epinoia* is continual. Elsewhere, he writes, "But in applying such appellations to the

---

[15] Ayres, "On Not Three People," 456.

Divine essence, 'which passeth all understanding,' we do not seek to glory in it by the names we employ, but to guide our own selves by the aid of such terms towards the comprehension of the things which are hidden" (*Cont. Eun.* 13, 265).[16]

Gregory notes that we use the name "Godhead" to describe God's activity (his nature is unknown to us) as watching over us, seeing, or beholding. The Three persons are ascribed to each of these activities in Scripture. In Psalm 84:9, David says, of the Father, "See, O God our defender," in which sight is a proper operation of God. In Matthew 9:4, Jesus sees the thoughts of those who condemn him, questioning his power to pardon sinners. In the classic passage of Ananias and Saphira lying to Peter (Ac 5:3), the Holy Spirit is the true witness of this act in that he was aware of their secret actions, sharing with Peter what he observed (*Ad Abl.*, 333). In Gregory's analyses of the term "Godhead," whereby each member of the Trinity is engaged in the same activity of seeing, he concludes that "if the activities are the same, then the power which gave rise to them is the same and the ineffable divine nature in which that power is inherent must also be one."[17]

But Gregory admits that his argument is not satisfactory. The "three Gods" claim remains relevant because mankind, having the same nature, does the same things proper to humanity, appropriately spoken of as three (e.g., three orators and three shoemakers). Understanding this issue, Gregory moves on to bring the apparent contradiction to a close. Regarding the common example of humanity, we know that each activity is done by separate individuals "according to the special character of [each one's] operation." Therefore, Gregory writes that these "pursuits" are considered many. However, as it pertains to the divine nature, Gregory writes,

> we do not similarly learn that the Father does anything by Himself in which the Son does not work conjointly, or again that the Son has any special operation apart from the Holy Spirit; but every operation which extends from God to the Creation and is named according to our variable conceptions of it, has its origin from the Father, and proceeds through the Son, and is perfected in the Holy Spirit. For this reason, the name derived from the operation is not divided with regard to the number of those who fulfill it, because the action of each

---

[16] Ayres, "On Not Three People," 457.

[17] Ayres, "On Not Three People," 459.

> concerning anything is not separate and peculiar, but whatever comes to pass, in reference either to the acts of His providence for us, or to the government and constitution of the universe, comes to pass by the action of the Three, yet what does come to pass is not three things. (*Ad Abl.*, 334)

Gregory is illuminating to us that the Trinity has an order, from which the divine activity (*energeia*) of the Three persons is *one motion*, communicated from the Father, through the Son, and to the Spirit. The divine nature is unknown, but we see the divine operations carried out by one power, leading to a conception of an undivided Godhead. Gregory deploys a helpful phrase from nature, which speaks of the power and action of God "issuing from the Father as from a spring, brought into operation by the Son, and perfecting its grace by the power of the Spirit" (*Ad Abl.*, 334).

In phrasing his understanding of God's divine activity and demonstrating his power and character, Gregory addresses the "Three Gods" problem: God's activity is not individuated as we would see in human natures. God's activity as observed in creation and narrated in Scripture, reveals one power, which always works without delay according to the motion of the Divine will "by a unitary causal sequenced activity of the three persons."[18] "Godhead" is a name. It is an appellation given to the unlimited and incomprehensible Divine nature. Gregory notes "that the Deity is above every name: and 'Godhead' is a name" (*Ad Abl.*, 335).

In revisiting the error—applying the name of a nature to denote a multitude—Gregory emphasizes that Scripture never speaks of God as Gods. Nature is indivisible; however, Gregory writes that Scripture names "men" in the plural "because no one is by a figure of speech led astray in his conceptions to imagine a multitude of humanities or supposes that many human natures are indicated by the fact that the name expressive of nature is used in the plural" (*Ad Abl.*, 336). As it pertains to Scripture's reference to God: "The Father is God: the Son is God: and yet by the same proclamation God is One, because no difference either of nature or of operation is contemplated in the Godhead." The Lord our God is one Lord, with Scripture declaring the Only-begotten Son as God from the Father, but we do not have two Gods. The reason for our proclamation that God is one, Gregory writes,

---

18 Ayres, "On Not Three People," 462.

is because "no difference either of nature or of operation is contemplated in the Godhead." Ayres succinctly puts it: "The sequence of the one divine action *ad extra* reflects the nature and order of God's internal generation, and in both the same sequence of causality is operative."[19]

As he ends his letter to Ablabius, Gregory addresses the matter of the distinction of persons. The matter looms overhead because of the *human* (weakness?) understanding of individuation. The persons are distinguished from each other: one, the Father, is the *without* Cause; the Only-begotten is directly from the First Cause, with the Spirit proceeding from the Father through the Son. Gregory notes,

> But in speaking of "cause," and "of the cause," we do not by these words denote nature (for no one would give the same definition of "cause" and of "nature"), but we indicate the difference in manner of existence. For when we say that one is "caused," and that the other is "without cause," we do not divide the nature by the word "cause," but only indicate the fact that the Son does not exist without generation, nor the Father by generation. (*Ad Abl.*, 336)

His point is that *generation* presents the MODE OF EXISTENCE, but the phrase *generation* does not indicate *what* exists. The phrase *unbegotten*, as applied to the Son, teaches us the mode of his existence and how we conceive of him, but it does not tell us *what* he is. And in recognizing as such, the *grammar of divinity* allows us to acknowledge a distinction in the Trinity, whereby One *is* the Cause, and another is *of the* Cause, and thus "we can no longer be accused of confounding the definition of the persons by the community of nature" (*Ad Abl.*, 336). Gregory concludes his letter to Ablabius:

> Thus, since on the one hand the idea of cause differentiates the Persons of the Holy Trinity, declaring that one exists without a Cause, and another is of the Cause; and since on the one hand the Divine nature is apprehended by every conception as unchangeable and undivided, for these reasons we properly declare the Godhead to be one, and God to be one, and employ in the singular all other names which express Divine attributes. (*Ad Abl.*, 336)

Gregory set out to delineate a Trinitarian doctrine that was logical yet derived from Holy Scripture. His dynamic line of argumentation, whereby the *energeia*—the activity and power of God as observed in a

---

[19] Ayres, "On Not Three People," 463.

causal "from–through–in" order by each of the persons, cogently and coherently articulated a *monarchial* formula of divine power and activity *from* God the Father, mediated *through* the Only Begotten Son, and perfected *in* the Spirit. The triune God, therefore, is not "three gods."

Gregory of Nazianzus

One of the Cappadocian fathers, Gregory of Nazianzus (c. 330–389), given the title "The Theologian," was instrumental in the development of Trinitarian theology, specifically the distinct terms to describe the persons of the Godhead (*Unbegotten, eternally begotten,* and **PROCESSION**). Gregory's main contribution to the development of Christology was in his opposition to Apollinarius. He argued that when Adam fell, all of humanity fell in him; therefore, that fallen nature must be fully united to the Son—body, soul, and mind, 'for the unassumed is the unhealed.' We will be looking specifically at his five *Theological Orations*, a set of sermons delivered in Constantinople in 380, showcasing Gregory's divine grammar in his articulation of the doctrine of God and the Trinity.

In his *Second Theological Oration*, 28 (Greg. Naz., *Orat.* 28),[20] Gregory expounds his doctrine of God, whereby he ascends to him through contemplation on the things he has created (Ro 1:19–20; Ps 8:1)—or going from the effect to the Cause. However, Gregory does not begin that way; rather, he reflects on the incomprehensible mystery of God, to which no one can ascend (*Orat.* 28.3). In contemplating the grandeur of God, no one can know what the Divine nature is, rather, the created things God has brought forth and governs (Ps 111:3; 145:5, 12), Gregory writes, are "indications of himself he has left behind," an "averted figure" (Ex 33:21–2). And this *averted figure* is impossible to describe. Gregory writes, "to grasp so great a mystery is utterly beyond real possibility even so far as the very elevated are concerned, never mind the slack and sinking souls" (*Orat.* 28.4). What we have right is a "scant emanation . . . a small beam from a great light" (*Orat.* 28.17). What was

---

[20] English translation of his *Orations* cited from: St. Gregory of Nazianzus, *On God and Christ: The Five Theological Orations and Two Letters to Cledonius* (Crestwood, NY: St Vladimir's Seminary Press, 2002); Gregory of Nazianzus, *St. Gregory of Nazianzus Select Orations*, trans. Martha Vinson, vol. 107 (Washington, D.C.: Catholic University of America Press, 2004).

seen in the time of the OT and NT, express visions of the Lord God, was his presence, not his essence. "None saw, none told, of God's nature" (*Orat.* 25.19). While Gregory is convinced of God's existence, it is a whole other matter to know *what* it is (*Orat.* 28.5).

As he moves toward contemplation of God, Gregory provides a simple apologetic regarding God's existence "as the creative and sustaining cause of all." He writes, "No one seeing a beautifully elaborated lyre with its harmonious, orderly arrangement, and hearing the lyre's music will fail to form a notion of its craftsman player, to recur to him in thought though ignorant of him by sight" (*Orat.* 28.6). The argument is not profound; it is not something that only elite intellectuals can understand; rather, it merely affirms what God's Word declares about God—he has "clearly" revealed himself in the creation of the world. However, as Paul indicates, *what can be known about* God is evident in creation. In other words, creation provides the grounds to know *that* God exists, but we cannot know *what* God is.

Affirming that this is the case, Gregory takes a deductive approach in forming a conception of God. He also formulates this as a manner of argumentation against those who think that God has a body. He writes, "Is it corporeal? How then can it be boundless, limitless, formless, impalpable, invisible? Can bodies be such? The arrogance of it! This is not the nature of bodies. Or is it corporeal without these properties? The grossness of it, to say that deity has no properties superior to ours! How could it be worth worship were it bound?" (*Orat.* 28.7). We see from Gregory a basic assumption that God is incorporeal, namely that God does not have composition. The logic is straightforward because Scripture attributes omnipresence, omnipotence, eternity, and infinity to God. Therefore, for God to be as such, "dissolution is utterly alien to . . . the prime nature." God's essence has no division and no composition; thus, he has no body. Though he did not explicitly use the word, his conclusion regarding God's non-composite nature is an affirmation of his simplicity.

Gregory writes that God's incorporeality does not explain his essential being. He further notes that the apophatic statements (i.e., *negative* theology), *ingenerate*, *unoriginate*, *immutable*, and *immortal* do not aid in this manner either (*Orat.* 28.9). It is important to note Gregory's affirmation and understanding of what negative theology does *not* intend to do, namely teach us something positive about God.

Gregory argues that one must provide negative statements, but also positive assertions of what God is to gain a proper understanding. However, in our case, it is much easier to "indicate all that something is *not* by indicating what it *is*, than to reveal what it *is* by denying what it is *not*" (*Orat.* 28.9). In his discussion up to this point, Gregory reveals his true intentions in taking up this exercise: "I wanted to make plain . . . the incomprehensibility of deity to the human mind and its totally unimaginable grandeur" (*Orat.* 28.11). There are two outcomes in contemplating the grandeur of God. Either we fall into the dangerous trap of idolatry—making the visible a deity when using earthly objects or concepts to describe *what* the Divine essence is, or we "discover God through the beauty and order of things seen, using sight as a guide to what transcends sight without losing God through the grandeur of what it sees" *Orat.* 28.13). The latter path of discovery is prescriptive of how we are to reflect on the Divine essence of God. Sight is intended to guide us to the transcendent, but what we see is not transcendent. The material reality is a metaphor for the spiritual reality. We run into gross error when we mistake the material for the spiritual.

God's nature is hidden behind God's ways. Gregory writes that there is nowhere for man to go when it comes to the fathomless depths of God's ways, of which Solomon, in all his wisdom, only drew further into an abyss the more he searched and pondered the profundities of God. The apostle Paul came to a standstill when approaching the impenetrably towering wall of God's judgments and ways—he had nowhere to climb. All he could do was revel in "impassioned wonder in acknowledgment of the incomprehensibility of God's judgments" (*Orat.* 28.21).

In sections 24–31, Gregory is captivated by the awe-inspiring and enigmatic creation surrounding him. Through this, he perceives the divine power and eternal nature of God (Ro 1:19–20) as unmistakably revealed in the things he has made. Gregory's "poetic account"[21] of creation, expressed through elegantly phrased questions about the smallest to the most magnificent elements within creation, is truly noteworthy. His descriptions of fish, birds, spiders, bees, fruit, trees, seas, oceans, the sky, the heavens, and the radiant sun reveal a clear sense of excitement and

---

[21] John Behr, *The Formation of Christian Theology: The Nicene Faith*, vol. 2, (Crestwood, NY: St Vladimir's Seminary Press, 2004), 351.

awe. In looking at all of creation, Gregory concludes that "reason has no explanation of what upholds the world except the will of God" (*Orat.* 28.26; cf. Re 4:11). In the face of "natural philosophers," Gregory jabs at their "futile cleverness" in their account of the vastness and powerful motion of the oceans though contained as bodies of water, providing a short and truthful answer—God commands a fence for the waters and his command binds them (*Orat.* 28.27). And as he brings this oration to a close, Gregory writes:

> What do you say? Shall we stop our preaching here at matter and objects of sight? Or, since Scripture recognizes the tabernacle of Moses as a symbol for the whole world (the world, I mean, of things "visible and invisible") shall we pass through the first veil, transcending sense, to bend our gaze on holy things, on ideal and heaven transcending reality? But not even this can we see as something free of body, even it if actually be so, since it has 'fire' and 'wind' for its name or created being (*Orat.* 28.31).

Gregory speaks of all the angelic creatures, powers, dominions, thrones, etc., yet each one of them is under God according to his ranking, "making all things obey the beck and call of him who alone fashioned them. They hymn God's majesty in everlasting contemplation of everlasting glory: not to make God glorious—God, whose fullness supplies all else with excellence, cannot be added to—but to leave beings supreme after God with no service undone" (*Orat.* 28.31).

Gregory's Doctrine of the Trinity

Because of the foundational importance of Gregory's doctrine of the Trinity in orthodox classical theism, a review of his Trinitarian doctrine is worthy of independent study (We will do the same when getting to Basil of Caesarea and Augustine). His clearest statement on the Trinity is found in his *Oration* 25.15–18 (Some of his other writings will be incorporated into our study). *Oration* 25 was part of the series of sermons delivered in 380. As a gesture of gratitude, Gregory dedicates *Oration* 25 to Christian philosopher Maximus the Cynic as a sort of 'charge' for him to push forward and remain strong in the orthodox teachings of the faith. And these sections are that orthodox articulation.

In creedal fashion, Gregory outlines the orthodox definition of the Trinity, stating:

God, unbegotten, the Father, and one begotten Lord, his Son, referred to as God when he is mentioned separately, but Lord when he is named in conjunction with the Father, the one term on account of his nature, the other on account of his monarchy; and one Holy Spirit proceeding, or, if you will, going forth from the Father, God to those with the capacity to apprehend things that are interrelated, but in fact resisted by the impious though so recognized by their betters and actually so predicated by the more spiritual. Neither should we place the Father beneath first principle, so as to avoid positing a first of the first, thus necessarily destroying primary existence; nor say that the Son or the Holy Spirit is without beginning. Thus, we shall avoid depriving the Father of his special characteristic. Paradoxically, they are not without beginning, and, in a sense, they are; they are not in terms of causation, since they are indeed from God although they are not subsequent to him, just as light is not subsequent to the sun, but they are without beginning in terms of time since they are not subject to it. Otherwise, that which is transitory would be antecedent to things that abide, and that which has no independent existence to things that do. . . . For what the Father and the Son and the Holy Spirit have in common is their divinity and the fact that they were not created, while for the Son and the Holy Spirit it is the fact that they are from the Father. In turn, the special characteristic of the Father is his ingenerateness, of the Son his generation, and of the Holy Spirit its procession. (*Orat.* 25.15, 16)

A key aspect of Cappadocian Trinitarianism is the *monarchial* order of the Godhead, whereby the Father is Source (*Principle, Unbegotten,* or *Ingenerated*), the Son is *begotten* (*generated*), and the Spirit *proceeds* from the Father. The Father as Source is his special characteristic, from which the Son and the Spirit find their causal origin. It is important that when reading Gregory's account, we understand that his use of *cause* is not temporal; rather, it is an implication of the oneness of God, according to Scripture's presentation of God (e.g., Ro 1:7; 1Co 1:9 [cf. 8:6]; 2Co 1:2; 13:13; Ga 1:1; Ja 1:1; 1Pe 1:3) in the Son and the Spirit being generated from the Father (as cause), which is an eternal act, with the *active* terms denoting relations as they both have the same divine nature. Their point of origin from the Father delineates their relation (thus a real distinction) to him. The Father is always Father; therefore, he has always had a Son (*Orat.* 25.15). The Son is not the Father, the Son is not the Spirit, the Father is not the Spirit, and the Spirit is not the Father.

Giving priority to the Father in the Godhead is what maintains Christian monotheism. Therefore, the Father has the primary causality in God, whereby the divine will is carried out in *one* divine act, not three wills carrying out three divine acts. The logic behind the monarchial ordering is that if the Son and the Spirit are given the same *characteristics* as the Father, we then have three sources, three distinct beings, and thus three Gods. However, that is not what we have; rather, the:

> Godhead exists undivided in beings divided. It is as if they were a single intermingling of light, which existed in three mutually connected suns. When we look at the Godhead, the primal cause, the sole sovereignty, we have a mental picture of the single whole, certainly. But when we look at the three in whom the Godhead exists, and at those who derive their timeless and equally glorious being from the primal cause, we have three objects of worship (*Orat.* 31.14).

Gregory affirms the eternality of the Son and the Spirit, "since there never was a time when he began to be a Son ; .. otherwise, there would be a time when the one was not a Father and the other not a Son." Elsewhere, Gregory writes, "[The Son] must share in the glory of the uncaused, because he stems from the uncaused" (*Orat.* 29.11). And the Spirit is "truly Holy in that there is no other like it in quality or manner and in that its holiness is not conferred but is holiness in the absolute, and in that it is not more or less, nor did it begin or will it end in time" (*Orat.* 25.16). The distinctions between the three are a matter of relational order, not nature. With the Father as the *only* source of the Trinity and his unique identity, Nicene orthodoxy stands opposed to Arianism and Sabellianism. It avoids the fatal errors of these aberrant theologies in that the Son is *not* a creature (according to Arianism), nor is God merely three different manifestations of one person (according to Sabellianism).[22]

With the monarchy of the Father, he is the source of the Trinity and the source of the three divine persons (*hypostasis*). For Gregory, the oneness of God is maintained "if both Son and Spirit are causally related to [the Father] alone without being merged or fused into him and if they all share one and the same movement and purpose," being identical in essence (*Orat.* 20.7). We avoid tri-theism because the Father as the Source (who is, importantly, without source) of divinity shares it with the Son

---

[22] Christopher A. Beeley, "Divine Causality and the Monarchy of God the Father in Gregory of Nazianzus," *Harvard Theological Review* 100, no. 2 (April 2007): 207.

and the Spirit by means of his eternal generation and procession. The Son, in the temporal sense, is the source of all things; thus, also he is the Lord of all things, including time (*Orat.* 20.7). The Father, in the eternal sense, is the cause of the Son, for he is the Father's Word, who speaks and brings creation into existence (Ps 148:5 LXX). This act of creation is ineffable; God's "act of will and its fulfillment are identical" (*Orat.* 20.9).

Scripture declares the divine qualities of the Son and the Spirit, which is in reference to their source being that of God the Father. When Jesus refers to the Father being greater than he is (Jn 14:28), Gregory interprets this statement to mean "the Father's superiority to the Son as the eternal source of his existence" (contrary to Augustine, who prefers to see it as the Son's economic inferiority as the incarnate Lord).[23] In *Oration* 29.14, Gregory does away with any notions of inferiority in the Son by those who emphasize the divine names, overlooking the unique, *equally shared* divine nature. In doing so, Gregory writes, you "rob the Son of it [unique deity] and make him subordinate. You give the Son a second level in quality and worship." We plunge into deep error when we mistakenly assume names indicate quality of nature or differing substance. The names designate relationships between the persons of the Godhead—all share in the same substance.

In *Oration* 23.11, Gregory offers a succinct definition of the Trinity. He writes:

> The Trinity, my brothers, is truly a trinity. Trinity does not mean an itemized collection of disparate elements; if it did, what would prevent us from calling it a decad, or a centad [a hundred], or a myriad, if the number of components so justified? The arithmetical possibilities are many; indeed, more than these examples. Rather, Trinity is a comprehensive relationship between equals who are held in equal honor; the term unites in one word members that are one by nature and does not allow things that are indivisible to suffer fragmentation when their number is divided.

In 25.17, Gregory addresses some of the errors that stem from a human understanding of a monarchial view of God. First, addressing worship,

---

[23] Beeley, "Divine Causality," 208. In *Orat.* 30:7, Gregory does take up the matter, stating, "the explanation that the Father is greater than the Son considered as a man is true, but trivial. Is there anything remarkable about God's being greater than man? Certainly this must be our answer to those who preen themselves on their 'being greater.'"

he notes the miraculous manner of its union as the Trinity; therefore, we are worshipping the one true God. As it pertains to the Son, again, the human mode needs to be dispelled, as being generated, he does not have *passions* as human generation entails (cf. *Orat.* 23.10), for the divine is impassible even in generation. Generation does not mean *creation*; therefore, generation is not temporal; otherwise, the Son would not be divine and thus not part of the Godhead. As of the procession, Gregory writes, we only know of proceeding by biological means; of the Spirit proceeding from the Father, "let us go mad for prying into God's secrets" (*Orat.* 31.8).

Gregory gives us a helpful reminder about the intention of the language being used in Trinitarian discourse. The names do not present any manner of shortcoming or deficiency in the Godhead; rather, they are for "safeguarding the distinctness of the three hypostases within the single nature and quality of the Godhead" (*Orat.* 31:9). For Gregory, "the monarchy of the Father is the foundational principle in trinitarian logic and the fundamental dynamic that contains and gives meaning to the grammatical aspects of consubstantial unity and relational distinctness."[24] We call the Spirit—*Spirit* because he is not the Son nor the Father. He has his own role in the divine economy, as revealed to us in the NT. All three have the full divine nature, each one complete in oneself, by identity of being and power. Gregory writes that this is how we can best explain and understand the Trinity; if it "is convincing, we ought to thank God for the insight. If not, we should look for a better one" (*Orat.* 31.16).

In conclusion, we must say something about the Father as Cause. Gregory's emphasis on the Father as the source of the Godhead, the Trinity, does not mean the Father is the originator of divinity, as in the cause of the divine nature. Rather, the Father as Source alone is *A se*—*self-existent*. He has life in himself and has shared it with the Son. And the Spirit eternally proceeds from the Source, being of the same divine nature from the Father but distinctly not the Son. All three manifest themselves in one divine act of redemption, "a truly golden chain of salvation. From the Spirit comes our rebirth, from rebirth comes a new creating, from new creating a recognition of the worth of him who effected it" (*Orat.* 31.28).

---

[24] Beeley, "Divine Causality," 209.

Basil of Caesarea

Basil of Caesarea (c. 329–379), also known as Basil the Great, was the foremost figure among the three Cappadocian fathers. He played a key role in defending Nicene orthodoxy against the Arians in the later fourth century. He thus became the chief architect of the Cappadocian doctrine of the Trinity, which became definitive for the East and the West. Basil denies that 'unbegottenness' is an adequate definition of the essence of God and defends the doctrine (inherited from Origen and Athanasius) of the eternal generation of the Son. The generation of creatures is physical and temporal. The generation of the Son is ineffable and eternal. Here, Basil makes a distinct contribution to Trinitarian doctrine.

Athanasius and the older Nicenes had defended the deity of the Son by insisting that he was consubstantial (*homoousios*) with/of the same essence or substance (*ousia*) as the Father. Basil made a distinction between *ousia* and *hypostasis* (which, confusingly, may also be translated as 'substance'). He spoke of one *ousia* of God, but three *hypostases*: the *hypostasis* of the Father, the *hypostasis* of the Son, and the *hypostasis* of the Holy Spirit. This became the definitive doctrine of the Trinity in the East.[25]

Two key works we will examine, further elucidating the theologically rigid Nicene orthodoxy of the Cappadocians, are *Against Eunomius*,[26] a refutation of the *Apology* of Eunomius, an Arian extremist, and *On the Holy Spirit*, which is one of the first treatises from the church fathers solely focused on the Spirit. The heresy of Arius not only lowered the dignity of the Son; he lowered the Spirit as well. During the Arian controversy, the attention centered mostly on the Son. The Arian creeds did not directly attack the divinity of the Spirit; however, they did not affirm his unity with the Father. The "doctrinal" status of the Spirit remained in the foreground, which created more confusion as the debate continued. Doctrinal unity on the Trinity regarding divine persons needed to be ironed out. Amphilochius, cousin to Gregory of Nazianzus

---

[25] Portions of the biographical info above are adapted from "Basil of Caesarea," T. A. Noble, in *New Dictionary of Theology*, 80–1.

[26] English translation cited: (*Eunom*) Basil of Caesarea, *Against Eunomius*, trans. Mark DelCogliano and Andrew Radde-Gallwitz, *Fathers of the Church* (Washington, D.C: The Catholic University of America Press, 2011).

and friend of Basil, visited Basil in 374 and urged him to do so. And Basil did; his work on the Spirit removed all doubt as to the nature and person of the Spirit—fully divine, God of God, and one with the Father and the Son.

Against Eunomius is divided up into three parts or books. The center of the debate is not on "whether we are to use names like Father, Son, and the Spirit or whether to apply the term 'God' to Father and Son, but rather it is about how to divide up or, to switch metaphors, how to map the territory: it is about what is meant when God is said to be the unbegotten or Father or good, not whether one should say these things in the first place."[27] The main themes of Basil's response are 1) the role of conceptualization in theology; 2) the distinction between positive and negative theological terms; 3) the distinction between names said in COMMON of the Father and the Son and names specifically of each; and 4) the distinction between what is true of God *in se* and from eternity and what God has done on behalf of humans whose perspective is inherently temporally structured" ("Introduction," *Against Eunomius*, 47).

Book I

Basil begins by engaging in argumentation about the nature of human speech about God, termed in the Greek *epinoia*, which we would call conceptualization. More defined, it is "the activity of reflecting on and identifying the distinct qualities or properties of something."[28] Eunomius asserts that we cannot know God by way of *epinoia*. Basil responds in detail, explaining this is a process that we do all the time. Basil aims to demonstrate how Scripture accommodates the *divine* to human capacities. He gives the example of grain. One looks at a simple grain seed and sees one little piece of grain. However, when examining it in detail, one can conceive, i.e., *conceptualize*, "different designations to indicate the different things that we have conceived" (*Eunom.* 1.6). The grain at one time is called "fruit," another, "seed," and "nourishment." These categories are assigned based on the different times or stages of the grain's life—planting, harvesting, and then consuming. Basil notes that such concepts do not dissolve after utterance (a similar phrase

---

[27] "Introduction," in Caesarea, *Against Eunomius*, 46.
[28] Ayres, *Nicaea and Its Legacy*, 191.

Eunomius used); rather, "the concepts remain settled in the soul of the one who has conceived them" (*Eunom*. 1.6). To sum it all up, Basil writes: "Generally speaking, all things recognized through sense-perception and which seem simple in substrate [i.e., the substance of the thing] but which admit of a complex account upon further consideration are said to be considering through conceptualization" (*Eunom*. 1.6).

Basil now moves into this practice, theologically speaking. In Scripture, Christ gave himself many designations, such as "the door," "the way," "the bread of life," "the vine," "the good shepherd," and "the light." While Christ is one, simple, not composite, he references himself by many other things, which differ from each other as well. He does so based on "his different activities and his relation to the objects of his divine benefaction [gift]" (*Eunom*. 1.7). To note a few, Basil writes that Christ calls himself "'the light of the world,' because he illumines those who have purified the eye of their soul with the splendor of his knowledge." And "'the vine' because he nurtures those who have been planted in him by faith so that they bear the fruits of good works" (*Eunom*. 1.7). In doing *epinoia*, we can conceive of God's redemptive work through the association of *real things* that we can sense in the world, thus enabling believers to grow deeper in their knowledge of Christ. John Behr, commenting on this passage, notes, "We do not reflect on the essence itself, but on the way in which it appears to us, the manner in which it presents or reveals itself, in other words, its activity (*energeia*)."[29] Therefore, Basil questions, why then can we not have a conceptual framework for the "unbegotten" God of the universe? The term 'unbegotten' is the focal point of the entire debate. Basil writes:

> We will discover that the name 'unbegotten' is said in no other way. For we say that the God of the universe is 'incorruptible' and 'unbegotten,' designating him with these names according to various aspects. Whenever we consider ages past, we find that the life of God transcends every beginning and say that he is 'unbegotten.' Whenever we stretch our mind forward to the ages to come, we designate the one who is without boundary, infinite, and comprehended by no terminal point as 'incorruptible.' Therefore, just as 'incorruptible' is the name we give him because his life is without an end, so too is 'unbegotten' the name given because his life is without a beginning, when we consider each through conceptualization. What reason could there be, then, for

---

[29] Behr, *The Formation of Christian Theology*, 2:286.

denying that each of these names is conceptualized and that they constitute a confession of what truly belongs to God? (*Eunom.* 1.7)

Eunomius argues that human conceptualization of God dishonors him; calling him "unbegotten" means confessing that he is what he is, which Eunomius says is God's *substance, which* is "unbegotten." And so, the issue in Eunomius' claim is that in asserting God's substance is *unbegotten*, the relational term of origin given to the Son—*begotten*—then situates the Son less than the Father because Eunomius erroneously univocally states *unbegotten* = *Divine essence*.

Basil unfolds the implications from Eunomius' reasoning, stating that if one is to avoid making conceptualizations about God because one profane's his holiness, then all things that one attributes to God are then references to his substance. However, would it not be absurd to refer to God's creative power, providence, and foreknowledge as his substance?[30] The problem is that when these designations all have the same meaning, it doesn't give us a way to differentiate aspects of God as the Scriptures do (cf. Ps 103:24, his creativity; 144:6, his encompassing providence; 17:2, his invisible nature; Ma 3:6, his Divine Substance is unchanging) [*Eunom.* 1.8]. Furthermore, Basil contends that if we follow Eunomius' logic, then he refutes himself because Scripture makes the same designations about the Son; therefore, according to Eunomius, such terms would be indicative of the Son's substance. However, he does not apply this method in reference to the Son, revealing that Eunomius' reasoning is arbitrary.

Utilizing *epinoia* allows us to meditate on the fullness of God's splendor, speaking of his attributes about what God is like while avoiding stating what God is. Furthermore, in *epinoia*, we deploy the use of apophatic theology, which gives us a framework of ascription that keeps us from "falling into inappropriate notions in or suppositions about God" (*Eunom.* 1.10). When we say that God is incorruptible, we are saying that God is not subject to corruptions; invisible, we are saying that God is not observed through our eyes; immortal, God cannot die. So, unlike Eunomius' claim that *epinoia* is blasphemous, Basil

---

[30] Interestingly, the classical doctrine of divine simplicity affirms that God *is* his attributes. But the reasoning behind it is to maintain that all that is in God is God; however, the distinctions are manifest to us through revelation. Illustratively, it is like a beam of light that manifests all its colors when refracted through a prism.

demonstrates that it is honoring of the Divine essence because it safeguards us from idolatry, in that it "forbids us from lowering our thoughts to the level of what is not appropriate" (*Eunom.* 1.10).

Basil reiterates Eunomius' error of "situating unbegottenness in the substance itself" (*Eunom.* 1.11). With that said, Basil affirms one side of the equation: "The substance of God is unbegotten," just not the inverse. Furthermore, Basil finds it important to remind Eunomius that "partlessness and simplicity are the same thing as far as the notion is concerned. For that which is not composed of parts is partless; similarly, that which is not constituted from many elements is simple" (*Eunom.* 1.11). Basil issues the rudimentary lesson because Eunomius has forgotten the doctrine of divine simplicity and its entailments.

To illustrate the absurdity of Eunomius' thinking, Basil discusses our limited rational knowledge about the earth, its components, its shape, and human sensations. He points out that while we can perceive the elements around us through our senses, we are unable to fully comprehend them in a rational sense. While we can distinguish between hard and soft, heat and cold, and other things, we would not attribute "softness" as its substance. Therefore, it is of the "utmost insanity" to think we can comprehend the Divine essence, attributing "unbegottenness" as its substance (*Eunom.* 1.12). But Basil returns to Scripture to demonstrate the mode of knowledge we attain about God and the way we attain it. He writes,

> It is to be expected that the very substance of God is incomprehensible to everyone except the Only-Begotten and the Holy Spirit. But we are led up from the activities of God and gain knowledge of the Maker through what he has made, and so come in this way to an understanding of his goodness and wisdom. For *what can be known about God is that which God has manifested* [Ro 1:19] to all human beings. (*Eunom.* 1.14, emphasis added)

The emphasis on the *activities* of God, in which the world was made, points us to the "way of causality," in that whatever effect is observed, the Cause has a relation to it. The effects that we see demonstrate goodness and beauty and bring us to the conclusion that God is good and beautiful. Scripture, thus God, expresses himself in figurative language so that we can associate what we can comprehend with what we cannot comprehend (the Divine essence). Basil notes that Eunomius' error of

directly applying anthropomorphic language in Scripture to God—
literally—is what the atheists do. And this is not what the Scripture
intends for us to do. If we do, Basil writes, then we would have to
conclude that God has loins of amber (Ez 8:2), he is a consuming fire
(Dt 4:24), and has hair like whitest wool (Da 7:9) (*Eunom.* 1.14).

Moving forward from such "idle curiosity," Basil draws our
attention to Hebrews 11:6, in which the inspired writer says: *One must
believe that God exists and that he rewards those who seek him.* Basil's point
in referencing this passage is in line with what I said earlier: the Divine
essence is incomprehensible and ineffable to human nature. Therefore,
we must examine unbegottenness itself; in doing so, Basil writes, "we
find that our notion of unbegottenness does not fall under the
examination of 'what it is,' but rather—and here I am forced to speak this
way—under the examination of 'what it is like.'" Thus, in this manner of
speaking, we consistently apply the distinction between positive and
negative terms in our God-talk. *Unbegottenness,* then, "does not signify his
'what' but that he is 'from no source'" (*Eunom.* 1.15). Luke's genealogical
account (Lk 3:23–38) demonstrates God's unbegottenness in that he starts
according to the flesh, working backward, tracing the lineage back to Adam,
and stopping there. And Basil says, "Is it not obvious in each one of our
minds that God came from no one?" Here, Basil sounds the death knell;
he writes:

> Clearly, that which is 'from no one' is 'without origin,' and that which is
> 'without origin' is 'unbegotten.' Therefore, just as being 'from someone'
> is not the substance when we are talking about human beings, so too
> when we are talking about the God of the universe it is not possible to
> say that 'unbegotten' (which is equivalent to saying 'from no one') is the
> substance. (*Eunom.* 1.15)

Having refuted Eunomius' point, Basil moves on to address "a most
harmful thing of all for his blasphemy against the Only-Begotten."
Eunomius says that God, as unbegotten, could never admit a begetting that
gives a proper share of his nature to the begotten.[31] His intention, writes
Basil, is to show that the Son is unlike the Father without using their
names—*subtle villainy,* he calls it. "Shameless and wicked blasphemy!"
(*Eunom.* 1.16). Eunomius argues that because God is uncreated and

---

[31] Eunomius, *Apol.* 9.1–3 (EW 42), R. P. Vaggione, trans., *Eunomius: The Extant
Works* (Clarendon Press, 1987).

cannot share his nature with a created being, there cannot be a genuine comparison between the two. The point is to divide the Father from the Son since Eunomius does not believe that the Son shares the same essence as God. Basil, however, retorts, stating such claims go against Scripture, which shows a proper comparison between the Son and the Father. Furthermore, to say otherwise, Basil writes, is to say that "the apostles are liars, and the gospels are liars" (*Eunom.* 1.17). Basil continues, "If he has no comparison whatsoever with the Father, how could [Jesus] say to Philip: *Have I been with you for so long a time and you do not see me, Philip* [Jn 14:9]? How could he say: *The one who sees me see the one who sent me* [Jn 12:45]?" Basil's point is that the Son, as the image of God, has the impression of the Father stamped on him. That which is unknown to us, the Father, has made himself known to us in the Son; therefore, the image of the invisible God must be like *that image*. And such is this likeness in Christ from the Father, that Jesus, also in John 14:9, says, "*The one who has seen me has seen the Father.*"

Basil offers other proof texts, Colossians 1:15 and Philippians 2:6, noting Paul's words about Christ having the form of God, revealing, without a doubt, "the distinctive feature of the divine substance (*Eunom.* 1.18)." Eunomius' antics lead him to sever the comparison between the begotten and the unbegotten, which cuts us off from attaining "upward knowledge that occurs through the Son." Basil's remark is crucial to observe in Eunomius' flawed theology. If the Son has no comparison to the Father, then statements of Christ having the radiance of the Father, the character of his subsistence (He 1:3), are meaningless.

Basil brings *Book I* to a close with a response to Eunomius' misunderstanding of *greater than I* language that the Son uses in John's Gospel. His mistake is a categorical one. For him, likeness is a question of form and equality, a question of mass, which is proper to that which has composition (*Eunom.* 1.23). But the Father is simple, and so is the Son, as Basil notes. So, for things that have composition, having shape and figure, "likeness is considered to be a question of identity of form." But for that which does not have form (i.e., God) but is *nature*, "the likeness is in the substance itself." Therefore, Basil writes, "In this case equality is not a question of comparing masses, but rather identity of power, as displayed in divine actions/activity. *Christ the power of God* [1Co 1:24]" (*Eunom.* 1.23). In Christ, all the Father's power is contained, which we see in John 5:19, in Jesus saying that whatever the Father does, the Son does likewise. Jesus criticizes the Jews for their misunderstanding, urging them to assess his claims of divinity based on his actions rather than just his words. His actions, powerful acts only achievable by God, serve as evidence of his divinity.

But for Eunomius, 'Father' signifies activity and not substance. So, when the Son says the Father is greater than I, this "activity is greater than the product" (*Eunom.* 1.24). The comparison then does not hold through because other passages speak of the Son as *the power of God* [1Co 1:24] and the Son and the Father are one [Jn 10:30], which refers to equality and identity in power. Therefore, *greater than* language, Basil writes, "is according to the account of cause," in that the "Son's principle comes from the Father [generation], [so] in this sense the Father is greater, as cause and principle" (*Eunom.* 1.25). And while the distinction is a relation of origin (the Father is unbegotten and the Son is begotten), because of the equality and identity in power, the Father's substance is not greater than the Son's substance because they share the same essence. We must conclude as much because God declares that he is one God. Basil's consistency pays off in that he does not confuse categories in his theological language, as observed in Eunomius.

Book II

Basil titles *Book II, On the Son*. He opens this work in response to Eunomius' blasphemies against the Son, whereby he refers to him as something begotten (Gk. *gennema*, i.e., "offspring") and something made (Gk. *poiema*, "product/work"). Basil states such a claim has never been made about the Son. He cites various passages that speak about the things that are made in creation (Ge 1:1; Ps 142:5; Ro 1:20). While there are passages that utilize metaphorical references or figurative language employing terms pertaining to things that are made (e.g., rock, river, door, etc.) about Christ, nowhere in Scripture do we see any writer referring to Christ as "something made" (*Eunom.* 2.2).

In the following section, we now see Basil unpack theology and economy, where he engages in discussion on Christ's eternal divine being apart from his works (i.e., *theologia*), in reference to the unfolding of the redemptive drama (i.e., *oikonomia*), is where we see the outworking of the Father, the Son, and the Spirit. Basil must move in this direction because Eunomius is trying to edge his argument based on the incarnation, the begetting of the Son in time and space, arguing that the apostles were communicating about his substance in his human manifestation (i.e., Ph 2:7; 2Co 13:4; Ac 2:36). Basil returns, stating, "he who said: *God made him Lord and Christ* [Ac 2:36] is speaking of his rule and power over all, which the Father entrusted to him. He is not describing his arrival at being" (*Eunom.* 2.3). Eunomius' mistake was to transfer the expression 'he created' to the original begetting of the Only-begotten; Lord does not denote his substance but the economy of Christ as Lord, possessing power and rule over all of creation.[32]

Basil outlines the absurdity of Eunomius' methodology in assuming names mean substance while also meaning different substance. Peter and John have different names, but both share the same substance; it is "their distinguishing marks considered in connection with each one of us that we are different, each from the other" (*Eunom.* 2.4). Names do not imply substance. Rather, the name determines the character of an individual, and Basil goes on to speak about biblical figures such as Paul and all the distinguishing marks we associate with him, encompassed in the name 'Paul.' Basil, in a *warm* tone, says, "There is no one so stupid and so inattentive to the common nature that he would be led to say this [names = substance]." For example, if we followed Eunomius' univocal designation method, then Basil notes when Scripture refers to human beings as 'gods' then we would be led to say that they have the same substance as the God of the universe—"sheer madness." Eunomius' "logic here is equally crazy" (*Eunom.* 2.4). Therefore, in line with the economy, the names Father and Son do not communicate the Divine essence but rather they "are revelatory of the distinguishing marks" of the divine persons (*Eunom.* 2.5).

Basil launches a powerful onslaught, honing in on key texts such as John 1:1 and Hebrews 1:3. His opponents stumble over a plain reading of these passages, which are grounded in a metaphysical framework that underpins his uwavering proclomations. Basil wholeheartedly embraces these claims as they form the foundation for a unified theology, both in terms of theology and interpretation. Here we see that theological grammar provides a consistent method of interpretation. When used to refute arguments, it can be quite confounding as it skillfully addresses errors with a straightforward and logical approach. This leaves us, 1700

---

[32] Behr, *The Formation of Christian Theology*, 2:291–2.

years later, scratching our heads at how anyone could have arrived at such absurd conclusions.

In *Eunom* 2.15, for example, Basil asks the question (rhetorically to Eunomius), "Was God the Word *with God in the beginning* [Jn 1:1], or did he supervene later?" Well, in John's account, *In the beginning was the Word, and the Word was with God, and the Word was God.* For Basil, this seems basic. He writes, "The Son's existence from eternity. His begetting without passion. His connaturality with the Father. The majesty of his nature. All these points he [John] covers in a few words. By including *was*, he guides us back to the beginning." Basil references other passages (Jn 1:4, 9) demonstrating the eternity of the Son. Eunomius rejects the Spirit's testimony about the Only-Begotten who *was* with God and *is* God. He was begotten, Eunomius will say, but it was not in *the beginning* according to a sensible reading of the Apostle John's words would have it.

Basil is passionate about giving the proper glory to the Son. He refers to the importance of avoiding "corporeal comparisons" and "material imaginations" and that we are to take our cue from the Spirit-authored Scripture, who has transmitted to us in his Holy Word "a begetting that is worthy of God, one without passion, partition, division, and temporality, being led to the divine begetting in a way consistent with the radiance that shines forth from light" (*Eunom* 2.16). And Basil directs us to the light of revelation in Colossians 1:15, that of the Son as the invisible image of God, "co-existent with and subsides with the who one who brought him into subsistence" (*Eunom* 2.16).

The harmony of the scriptural texts, Basil notes, does not, however, perfectly bring together the temporal and eternal realities; rather, we are to take them as the Spirit has given them to us, even if we cannot apprehend begetting in our minds in a manner that "does not involve passion." Basil supplies other classic texts that support the unity of being and the sameness of the Divine essence the Son has with the Father, in that he is the power, wisdom, and righteousness of God (1Co 1:24, 30), though not as a possession of God but rather as *the* essence of the one simple being of God. He is the radiance of the glory of God, revealing "the Father in his entirety, as he is *the radiance of his glory* in its entirety."

It is absurd to think, Basil writes, "that the glory of God is without his radiance? And that at some point the wisdom of God was not with

God?" (*Eunom* 2.17). So then, to answer the ineffable but providing the proper *logical* location of the Son's point of origin, Basil, asks, "When was he brought into being by the Father? From whatever point the Father exists." The Father is from eternity; the Son is from eternity, "connected in a begotten way to the unbegottenness of the Father" (*Eunom* 2.17). Eunomius denies these notions because, to him, the Father as eternal is the same as "without beginning," thus he is unbegotten, having no cause of his own being. But because the Son is said to be begotten, thus he has a cause to his being, he is not eternal. Eunomius' blasphemous views, as noted here, agitate Basil: Eunomius writes, "We do not construe the Only-Begotten as having a substance in common with those which have come to be from nothing. For that which is nothing is surely not a substance. Rather, we allot him as much superiority as the maker necessarily has over the things he himself has made."[33] The "we allot him," Basil finds deplorable.

A few pages later, Basil offers a quick but insightful logic of how God commanded creation to be (Ps 148:5), intending to demonstrate to Eunomius that the Word is not some "lifeless instrument" (*Eunom* 2.22). He writes, "How do *we* say that all things come into being from the Son? In this way: the divine will, taking its origin from the Primal Cause as from a kind of spring, proceeds to activity through his own image, God the Word" (*Eunom* 2.22). This contrasts with Eunomius who thinks of the Son as some kind of minister, administering the things that have been assigned to him.

Basil catches Eunomius in reasonless sophistry. He mentions the distinction between the Son and the Father, begotten and unbegotten, stating that one differs from the other as "the light from the light, the life from the life, and power from the power."[34] Basil's reaction: "Behold and grasp the horrible blasphemy!" (*Eunom* 2.25). How can one differentiate the concept of light from light? It makes no sense. Such comparisons cannot be measured. Basil, seeing the inconsistency, unravels Eunomius' entire position. The Son is the true light (Jn 1:9); if the Father is the true light, then how can one be a lesser true light? Is the Son a dimmer light than the Father? Christ is the Life (Jn 14:6); the Father is the Life as

---

[33] Eunomius, *Apol.* 15.7–11 (EW 52), cited from *Eunom* 2.19 .

[34] Eunomius, *Apol.* 19.9–15 (EW 56–58), cited from *Eunom* 2.25.

well, right? Can there be a lesser life? As noted, it makes no sense and, with ease, Basil pulls apart his argument.

Basil tones it down a bit, providing a precise articulation that identifies the error and articulates the Divine essence and economy without any semblance of contradiction. I will quote him at length:

> If anyone wants to accept that which is true, namely, that begotten and unbegotten are distinctive features that enable identification and are observed in the substance, which lead to the clear and unconfused notion of the Father and the Son, then he will escape the danger of impiety and preserve logical coherence in his reasoning. The distinctive features, which are like certain characters and forms observed in the substance, differentiate what is common by means of the distinguishing characters and do not sunder the substance's sameness in nature. For example, the divinity is common, whereas fatherhood and sonship are distinguishing marks: from the combination of both, that is, of the common and the unique, we arrive at comprehension of the truth. Consequently, upon hearing 'unbegotten light' we think of the Father, whereas upon hearing 'begotten light' we receive the notion of the Son. Insofar as they are light and light, no contrariety exists between them, whereas insofar as they are begotten and unbegotten, one observes the opposition between them. (*Eunom* 2.28)

Of central importance in the discussion, or rather, refutation, is the necessity of maintaining proper categories—Eunomius' fatal mistake—that of nature and person, *theologia* and *oikonomia*. Confusing these categories can lead to various risks, notably a composite view of God. Allowing the language of economy, the engagement of the divine in the temporal, creaturely world, to function as a suitable *and guiding* grammar for the Divine essence, blasphemy ensues! Those who reject the doctrine of divine simplicity, do so not realizing (at least, I do not think) they lose the oneness *and* the threeness of God.

The confusion of terms, in Eunomius' case, the separation of Unbegotten from Begotten in the Divine essence, leads to a composite God. When Scripture uses figurative designations, such as light, for the divine persons, the purpose is to express a divine reality that communicates to our minds something about the essence of God. If we see these designations about the Son and the Father (and the Spirit), we must keep them united, otherwise, we compromise our monotheism.

Basil notes, that if we are to retain the simplicity and partlessness of God, the names we attribute to God, "invisible, incorruptible, immutable, Creator, judge," and all the names to reference his glory, we would have to omit them or apply all of them to his substance. If we were to make that move, Basil asserts we would essentially be showing that God is composed of different and unlike parts, as each of these names signifies different things (*Eunom* 2.29). Therefore, it is clear that upholding the doctrine of divine simplicity is essential to maintain the scriptural affirmation of the unity of God's divine being.

Book III

In this final act, against Eunomius, Basil considers the Spirit. Eunomius sees that the Spirit is from the Begotten, making him third in dignity and rank and thus third in nature. And this perspective, Eunomius claims, is the sacred teaching handed down and believed by the saints. Basil begins his response in bewilderment at Eunomius' claims of catholic fidelity to this view of the Spirit. Basil asks from where and what writings did he learn such blasphemy? (*Eunom* 3.1).

Basil offers agreement as it pertains to the rank of each person but contends that nowhere in Scripture do we see that rank indicates nature. He makes his argument referring to angels, in that they share a single designation and nature, but some angels have greater responsibility as overseeing and presiding over nations, whereas some are designated as personal angels to God's children (Mt 18:10). Basil quotes OT passages showing angels that have greater dignity as well as legions of angels at the call of Christ if the Father so wills it (Mt 26:53). His intention is to show that there are angels who are princes and others who are servants, and "all are angels in nature: while they differ in dignity, there is communion in nature" (*Eunom* 3.2). And therefore, the Spirit, likewise even if he is subordinate in rank, numbered third in the baptismal confession of salvation (Mt 28:19), nowhere in Scripture do we see that the Spirit is a third (*foreign*) nature.

To further support his argument, Basil refers to the dividing line, the "two realities: divinity and creation, sovereignty and servitude, sanctifying power and sanctified power," of which the former reality belongs to one by virtue of its nature; the latter is by virtue of freewill (*Eunom* 3.2). He then poses the question, Which reality belongs to the Spirit? Scripture testifies that the Spirit, by nature, belongs to the first reality (Jn 14:17; 15:26; 16:13). Holiness, by nature, "is observed in three subsistences" [Jn 4:24; Lam 4:20; 2Co 3:17] (*Eunom* 3.3). While the names given or in reference to the Spirit reveal his divine nature, Basil goes on to discuss his activities. He is the Creator of the heavens and the earth (Ps 32:6); he perfects creatures (Jb 33:4); the power of the Spirit "pervades the universe" (Ps 138:7). The Spirit is the seal of adoption for believers (Ro 8:15), is the true teacher just like the Lord (Jn 14:26; cf. Mt 23:9–10), distributes gifts to those who he wills (1Co 12:4–6), knows the mind of God and therefore can rightly judge the secrets of man (Ac 21:11; 1Co 2:11–2), and lavishes eternal life on us through and in Christ (1Ti 6:3; 8:11) (*Eunom* 3.4). In light of the scriptural testimony to the nature and activity of the Spirit, he does not have a third nature but has the one and only divine nature, shared by and in the Father and the Son.

Eunomius insists that the Spirit was created by the Begotten, "bereft of divinity and creative power."[35] Basil takes note of the Spirit's indwelling in us, the body of Christ, which Scripture says that the Spirit *of God* dwells in the body; therefore, to deny that he shares in divinity is impious (*Eunom* 3.5). And then Basil makes a comparison between the Spirit's divine quality and the creature's divine quality, which touches on the doctrine of deification. Basil writes:

> Moreover, it is impious to say of the Spirit, as one can say of human beings, that the divinity honored in him comes by participation and does not coexist with him by nature. For the one divinized by grace possesses a nature subject to change and falls away from the better state whenever he is careless. (*Eunom* 3.5)

The baptismal formula of saving faith is a creature's "assent to divinity." So, while there is a ranking in the formula, nevertheless, it is in this formula that one is saved and made holy. Because Eunomius cannot comprehend that the Spirit is beyond creation, he utters blasphemous assertions. Basil appeals to our finitude and inability to know the spiritual things. However, in our ignorance and lack of epistemic breadth of all of reality, even the things we can see, we have been taught through divine revelation that the Spirit is one with the Father and the Son, which we confess as the blessed Trinity, thus also preserving the singleness of the Trinity (*Eunom* 3.5). Basil's last book about the Spirit

---

[35] Eunomius, *Apol.* 25.22—26 (EW 68) cited from *Eunom* 3.4.

is short, but he has another treatise on the Spirit, which is much more theologically rigorous and detailed in its exegesis. It is one of the first works to focus expressly on the Spirit.

On the Spirit

While this book is titled *On the Spirit*, Basil does not heavily engage in his arguments about the Spirit until chapter 9. He begins this work by examining the heretics' (Arians) "use of syllables" to distort the doctrine of the Trinity. They posit that when Scripture uses prepositional phrases (i.e., syllables) speaking of the activity of God, these phrases create a subordinate ranking, which makes the Son and the Spirit of a different nature from the Father. The heresy is promoted as such: In the words of the apostle: "'One God and Father of whom are all things . . . and one Lord Jesus Christ by whom are all things' (1Co 8:6). 'Whatever, then,' he goes on, 'is the relation of these terms to one another, such will be the relation of the natures indicated by them; and as the term 'of whom' is unlike the term 'by whom,' so is the Father unlike the Son" (*Spir.* 2.4). And following this manner of thought, the differing prepositions taxonomize the Father from the Son and the Spirit from the Son and Father. The Son is a subordinate agent or instrument *through whom* the Father creates, and the Spirit is subordinate to the Son *in whom* the Father creates, whereby the Spirit "may appear to be adding to existing things nothing more than a contribution derived from place or time" (*Spir.* 2.4).

Basil takes a moment to address the *heathen philosophy* underlying this flawed logic. The heretics have embraced a mode of thinking in which "heathens" attribute specific natures or assign particular meanings when discussing causality, including the four causes (Formal, Efficient, Material, and Final). Briefly, Formal is the form or idea *according to which* a thing is made; Efficient is the agent *acting on* the thing made; Material is *out of which* a thing is made; Final is the *end to which a thing is made* or purposed. Romans 11:36 and First Corinthians 8:6 affirm the centrality of the triune God in creation, whereby God is the source (*ek*), sustainer (*dia*), and goal (*eis*) of all things. Paul understood this was common language in Greek stoicism, which Hellenistic Jews adopted and applied to Yahweh. Paul then borrows and applies it to the triune God (spec. Ro 11:36).[36]

In his opponents' adaptation of the four causes, they assert "*by whom*" is proper to the Father, thus he is the carpenter, "*through* which" signifies the instrument, thus the Son, and "*of which*" the material of the thing that is made, and "*in* which" refers to somewhere in time and space. It is this last element of causality that they designate to the role of the Spirit. And so, we see that they have made an "unpractical philosophy" and "belittling" doctrine of the Spirit (*Spir.* 2.3.5). What is the result, Basil asks? "There is one nature of Cause; another of Instrument; another of Place. So, the Son is by nature distinct from the Father, as the tool from the craftsman; and the Spirit is distinct in so far as place or time is distinguished from the nature of tools or from that of them that handle them" (*Spir.* 4.6). Basil, however, does not continue looking for scriptural proofs; rather, he wants to engage in a discussion about "the identity of language." His adversaries contend that the difference in language indicates a difference in nature. However, Basil is confident that they will "confess with shame that the essence is unchanged" (*Spir.* 5.11).

In the next chapter, Basil outlines his opponents' heretical notions, as mentioned already, challenging their assertion that the Son is "after the Father." Their interpretive mistake in delineating an ontology is in using the divine *oikonomia*, the redemptive revelation of God in time and space, to formulate their doctrine of God. The Arians' interpretation is defective because they allow an anthropomorphic reading of the text to govern their ontology. In refutation, Basil looks to a plain reading of John 1:1, observing the two words *beginning* and *was* keep us tethered to the text in that we have nowhere to go conceptually, leaving us with the notion that "it is impossible to get further than the beginning," . . . which teaches us to think that the Son was together with the Father *in the beginning* (*Spir.* 6.14).

The controlling *skopos*[37] of the Bible, teaches that Scripture, as a whole, reveals that Christ is fully human and fully divine. The *skopos*, then, is the leading principle forming the unity of Scripture. This unifying theme that makes individual texts of Scripture appear to be

---

[36] Douglas J. Moo, *The Epistle to the Romans* (Grand Rapids, MI: Wm. B. Eerdmans Publishing Company, 1996), 743.

[37] *Skopos* (Gk.) literally means *goal* or *mark* ("σκοπός," BDAG, 931).

contradictory is *complementary* of one another because Scripture is a product of the One, Divine mind.[38] Khaled Anatolios identifies the key aspects of this unifying *skopos* about Christ—the central figure of Scripture. He notes this unifying principle is based on the names and language about Christ observed in the NT authors, such as the Wisdom and Power of God (1Co 1:24), the brightness of his glory (He 1:3). The related or shared language throughout all of Scripture the biblical writers employed to speak of the Divine essence (i.e., The radiance of Light; he is a speaker of a Word; Wisdom and Power) are then lexically extended to include Christ. And this governing principle, "seemingly oversteps the contextual distance between different usages. The principle of the unity of Scripture is assumed to legitimate the meaningfulness of its intertextual relations."[39]

Basil notes his opponents' mistake in applying corporeal designations to the incorporeal essence, such as interpreting the expressions from Psalm 110:1, "Sit at my right hand," and Hebrews 1:3, "he sat down at the right hand of the Majesty on high," as God having a physical right hand and that it indicates a lower rank, but rather "equality of relation." The Son's act of standing and sitting is not of inferiority; rather, Basil writes, it is indicative of the "immutability and immobility of the Divine mode of existence" (*Spir.* 6.15). And then we see the lexical extension, thus Christ's inclusion in the Divine essence, spoken of above. Basil writes, "Scripture puts before us the magnificence of the dignity of the Son by the use of dignified language indicating the seat of honor" (*Spir.* 6.15). And then he references First Corinthians 1:24, Colossians 1:15, Hebrews 1:3, and John 5:27 asking his opponents if the language referring to Christ that presumes his inherent relation to God signifies "inferiority of rank." If Christ is the Power and Wisdom of God, how could he be anything less than the all-powerful and all-wise God? If Christ is a mere creature, then Paul has committed a heinous act of blasphemy.

Basil demonstrates his opponents' error in their assumption that the phrase "through Him" makes the Word an instrument of God, thus inferior to God, by the role of the Word in the creative and providential

---

[38] Carter, *Contemplating God*, 35.
[39] Anatolios, *Retrieving Nicaea*, 111.

acts, which alone belong to the Creator. Scripture credits the Son, the Word, with having brought forth "all created nature," the visible and invisible, which cannot be sustained and upheld apart from the "Creator Word, the Only begotten God" (*Spir.* 8.19). Basil notes the Son enlightens those in ignorance (Jn 1:9); He judges, for the Father has given all judgment to him (Jn 5:22); He is the Resurrection (Jn 11:25), raising those who have fallen. And "effectually working by the touch of His power and the will of His goodness He does all things" (*Spir.* 8.19). And then from the glory, power, and goodness of his *touch*, in a foray, Basil attributes all the excellencies of the Divine essence to Christ:

> He shepherds; He enlightens; He nourishes; He heals; He guides; He raises up; He calls into being things that were not; He upholds what has been created. Thus, the good things that come from God reach us "through the Son," who works in each case with greater speed than speech can utter. For not lightnings, not light's course in air, is so swift; not eyes' sharp turn, not the movements of our very thought. Nay, by the divine energy is each one of these in speed further surpassed than is the slowest of all living creatures outdone in motion by birds, or even winds, or the rush of the heavenly bodies; or, not to mention these, by our very thought itself. For what extent of time is needed by Him who "upholds all things by the word of His power," and works not by bodily agency, nor requires the help of hands to form and fashion, but holds in obedient following and unforced consent the nature of all things that are? (*Spir.* 8.19).

The work of the Son is to reveal the Father, "guiding us to the knowledge of the Father, and referring our wonder at all that is brought into existence to Him, to the end that 'through Him' we may know the Father" (*Spir.* 8.19). Basil's cogent and clear elucidation of the Word is the summation of Scripture about Christ. The unifying theme of Scripture is that the triune God has revealed himself in Christ. Therefore, the triune God is neither tethered to time nor confined to any page, book, or testament of Scripture. It is a canonical revelation that should guide our interpretation and formulation of our doctrine of God.

The divine activity of God is the divine activity of the Father, Son, and the Holy Spirit. The divine *energeia*, though manifesting the persons of the Trinity in distinct modes and activities—*oikonomia*, nevertheless must always be understood that there is no variation or separation in the

Divine essence or in the divine operations. Basil writes, "The Word is full of his Father's excellences; He shines forth from the Father and does all things according to the likeness of Him who begat Him." Therefore, if he is the same in essence, he is the same in power (*Spir.* 8.19). The power and operation are always equal because of the One, Divine will. The Son comes to execute the Father's command, but what we see in the divine *economy* is not a denigration of the Son.

Basil is keenly aware of Arian errors, noting that the interaction between the Father and the Son does not imply the Son's ontological subservience to the Father. Rather, Basil emphasizes that we must theologize according to what is befitting of the Godhead—who is Spirit; the Father and the Son "perceive a transmission of will, like a reflection of an object in a mirror, passing without note of time from Father to Son." Keeping the distinction between *economy* and *theology*, Basil notes, when the Son announces that he only speaks what he hears the Father speak, or he only does what the Father commands him to do, the purpose is to "make plain" that the Son has an "indissoluble union with the Father" (*Spir.* 8.20). So, when Christ tells Philip, "The one who has seen me has seen the Father" (Jn 14:9), it is not the express image or the form of God that Philip sees, because "the divine nature does not admit of combination." Rather, to see the Father in Christ is to "see the goodness of the will of God, being concurrent with the essence, beheld as like and equal, or rather the same, in the Father as in the Son" (*Spir.* 8.21).

In conclusion, Basil expresses that the Father's act of creating *through* the Son is the "confession of an antecedent Cause and is not adopted in objection to the efficient Cause." What does that mean? The revelation of God as Creator and Cause in Scripture is the expressive act of the Divine essence (*theologia*), whereby the modes and operations of the triune God are manifested in creation (*oikonomia*) to display the glory of God to creatures. The identity of language shared between the Father and the Son is to indicate the one will of God in creation and providence. The prepositional phrases (Basil terms *syllables*) by, through, and in ascribed to the persons of the Godhead do not imply taxonomic degradation; rather, it is a formulaic expression of divine accommodation.

Basil's attention to the inseparable union of the Father and the Son in essence and activity sets the foundation to seamlessly shift into his argumentation about the Spirit. If he manages to convince his critics that the Son and the Father are one, then he won't need to present extensive argumentation about the Spirit's inseparable connection with the Father and the Son. Delineating the identity of language, whereby a clear *rule* emerges, a lexical extension/sharing of terms proper to the Divine essence and inclusive of the Son, which will also extend to the Spirit because the terms of excellency, likewise, are attributed to him in Scripture. Simply put: if Basil has proven that the Son is fully divine as the Father, then adding another person "to the mix" should not be problematic.

In chapter 9, Basil outlines the "common conceptions" in Scripture about the Spirit, along with the divine epithets properly belonging to the Spirit. The Holy Spirit is the "Spirit of God" (Mt 12:28) and the "Spirit of truth," who proceeds from the Father (Jn 15:26). He is termed the Holy Spirit because he is without form, not "subject to change and variation" as creatures are. He is of the supreme nature of the Father, since Scripture says, "God is Spirit" (Jn 4:24). Therefore, considering the scriptural teaching about the Spirit, Basil then says, "We are compelled to advance in our conceptions to the highest, and to think of an intelligent essence, in power infinite, in magnitude unlimited, [and] unmeasured by times or ages." Basil proceeds to list all the designations of God that belong to the Spirit, concluding that the Spirit is "in essence simple," fully coinhering in the Godhead, "impassively divided," is shared in fullness without loss, like a sunbeam "whose kindly light falls on him who enjoys it as though it shone for him alone," and sending "forth grace sufficient for all mankind" (*Spir.* 9.22).

Basil seems to prefer the analogy of a sunbeam concerning the Spirit to denote his effects on those to whom God extends his grace. These "become spiritual" in that the Spirit indwells and illuminates them, revealing the will of God. The telos of the Spirit in creatures is to disclose the foreknowledge of the future, reveal hidden divine mysteries (Basil notes is "the peculiar function of the Spirit;" *Spir.* 16:38), distribute gifts, which belong to those who are citizens of heaven. The Spirit's abiding in creatures is to bring them "joy without end." The grace of fellowship is the work of the Spirit, whereby a creature, through participation, is "being made God" (*Spir.* 9.23). Basil's remarks reflect the same teachings of Athanasius, with his famous expression that "Christ was made like man so we could be made God," (*de Incar.* 54), and Gregory of Nazianzus, similarly states by the "power of the Incarnation he makes me God" (*Or.* 3.14). Through the work of the Spirit, "comes our restoration to paradise," in that we have been brought to glory, being made partakers of the grace of Christ, called children of light, in which now and forever we live in a state of fullness of blessing and enjoyment in God (*Spir.* 15.36).

In chapter 16, Basil reiterates his primary intention of this treatise: to demonstrate that the Spirit is inseparable from the Father and the Son as observed in his operations. Basil refers to Paul's teaching about spiritual gifts, emphasizing that while they are diverse, they come from the "same Spirit" and the "same Lord" (1Co 12:3–5). Every operation of the Spirit is "conjoined with, and inseparable from, the Father and the Son." Not only is the Spirit present of his own will in dispensing gifts to the church, but he was also fully present in the creation of all things. Basil notes that while the mode and manner of creation are left a mystery, in that we can only perceive the creation through our senses, nevertheless, through *epinoia*, we "can form an analogy of the unseen, glorify the Maker by whom all things were made, visible and invisible, principalities and powers, authorities, thrones, and dominions, and all other reasonable natures whom we cannot name" (cf. Col 1:16) (*Spir.* 16.38). From this analogy, we conceive that the Father is the original Cause—*by his will* all things subsist; that the Son is the creative Cause—*through whom* all things are brought into being; and the Spirit is the perfecting Cause—*in whom* the Spirit's presence perfects. But Basil quickly qualifies that in the operations, though delineated in what appear to be distinct, separate actions, a thing's coming into existence and the sustaining of a thing's subsistence is carried out by "One, creating through the Son and perfecting through the Spirit" (*Spir.* 16.38).

Following this understanding of the *economy*, Basil interprets passages in a manner that gives shape to the metaphysical reality of the triune operations disclosed in metaphorical and/or figurative expressions. Citing Psalm 33:6, which says, "The heavens were made by the word of the Lord, and all the stars, by the breath of his mouth," Basil notes, "the Word then is not a mere significant impression on the air, borne by the organs of speech; nor is the Spirit of His mouth a vapor, emitted by the organs of respiration; but the Word is He who 'was with God,' [Jn 1:1] and the Spirit of the mouth of God is 'the Spirit of truth which proceeds from the Father' [Jn 15:26]." Basil's interpretive maneuver—*epinoia*—is key to understanding the oneness of God in his operations, showing that the figurative contains a metaphysical *literalness* in the divine work of God. Our interpretation of Psalm 33:6 reveals that the Lord gives order; the Son creates; the Spirit confirms. Basil clarifies the work of the Spirit, observed earlier as a work of perfecting, stating it is the confirming "of firmness, unchangeableness, and fixity in good" (*Spir.* 16.38). His designation of the Spirit in creation and sustaining of the universe is the act of God that makes his creation good, i.e., a work of sanctification.

To avoid confusion, it's important to understand Basil's use of the term "sanctification" in relation to a believer's sanctification and conforming to the image of Christ. Basil uses this term to illustrate the order of goodness or purpose for each created thing. This order is demonstrated through a "communion" with the Spirit, which enables the full presence of the Spirit in a created thing, empowering it to act in accordance with its nature. Challenging his opponents who claim the Spirit is not the Divine essence, Basil writes:

> It results that, if by your argument you do away with the Spirit, the hosts of the angels are disbanded, the dominions of archangels are destroyed, all is thrown into confusion, and their life loses law, order, and distinctness. For how are angels to cry "Glory to God in the highest" [Lk 2:14] without being empowered by the Spirit? For "No man can say that Jesus is the Lord but by the Holy Ghost, and no man speaking by the Spirit of God calls Jesus accursed;" [1Co 12:3].

In chapter 18, Basil contends for the *monarchia* of God, as opposed to the error of tritheism and polytheism. In the *monarchia*, Basil specifies the Trinitarian formula: "There is one God and Father, one Only-begotten, and one Holy Ghost. We proclaim each of the hypostases singly; and, when count we must, we do not let an ignorant arithmetic carry us away to the idea of a plurality of Gods" (*Spir.* 18.44).

In this confession, Basil notes the affirmation of the persons but within a monarchial schema. The Son is in the Father and the converse, one Form or Nature, both one in essence and will. The monarchy is not two Gods, writes Basil, because "we speak of a king, and of the king's image, and not two kings. The majesty is not cloven in two, nor the glory divided," both exercising sovereignty as one and receiving praise and glory as one. The Spirit, likewise, is singly, conjoined to the *monarchia*, consisting of the blessed Trinity. The Spirit is not of rank among creatures but is fully God of God, one with the three, though the one is distinctly the Father, the Son, and the Spirit.

The Scripture speaks of the Spirit's origin as that of procession from God, not as a creature who comes into being from God through his creative agency, but he proceeds from God. His procession is not generation like that of the Son, otherwise there would be two Sons. Rather, the Spirit proceeds or is spirated from the "mouth" of God. These attributions of the persons are relations of origin, which indicate the identity of each person by the imminent relations to one another. We must not refer to a human mode of relations, seeing that the relations of the persons are indicative of a time when the relations did not exist and then came into existence at some point. Rather, the eternal essence has always been, and the relations have always been as well. The imminent relations are ineffable, nevertheless, we speak of them in this manner so that they are safeguarded.

The Spirit works by illuminating creatures to fix their gaze on Christ, the beauty of the image of the invisible God. As the Spirit enlightens us, we are drawn up to the glory of Christ. The inseparable Spirit of the Trinity bestows on creatures the love and the vision to know God, which is a knowledge from within, not a natural knowledge of God as attained through nature. In this intimate knowing, the Spirit "shows the glory of the Only begotten, and on true worshippers He in himself bestows the knowledge of God." Basil sees the Spirit's work as a conduit of relations between the triune God and creatures, whereby the goodness, glory, holiness, and dignity of the Father and the Son extend through the Spirit. The result of this reveals the hypostases of the Godhead, while retaining the oneness of the Divine essence (*Spir.* 18.46–47).

The operations of the Spirit are ineffable, and it is through the operations that we perceive the *energeia* of the Divine essence. And our ability to contemplate God, in the blessed Trinity, is a specific work of the Spirit, who is inseparable from the Father and the Son, and is why we can only know and predicate anything about God, as the Apostle Paul writes: "Now God has revealed these things to us by the Spirit, since the Spirit searches everything, even the depths of God. For who knows a person's thoughts except his spirit within him? In the same way, no one knows the thoughts of God except the Spirit of God" (1Co 2:10–11). Because only the Son and the Spirit fully know God, it is only by the Son in the Spirit that creatures come to truly, though not fully, know God.

Hilary of Poitiers

Hilary (c. 315–367) was bishop of Poitiers in west-central France. He was the leading orthodox Latin church father during the peak of the Arian power. He is one of the greatest of the Western church fathers, but he is the least studied. His work *De Trinitate*, in response to Arianism (and Sabellianism), is a meticulously profound piece of theology, constructed with great passion and enthusiasm for the clear teaching of the Faith—the triune God. So, why then is he not as well-known nor well-received as others? For one, he was a Westerner, so his Latin tongue could not permeate the Eastern church walls. His work on the Trinity seemed more of a detailed and lengthy response to an epistle from an Arian, which soon deteriorated and was forgotten about. His writing style and form of argumentation are challenging to follow and use for instruction. Furthermore, Hilary's work was soon overshadowed by a later, masterful work on the Trinity from none other than St. Augustine.

Hilary, though an original thinker, was not a great systematician nor did he order his thoughts in a clear and organized manner.[40] Lastly, and rather unfortunately, Hilary has gone down in infamy as the orthodox theologian who claimed that Jesus did not feel pain, though he suffered unto death. And because of such views, those to follow found it hard to look to Hilary as a bulwark of sound theology when he affirmed ideas that evacuated the faith of Christ, our redemption, and even Christ of himself.[41]

While Hilary lacks a following, even today, his *De Trinitate* has much to offer. He has penetrating insights, whereby he tackles a subject exhaustively, leaving the reader depleted of mental acuity. At times I found myself asking Hilary to leave it alone already. He does not know

---

[40] Statements are a summary from the Introduction on Hilary in *NPNF, 2nd Series*.
[41] Carl L. Beckwith, "Suffering without Pain: The Scandal of Hilary of Poitiers' Christology," in *In the Shadow of the Incarnation: Essays on Jesus Christ in the Early Church in Honor of Brian E. Daley, S.J* (Notre Dame: IN, 2008), 71.

when to stop kicking a dead horse. My exposition of his theology comes directly from his *De Trinitate*, though he has other writings. The goal is to outline his doctrine of God, noting the classical strand of thought representative of his work.

De Trinitate is a hefty tome, divided into twelve books. I aim to provide the contours of Hilary's doctrine of God, with an eye to the classical expressions of God showing the continuity of thought within the Christian tradition. I will conclude my exposition with Hilary's views on Jesus' painlessness—his departure from the continuity of Christian tradition.

Hilary commences his work by expressing his intentions to refute particular Arian and Sabellian heretics. (We will see in his writing a strong emphasis on the understanding that the Son's birth [generation] from the Father guarantees a sharing of essence yet a *real* distinction within the Godhead).[42] These teachers have degraded our Holy Savior, Son, and God by declaring him the greatest of all creatures (Arianism) or stating that there are no instantiations or modes within the being of God and that the designations of Son, Lord, and Savior, are mere names of the same God (Sabellianism). Both, therefore, deny the triune God. Through revelation of the Scriptures, God has demonstrated that he is the blessed Trinity, and it is through the Scriptures that Hilary will assert the veracity of this truth, in which he lambastes his opponents for not taking Scripture at its very Word. If God says he has a Son, then he has a Son. We need to then discern the mystery of God, who is one, yet three.

Hilary reminiscently reflects on his thoughts of God in the initial stages of his coming to behold the God of the Hebrew Scriptures. He affirmed a Philosopher's god, of which "omnipotence and eternity are the possession of the One only, for omnipotence is incapable of degrees of strength or weakness, and eternity of priority or succession. In God we must worship absolute eternity and absolute power" (*De Trin.* 1.4). He then "chanced upon" Hebrew books written by Moses and the prophets, where he came face-to-face with God the Creator, the given testimony of the "I AM" who *is*. Hilary writes that nothing is more unattainable to our understanding yet so characteristic of the mysterious Divine nature than his existence. The Divine nature "can neither be originated or

---

[42] Ayres, *Nicaea and Its Legacy*, 179.

destroyed" (*De Trin.* 1.5). God communicates of himself in Holy Scripture that he has no beginning or end, thus he is eternal, and holds the heavens and the earth in the palm of his hand (Is 66:1–2). Heaven is his throne and earth is his footstool, and Hilary says God declares these things in metaphors not as one who sits, but rather as one who has "extension in space," in which his throne and footstool are also held in the hand and palm of "infinite Omnipotence" (*De Trin.* 1.6).

God's presence is revealed in such a manner to manifest to every born and created thing that "God might be known within and without, overshadowing and indwelling, surrounding all and interfused through all. . . . In this wise does God, from within and from without, control and correspond to the universe; being infinite He is present in all things, in Him Who is infinite all are included." God's boundless infinity, as observed in Psalm 139:7–10, means that there is no place or space in which God does not exist, and nothing exists apart from him; he "embraces, and is embraced by, the universe, confined to no part of it but pervading all" (*De Trin.* 1.6).

Hilary recalls his soul trembling as God unveiled himself to him, in beholding him first as God the Father, learning about his eternal and infinite beauty, through which we come to know God as Creator by the things he has made. God is God and there are no others; yet, further revealing of the nature of God, was that of grace and truth, who was with God in the beginning and who is *also* God (*De Trin.* 1.11). God revealed his divine gift to the world: "God the Word became flesh, [and] that through His Incarnation our flesh might attain to union with God the Word" (*De Trin.* 1.11). The Divine mysteries, Hilary writes, were "gladly welcomed by my soul." The mighty workings of God were measured by "boundless faith" not by his "own powers of perception." Hilary says he "refused to *dis*believe because [his soul] could not understand that God was in the beginning with God" (*De Trin.* 1.12). His confession, though not as elegant, reminds us of Augustine, who writes, "For understanding is the reward of faith. Therefore, do not seek to understand in order to believe, but believe that you may understand."[43] Anselm's motto: "For I do not seek to understand that I may believe, but I believe in order to understand. For this I believe,—that unless I believed, I should not

---

[43] Augustine, *Tract.* 29.6, John 7:14–18.

understand."[44] For Hilary, his belief was strong because his understanding was not.

God is beyond our comprehension: God became man—the Immortal died—the Eternal was buried (*De Trin.* 1.13). These cannot be grasped through reason. And therefore, we must not venture beyond what Scripture reveals, which is what heretics attempt to do. Heretics question not so much of *what* is given in Scripture but rather *how* it can be what it says. They want to gauge the Divine mysteries for themselves (*De Trin.* 1.18). And they want to give priority to analogies from nature and anthropomorphic statements in Scripture, giving them control over their interpretation of it. To those who want to hinder God's glorious self-revelation in Scripture, Hilary writes:

> For he is the best student who does not read his thoughts into the book, but lets it reveal its own; who draws from it its sense, and does not import his own into it, nor force upon its words a meaning which he had determined was the right one before he opened its pages. Since then we are to discourse of the things of God, let us assume that God has full knowledge of Himself, and bow with humble reverence to His words. For He Whom we can only know through His own utterances is the fitting witness concerning Himself. (*De Trin.* 1.18)

Hilary recognizes the limitations of using nature metaphors to explain spiritual concepts. This theme is mentioned throughout the rest of his treatise.

In *Book II*, Hilary begins by stating the baptismal command (Mt 28:19) as the summary of the Faith, where Christ commands us to baptize "in the *name* of the Father, the Son, and the Holy Spirit." But the heretics mangle Christ's words. They question the meaning of the divine utterance, and then dogmatically assert some arbitrary interpretation, which, Hilary writes, then "forces us to deal with unlawful matters, to scale perilous heights, to speak unutterable words, to trespass on forbidden ground" (*De Trin.* 2.2). This passage, as simple as it is spoken, heretics easily pervert. Hilary writes:

> Heresy lies in the sense assigned, not in the word written; the guilt is that of the expositor, not of the text. Is not truth indestructible? When

---

[44] Anselm, *Proslogion*, I, 7. In Anselm and Charles Hartshorne, *St. Anselm Basic Writings: Proslogium, Monologium, Gaunilo's In Behalf of the Fool, Cur Deus Homo*, trans. S. N. Deane, 2nd Revised (LaSalle, IL: Open Court, 1998).

we hear the name Father, is not sonship involved in that Name? The Holy Ghost is mentioned by name; must He not exist? We can no more separate fatherhood from the Father or sonship from the Son than we can deny the existence in the Holy Ghost of that gift which we receive. (*De Trin.* 2.3)

In having to respond to the heretic's treasonous actions, Hilary notes, we are compelled to move beyond Scripture. Although language may struggle to capture the ineffable, it is essential to recognize that God has provided precise terms to describe himself. Venturing into greater precision carries inherent risks. Hilary says it fills him with anxiety to consider tearing up Perfection, making laws for Omnipotence, and limiting Infinity (*De. Trin.* 2.5).

Next, Hilary considers the Ineffable, beginning with the divine *simple* nature of God. Our study, thus far, has demonstrated that divine simplicity is foundational in contemplating the Divine essence. One must begin with simplicity to establish a cogent and consistent view of God.[45] Hilary's expression of the simple essence is accompanied by negative terms, with a profound sense of awe of the limitlessness of God, which is what the heretics defile in their perverted doctrines. He writes:

> It is the Father to Whom all existence owes its origin. In Christ and through Christ He is the source of all. In contrast to all else He is self-existent. He does not draw His being from without, but possesses it from Himself and in Himself. He is infinite, for nothing contains Him and He contains all things; He is eternally unconditioned by space, for He is illimitable; eternally anterior to time, for time is His creation. Let imagination range to what you may suppose is God's utmost limit, and you will find Him present there; strain as you will there is always a further horizon towards which to strain. Infinity is His property, just as the power of making such effort is yours. Words will fail you, but His being will not be circumscribed. Or again, turn back the pages of history, and you will find Him ever present; should numbers fail to express the antiquity to which you have penetrated, yet God's eternity is not diminished. (*De. Trin.* 2.6)

Hilary's apophatic statements of glory bring us to the edge of a great chasm that we cannot cross. But because the Son who reveals God has

---

[45] However, some would argue starting with simplicity is a debatable point, in that later writers begin with the triunity of God rather than the oneness of God.

complete knowledge of him, Hilary admonishes us to "let our thoughts of the Father, be at one with the thoughts of the Son," in that he is the faithful witness of the ineffable Creator. To know God, we go to Christ.

Hilary's utilization of apophatic theology serves as a compelling illustration of its significance: to articulate the magnificent transcendence of God. Despite the reluctance of contemporary theologians to employ negative descriptions, Hilary's approach to discussing the Divine essence starkly highlights the disparity between the portrayal of the divine nature in Scripture and the teachings of the heretics. A classical view of God (to use the term anachronistically) is the most consistent approach to properly express and uphold that transcendent distinction.

In articulating the doctrine of the Trinity, Hilary leans toward a monarchian view, whereby the Son draws his life from the Father (Jn 5:26) because "the Father is His sole Origin" (De. Trin. 3.4).[46] Again, this is an eternal relation, with no division or separation of the Son from the Father; rather, the distinction is made by relation (we cannot impose our thoughts of distinction in human terms, which implies distinct centers of consciousness and also bodily divisions), thus upholding Scripture's revelation, or the economy of the Trinity, with the Father as source, ensuring a logical monotheism. The relations of the Trinity, which are the persons, are "mutually Each in the Other, for as all is perfect in the Unbegotten Father, so all is perfect in the Only-begotten Son" (De Trin. 3.4). Hilary clarifies that the Son is the perfect offspring of the Father "with no lessening of the Father or subtraction from His Substance, but he Who possesses all things begat an all-possessing Son; a Son not emanating nor proceeding from the Father, but compact of, and inherent in, the whole Divinity of Him Who wherever He is present is present eternally" (De Trin. 2.22).

---

[46] In 4.33, commenting on Ex 3:2–6, Hilary writes, "For He is God the Only-begotten, and the title 'Only-begotten' excludes all partnership in that character, just as the title 'Unoriginate' denies that there is, in that regard, any who shares the character of the Unoriginate Father. The Son is One from One. There is none unoriginate except God the Unoriginate, and so likewise there is none only-begotten except God the Only-begotten. They stand Each single and alone, being respectively the One Unoriginate and the One Only-begotten. And so They Two are One God, for between the One, and the One Who is His offspring, there lies no gulf of difference of nature in the eternal Godhead."

John 1:1–3 provides the substance of Hilary's understanding of the mysterious generation of the Son, which we will observe. His aim is apologetic; Scripture provides its own explanation, from which we derive such doctrines. Hilary, sarcastically, writes, "From what books shall I borrow the terms needed to state so hard a problem? Shall I ransack the philosophy of Greece? No! I have read, *Where is the wise? Where is the enquirer of this world?* [1Co 1:20] In this matter, then, the world's philosophers, the wise men of paganism, are dumb: for they have rejected the wisdom of God" (*De. Trin.* 2.12). To further demonstrate that one does not need to venture into vain philosophy to arrive at these *truths* of God, Hilary looks to the "poor fisherman, ignorant, uneducated," to whom Christ revealed such mysteries. Hilary is not being disrespectful about John, rather, he is demonstrating that such profound mysteries do not come from the elite, the philosophers of the age; rather, they are revealed to us by the lowly, the common, the uneducated of the world. God has chosen that which is not wise, noble, or powerful from a human perspective to shame the wise, the noble, and the powerful (1Co 1:26–31).

The fisherman, unlettered and unread, writes of the fixed moment of creation with time, *In the beginning . . . was* the uncreated and timeless *Word.* But what if this fisherman's teaching is a departure from the incarnation, Hilary asks? Look to the very next sentence: *And the Word was with God.* We see that the Word *was* and the Word *is* with God in the beginning. He is with the Creator *at* the beginning of creation. Our fisherman, writes Hilary, "has escaped; perhaps he will succumb to the difficulties which await him" (*De Trin.* 2.14). The difficulties Hilary speaks of are in the assertion that the Word is merely an utterance from God, the sound of his voice. But that is not what we see. Granted, there is a mode of understanding in which we do say the Word is the "expression of the eternal Thinker's thoughts," which must also be eternal. However, the Word is not just an expression of God's thoughts; rather, he is a distinct mode or instantiation of the Divine essence (not in the Sabellian sense). While human words come into existence when uttered and then fall out of existence at the completion of the word, John's words declare the Word was in the beginning before words existed, with God, not *in* God as words and thoughts reside in our minds. What are we to see of this Word? Hilary writes: "The Word is a reality, not a sound, a Being, not a speech, God, not a nonentity" (*De. Trin.* 2.15).

Hilary continues his exposition of key texts of John's Gospel with meticulous resolve. But we must move forward. In *Book III*, Hilary takes up John 10:38, *The Father is in me, and I am in the Father*, expounding on the implications of this text in the divine Godhead. Because Hilary begins with the doctrine of simplicity, he can move into articulating what consists (speculatively speaking) within the Godhead. Later in his treatise, Hilary provides a few concise statements on simplicity, stating, "God is God, and it is God in Whom God dwells" and "He abides in One Who is His own, born from himself. God is in God, because God is from God" (*De Trin.* 4.40). The properties that belong to the Father are endowed to the Son, in their fullness. The Son has the fullness of the Godhead. And because God is Spirit, then the Father and the Son indwell each other.

The distinction between the Son and the Father is relational not essential. It is a true substantial existence, as the Divine essence does not have mixture or separation. I am going to jump ahead a bit in Hilary's treatise to flesh out the distinction. Hilary grounds his argument for the divinity of Christ in the fact that he is described by the divine properties and actions of God. He notes that we see the distinction consigned in the name, *The Word*, who is indistinguishable from the Father in nature and thus inseparable but is revealed to us as the divine utterance (Jn 1:1–3) and in the names *Power* and *Wisdom* of God (1Co 1:25), to show that the Word was not alien from the divine nature (*De Trin.* 7.11). Hillary's argument refutes heretical appeals to Exodus 7:1 and Psalm 82:6 to deny that Christ is God of God. Starting with Exodus 7:1, where God says he has made Moses *a god to pharaoh*, Hillary asks, "Does not this addition *to pharaoh* account for the title? Did God impart to Moses the Divine nature? Did he not rather make Moses a god in the sight of pharaoh?" In Psalm 82:6, where God says, "You are gods," Hillary notes this designation is a granting of favor, not a definition. A definition provides us "knowledge of the object," whereas, a description or title, as in 82:6, "has its origin only in the speaker's words, not in the thing itself." God provided the definition of his nature in Exodus 3:14, and we see it in Christ, in John 1:1, in the eight "I am" passages in John's Gospel, and in the names *Power* and *Wisdom* in First Corinthians 1:25.

Nowhere else in Scripture do we see the divine properties of God ascribed to creatures; rather, Scripture gives such designations to Christ to demonstrate that he is not a mere creature.

Following this discussion, Hilary addresses the question of how or what is it to glorify one who has all glory. Hilary's argumentation is lucid, starting from the essence and attributes of God, as derived from Scripture, whereby, Hilary writes, "God is subject to no change; His eternity admits not of defect or amendment, of gain or of loss. It is the character of Him alone, that what He is, He is from everlasting" (*De Trin.* 3.13). While one might think we are at a standstill, the Evangelist (John) does not fail to provide the answer. He writes: "Since you gave him authority over all people, so that he may give eternal life to everyone you have given him. This is eternal life: that they may know you, the only true God, and the one you have sent—Jesus Christ" (Jn 17:2–3).

Hilary's explanation from this text reveals an important and often forgotten aspect of how we are to understand the relationship between God in his essence and God in revelation, or rather, the divine economy. For example, God's glory. He cannot lose glory nor can more glory be added to him. But God glorifies himself through the Son, by being made known to us in the flesh, being charged with restoring eternal life....."He is glorified through the Son in the sight of us, ignorant, exiled, defiled, dwelling in hopeless death, and lawless darkness" (*De Trin.* 3.13). Hilary shows the full circle of this glory between the Father and the Son, who are both full in glory in the Divine essence but revealing that glory in time and space. He writes:

> It is through this work of the Son that the Father is glorified. So, when the Son received all things from the Father, the Father glorified Him; and conversely, when all things were made through the Son, He glorified the Father. The return of glory given lies herein, that all the glory which the Son has is the glory of the Father, since everything He has is the Father's gift. For the glory of Him who executes a charge redounds to the glory of Him Who gave it, the glory of the Begotten to the glory of the Begetter. (*De Trin.* 3.13)

In *Book IV*, Hilary delves into the core tenets of his doctrine. Early on, he examines the creation accounts in Genesis 1 and John 1, drawing connections between them to demonstrate that the act of creation occurs through divine dialogue of the Father saying to the Son, "Let there be . . ." and the Son executes his Father's will and brings about creation through him—*ex nihilo*. In Proverbs 8, the quintessential patristic creation passage, Hilary remarks on the wisdom of God; "she" was with him, not only present with him in the beginning but setting things in order. Hilary writes, "The Father, by His commands, is the Cause; the Son, by His execution of the things commanded, sets in order. The distinction between the persons is marked by the work assigned to Each. When it says, *Let us make*, creation is identified with the word of command; but when it is written, *I was with Him, setting them in order*, God reveals that He did not do the work in isolation" (*De Trin.* 4.21). The divine economy reveals the distinction of persons within the Godhead bringing about a greater understanding for us in the reading of God's activity. What initially sounds like God is just talking out loud to himself, is the Father talking to the Son as they rejoice in the manifestation of their divine will in creation.

Hilary delves further into theological proofs of the divine nature of the Son, whereby the Father and the Son, the one who commands and the one who creates are both true God. The logic of this assertion, Hilary notes, is that when God says let there be a firmament and the text says, "And God made the firmament," only the distinction of persons not a difference of power and nature is being asserted. Under the title of God, he reveals first the thought of him who spoke, then the action of him who created. Thus, the activity of the Godhead demonstrates that "the power to give effect to the word of creation belongs only to that Nature with Whom to speak is the same as to fulfill" (*De. Trin.* 5.5). And from this unity of divine dialogue and activity, Hilary formulates a definition of absolute power, with it being proper to both God the Father and the Son:

> Absolute power is this, that its possessor can execute as Agent whatever His words as Speaker can express. When unlimited power of expression is combined with unlimited power of execution, then this creative power, commensurate with the commanding word, possesses the true nature of God. Thus, the Son of God is not false God, nor God by adoption, nor God by gift of the name, but true God. (*De Trin.* 5.5)

Of the power displayed in the incarnation, Hilary writes, it is "a great work the unbelieving soul cannot grasp" (*De Trin.* 5.18). The godless[47] just see the feeble flesh in Jesus' helpless state at birth, growing into manhood, living as a carpenter, who is then arrested, scourged, and hung on a cross to suffer and die. The mystery of God was hidden beneath this flesh, in that the Logos added these capacities of humanity to his divinity, which the divine nature could not and did not possess. And he did so while retaining his full divinity, never ceasing to be God when he took on man. Hilary notes the display of divine power in the display of weakness and suffering, as he came to be what he previously was not. The person of Jesus Christ is folly for the faithless but the wisdom of God. In that, they cannot see that Christ is the power of God. Hilary writes, "So Christ in your eyes is not God because He, Who was from eternity, was born, because the Unchangeable grew with years, the Impassible suffered, the Living died, the Dead lives . . . is not all this simply to say that He, being God, was omnipotent?" (*De Trin.* 5.18).

To understand God's wisdom, to grasp his glory, Hilary writes, "God cannot be apprehended except through God; even as also God accepts no worship from us except through God."[48] A few sentences later, he writes: "We must learn from God what we are to think of God; we have no source of knowledge but Himself" (*De Trin.* 5.20, 21). In his concluding paragraphs of *Book V*, Hilary sums up his exposition of the Godhead in the Godhead itself. He writes,

> That true and absolute and perfect doctrine, which forms our faith, is the confession of God from God and God in God, by no bodily process but by Divine power, by no transfusion from nature into

---

[47] "Blasphemy is incompatible with wisdom; where the fear of God, which is the beginning of wisdom, is absent, no glimmer of intelligence survives" (*De Trin.* 5.26).

[48] In a later statement in this treatise, Hilary writes: "God is a simple Being: we must understand Him by devotion and confess Him by reverence. He is to be worshipped, not pursued by our senses, for a conditioned and weak nature cannot grasp with the guesses of its imagination the mystery of an infinite and omnipotent nature. In God is no variability, no parts, as of a composite divinity, that in Him will should follow inaction, speech silence, or work rest, or that He should not will, without passing from some other mental state to volition, or speak, without breaking the silence with His voice, or act, without going forth to labour. He is not subject to the laws of nature, for nature has received its law from Him: He never suffers weakness or change when He acts, for His power is boundless, as the Lord said, *Father, all things are possible unto Thee*" (*De Trin.* 9.72).

nature but through the secret and mighty working of the One nature; God from God, not by division or extension or emanation, but by the operation of a nature which brings into existence, by means of birth, a nature One with itself. (*De Trin.* 5.37)

Heresy often arises when thinkers let figurative language shape their interpretation of Scripture, leading to teachings that deviate from biblical orthodoxy. Hilary makes this observation multiple times, noting the error of taking analogies too far, in that "human analogies are not a perfect application for the mysteries of Divine power," rather, their value is in their comparison between the material and spiritual, intending to raise us closer to apprehend the majesty of God (*De Trin.* 6.9). However, and here is where the folly rushes in hard when we do not accept what Scripture says, "when we are told that God was born from God, we must accept it as true that He was born, and be content with that" (*De Trin.* 6.9). The lack of discernment in handling such passages, whereby one gives priority to the earthly manner of discourse in one's interpretation of Scripture, is disastrous when it comes to contemplating the Divine Essence.

Hilary is correct when he says we need to accept what Scripture says about the procession of the Son from the Father, but we must not assign the Father's act of begetting the Son according to human, bodily categories. Nothing bodily, lifeless, or material has a place in the essence of God; rather, "being immutable, [the Divine essence] has no incongruities, within it. God, because He is God, is unchangeable; and the unchangeable God begat God" (*De Trin.* 6.12). Hilary concludes using creedal language to express this mystery that the birth of the Son from the Father is not a "prolongation of God in space," not an extension, but rather "Light from Light." Light from light shows a unity and continuity in expressing the Divine essence.

In *Book VII*, Hilary continues advancing his arguments "against the wild extravagance of modern heresy" (*De Trin.* 7.1). In summarizing what has been discussed and refuted, Hilary confesses that "the straight path of truth" is that "each divine person is in the Unity, yet no Person is the One God." It has been shown that Christ has the full deity of the Father, whereby "His name, His birth, His nature, His power, and His own assertion" as found in Scripture leaves us without a doubt of his origin. "Two truths are combined in one proposition," writes Hilary;

"that His works are done likewise proves His birth; that they are the same works proves His nature" (*De Trin.* 7.18). Against the raging and cunning heretics, Hilary says his position is impregnable! John 5:19–23 demonstrates the divinity of Christ, God of God, in that he "is the Son, because He can do nothing of himself; He is God, because whatever the Father does, he does the same; They Two are One because He is equal in honor to the Father and does the very same works; He is not the Father, because he is sent" (*De Trin.* 7.21)

The foundation of Hilary's doctrine of the Trinity lies in the ultimate oneness that serves as the means of articulating the triunity of God, rather than just conferring a title. If the triunity of God were derived from the diversity of God, the error of tri-theism would be constantly nipping at our heels. Having the oneness of God as our anchor point places restrictions on our language and interpretation. When we see distinctions of the Father, the Son, and the Spirit, the unifying force of oneness compels us to base our doctrine on the simple oneness of God. Hilary follows that path. He notes that God's attributes are not attached to different portions of him; rather, "God, Who is Life, is not a Being built up of various and lifeless portions; He is Power, and not compact of feeble elements, Light, intermingled with no shades of darkness, Spirit, that can harmonize with no incongruities. All that is within Him is One; what is Spirit is Light and Power and Life, and what is Life is Light and Power and Spirit" (*De Trin.* 7.27).

Interestingly Hilary says that God's nature "cannot suffer change" but is "capable of increase, not of diminution." He speaks of the analogy of fire to express his point, casting light (no pun intended) on this meaning. The flame of a fire kindles another but without division, separation, or change to the property of fire itself. But in the second flame, the first flame lives on. The two are one, deriving light from light, though physically impossible to divide or distinguish the two. The eternal Divine essence did not exist at "a time" when the Son was not one with the Father; however, with the analogy of the flame, we can observe a material comparison that shows us the possibility within created matter of two objects united as one without a visible distinction or division. Hilary sees that the nature of God increases in that giving birth to the Son is comparable to a flame begetting another flame. However, as Hilary notes often in scrutiny, such analogies are meant as an aide for apprehension of the Faith.

Throughout our study of Hilary, it is readily apparent that the Holy Spirit has remained in the shadows. But in *Book VIII*, he devotes some attention to the Spirit, specifically, seeking to "expose their [the heretics] license of speculation" of the origin of the Spirit, the Paraclete. Scripture is quite clear on this, writes Hilary. Quoting John 16:12–15, Hilary says of the Spirit, "Accordingly He receives from the Son, Who is both sent by Him, and proceeds from the Father" (*De Trin.* 8.20). However, Hilary notes that this raises a question: "Now I ask whether to receive from the Son is the same thing as to proceed from the Father. But if one believes that there is a difference between receiving from the Son and proceeding from the Father, surely to receive from the Son and to receive from the Father will be regarded as one and the same thing" (*De Trin.* 8.20). They are the same because Christ says that everything the Father has is his. The unity of the Father and the Son writes Hilary, makes no difference from whom the Spirit is received because that which is given by the Father, according to Scripture, is also given by the Son.

Hilary's position on this point is another reason why the Eastern church was unreceptive to his Trinitarian doctrine. Hilary has made the unity of God so absolute that it dissolves the key feature of the Cappadocian [thus Eastern] doctrine of the Trinity, the hallmark of logical Trinitarian thought, the monarchy of the Godhead (even though Hilary sees the Father as the origin/source). According to the Eastern doctrine, if the sending of the Spirit is ascribed to the Father and equally to the Son, then we have two Gods. Eastern thought says the Father is the source, with the Son generating from the Father and the Spirit's **SPIRATION** from the Father through the Son. With the Father designated as the source of the Godhead, we can maintain monotheism and affirm a triune expression of it.

For Hilary, the notion of the Spirit of God in respect of each person of the Trinity is to distinguish God from composite matter. Only incomposite matter can be omnipresent (not that God is "matter"), thus God is omnipresent. Hilary writes, He, "in his infinite power, is present everywhere and nowhere absent, and manifests His whole self through His own, and signifies that His own are nought else than Himself. So that where they are, He may be understood to be Himself" (*De. Trin.*

8.24) With consistency, Hilary resorts to the simplicity of God to provide a metaphysical grammar to the biblical doctrine of divine omnipresence. He is everywhere present, all of him in every place but not located in every place; God cannot be located in a place because God is everywhere present.

Hilary now delves into the topic of the coinherence of the Godhead. If our doctrine is not clear and consistent with the Divine essence, then we are in jeopardy of landing into tritheism. The challenge is put forth regarding the Spirit of God and the Spirit of the Son indwelling in those who believe. A brief side note: The concept of omnipresence pertains to the pervasive nature of God's presence, encompassing all of creation while maintaining a clear distinction from it. His immediate presence denotes God's specific activity within his creation. This distinction aids us in differentiating the two aspects of God's relation to his creation. For example, we know the Scripture that says God cannot be in the presence of sin (Hb 1:13; cf. Ps 5:4), but that cannot mean God cannot be present around sinners otherwise God would not be in the world. Given that no creature can evade the Divine gaze, we assert that God's presence is mediate to all creation (everywhere known). However, because of his holiness, God refrains from communing with sinners. The immediate presence of God is an inward work, known only to those whom God wants to reveal himself.

Getting back to Hilary, he writes that the indwelling of God in the believer is not a "joint dwelling; it is one indwelling: yet an indwelling under the mysterious semblance of a joint indwelling, for it is not the case that two Spirits indwell, nor is one that indwells different from the other" (*De Trin.* 8.27). And we can again use the analogy of fire to shed light (again, no pun intended) on how this could be so. Logically, Hilary asserts Christ's oneness with God's Spirit, in that "what is of God is also of Christ, and what is of Christ is also of God, Christ cannot be anything different from what God is. Christ, therefore, is God, one Spirit with God" (*De Trin.* 8.27). Hilary continues further in his scriptural proofs demonstrating the deity of the Spirit, looking to such passages as Ac 1:4–5, 8; 1Co 8:4–6; 12:3, 8, 11; Ep 4:5–6; Jn 6:40, and others.

In the closing of *Book VIII*, Hilary offers an exposition of Colossians 1:15–20, which is worthy of close study. He aims to demonstrate that the unity and the fullness of the Godhead remained unbroken in Christ's birth. In his examination of Philippians 2:6–7, Hilary shows how the apostle does not perceive Christ's "being in the form of God" prior to his incarnation as a form of another god. Rather, the apostle assumes that this God, of which Christ was in the form, is the one, true God of the Bible. He who is in the form of God is God and cannot be other than God since God is the necessary being. The Son "possesses naturally from Him in Who glory He is, the property of divinity" (*De Trin.* 8.47).

Specifically, Hilary seeks to answer two questions: Is Christ the visible likeness of the invisible God? And can the infinite God be presented to view under the likeness of finite form? (*De. Trin.* 8.48). Hilary writes that we know that "Christ is a Spirit and God is a Spirit," so if we bound his Spirit in corporeal form then he cannot be the likeness of the invisible God because a finite representation cannot bear the "image" of the infinite. But we are not left without an answer. Christ told his disciples that he who sees him sees the Father, and this is evident in the works he does. If he does the work of the Father, then he has the same nature as the Father, since only divinity can do that which is proper to divinity. From his reading of Colossians 1:15–20, Hilary concludes that through the power of these works, as in the power perceived from which such activity occurred, Christ, therefore, is the image of God. As the image of God, Christ is meant to express the nature of divinity, not the form of God materially speaking, so "that by his exercise of the powers of the divine nature, that that nature is in [Christ]" (*De Trin.* 8.49).

The divine nature is perceived in the things that have been made (Ro 1:20). In Colossians 1:16–17, Hilary sees the origin of created things being described, *in, from, through,* and *for* Christ. In vv. 18–20, which Hilary refers to as the dispensation of Christ assuming a body, "the Apostle has assigned the spiritual mysteries their material effects." Hilary sees two aspects of the divine economy represented by the image of God in Christ. As the image of the invisible God, Christ is the head of his body, the church. And as he is called "the beginning," he is the first-born of every creature from the dead, for the express purpose that in all things "He might have the pre-eminence, being for us the Body, while He is also the image of God, since He, who is the first-born of created things, is at the same time the first-born for eternity" (*De Trin.* 8.50). What Hilary is getting at is that by Christ being the first-born of every created thing, since he possesses in himself the origin of all of creation, and being head of his body, the church, the first-born from the dead, Christ has preeminence because all things consist for him, in him, and are reconciled in him. Therefore, Christ, as the image of God is the origin of creation and the origin of recreation.

In conclusion, Hilary asks: "Do you now perceive what it is to be the image of God? It means that all things are created in Him and through Him." But there is a greater redemptive-cosmological reality to be observed. He writes:

> Whereas all things are created in Him, understand that He, Whose image He is, also creates all things in Him. And since all things which are created in Him are also created through Him, recognize that in Him Who is the image there is present the nature of Him, Whose image He is. For through Himself He creates the things which are created in Him, just as through Himself all things are reconciled in Him. Inasmuch as they are reconciled in Him, recognize in Him the nature of the Father's unity, reconciling all things to Himself in Him. Inasmuch as all things are reconciled through Him, perceive Him reconciling to the Father in Himself all things which He reconciled through Himself. For the same Apostle says, But all things are from God, Who reconciled us to Himself through Christ, and gave unto us the ministry of reconciliation: to wit, that God was in Christ reconciling the world unto Himself. Compare with this the whole mystery of the faith of the Gospel. For He Who is seen when Jesus is seen, Who works in His works, and speaks in His words, also reconciles in His reconciliation. And for this cause, in Him and through Him there is reconciliation, because the Father abiding in Him through a like nature restored the world to Himself by reconciliation through and in Him. (*De Trin.* 8.51)

What implications can we draw from Hilary's statement? Christ, as the image, in whom all the fullness of deity dwells bodily, in him, through him, from him, and for him all things have been created. In Christ taking on flesh and reconciling the world to God, in a consummative manner, the fullness of the Godhead is present in bodily shape, being fully present in his body, the church. In this way, Hilary can say that in Christ's birth, him taking on flesh, the Godman is true God. The Godhead fully dwells "wholly" in the person of Christ, "so dwelling that the Two are one, and so one, that the One Who is God does not differ from the Other Who is God: Both so equally divine, as a perfect birth engendered perfect God" (*De Trin.* 8.56).

The Painlessness of Christ

For many, *Book X* is where Hilary's brilliant theology finds its end. It is here, some say, that Hilary loses his orthodoxy, thus losing Christ and the Faith. In *Book X* Hilary takes up the notion of Christ's suffering in the flesh. Hilary believes that while he suffered, he did not feel pain. Why does Hilary think that? Before his discussion on it, Hilary responds to heretical claims against Christ having an impassible nature because of the fear he demonstrated during his Passion week, thus ultimately submitting to suffering (*De Trin.* 10.9). He challenges their reading of specific texts (Mt 26:38–39, 46; Lk 23:46), asking why would he, who drove away the fears of death in his apostles with the inheritance of glory to come, fear suffering and death? If death is life (i.e., Mt 10:38–9), "what pain can we think He had to suffer in the mystery of death, Who rewards with life those who die for Him?" (*De Trin.* 10.10). Hilary questions, Why would Christ, whose life and act of death that were by his choosing, according to the plan of God, be stricken with fear, as the one who has the power to lay down his life and to take it up again? He concludes, stating, "If Christ died of His own will, and through His own will gave back His Spirit, death had no terror, because it was in His own power" (*De Trin.* 10.11).

Hilary's remarks are thought-provoking (and alarming). He continues his dialectical monologue, asking that if Christ did fear death, was it terrible to his Spirit or his body? It cannot be to his body because the Holy One will not see corruption as Scripture foretold (Ps 15:10), nor can it be his Spirit, in that we see Lazarus rejoicing in Abraham's bosom, and Christ is supremely greater than them; therefore, the abyss of hell is not waiting for him, and so he has nothing to fear (*De Trin.* 10.12). In conclusion, Hilary pointedly states:

> It is foolish and absurd, that He should fear death, Who could lay down His soul, and take it up again, Who, to fulfill the mystery of human life, was about to die of His own free will. He cannot fear death Whose power and purpose in dying is to die but for a moment: fear is incompatible with willingness to die, and the power to live again, for both of these rob death of his terrors. (*De Trin.* 10.12)

But Hilary questions the issue further, enquiring about the kind of body "the Man Jesus was, that pain should dwell in His crucified, bound, and pierced body." The human body, writes Hilary, is endued with life and feeling, in conjunction with a sentient soul. Thus, it is the soul that feels various sensations (cold, heat, pleasure, hunger, paint, etc.). And through a "transfusion of the soul" with the body, when the body is pierced, for example, it is the soul that feels and suffers pain. This psycho-somatic pathology implies that when a limb becomes diseased, it loses the feeling of living flesh, and it can be cut or burnt, and no pain is sensed "because the soul is no longer mingled with it" (*De Trin.* 10.14). And when a limb needs to be cut off, drugs can lull the soul to sleep, whereby the limb can be removed without pain. Hilary's estimation of this phenomenon leads him to conclude that "the body lives by admixture with a weak soul, that it is subject to the weakness of pain" (*De Trin.* 10.14).

In contrast to the nature of the human body, Jesus' body, which is of true humanity after the likeness of our flesh, Hilary writes, "when it was struck with blows, smitten with wounds, or bound with ropes, or lifted on high, He felt the force of the suffering but without its pain" (*De Trin.* 10.23). Hilary identifies a key distinction between Christ's body and our bodies: "His conception was in the likeness of our nature, not in the possession of our faults" (*De Trin.* 10.25). In Christ taking on flesh, his sinlessness, due to his divine nature, meant that the body he took "possessed a unique nature of its own" (*De Trin.* 10.23); it could suffer, but it could not feel pain.

Hilary's perspective is informed by his comprehension of the term *likeness*. For Hilary, *likeness* implies the truth of his birth, but it removes sin and human weakness from him. In his decision to take on flesh in the form of a servant, Hilary distinguishes the incarnation, separating the human and the divine natures of Christ, stating that "Christ as man submitted to a human birth; yet as Christ, He was free from the infirmity of our degenerate race" (*De Trin.* 10.25). For Hilary, Christ must maintain the fullness of each nature in his person, with the distinction noted above. The Word taking on flesh, because he is the Word and is not of human origin, does not "vacate the nature of His Source." And while we must believe that the Word *is* flesh (which he made), in his dwelling among us, "the flesh was not the Word, but was the flesh of the Word dwelling in the flesh" (*De Trin.* 10.25). And because of the unique nature of his body, brought forth through "spiritual conception," not a natural one, the Word had the power to expel the infirmities of the body (*De Trin.* 10.35).

Hilary is confident that he has proved his point. But, in the very last few sentences of *Book X*, he writes:

> He was born for us, *suffered for us*, died for us, rose again for us. This alone is necessary for our salvation, to confess the Son of God risen from the dead: why then should we die in this state of godless unbelief? If Christ, ever secure of His divinity, made clear to us His death, Himself indifferent to death, yet dying to assure that it was true humanity that He had assumed: why should we use this very confession of the Son of God that for us He became Son of Man and died as the chief weapon to deny His divinity? (*De Trin.* 10.71, emphasis added)

In our analysis of Hilary, we encountered a profound demonstration of theological expertise and resolute apologetic dedication. His deep engagement with the subject matter was accompanied by a remarkable capacity to meticulously delineate arguments and establish cogent, logical connections. Therefore, it is perplexing to see how someone of his intellectual stature could come to the conclusion that Christ did not experience pain. On the one hand, there is a speculative logic that makes sense, but on the other, if Christ is to redeem man, then he had to take up man—all that is proper to man (minus the sinfulness). Pain is a distinct aspect of the human condition that can drastically impact what we do. Fear of pain and actual pain in the flesh can cause us to cave into our sinful desires and turn away from the Lord. If Jesus was to redeem man for his weakness, then he must also overcome the pain of the body to be obedient to the Father. No human can look at the passion of Christ without first intuitively considering the pain he went through. And that is one of the glorious aspects of the resurrection—no more pain.

Ambrose

Ambrose (c. 339–397) was the Bishop of Milan and played a crucial role in the spiritual journey of Augustine. Ambrose's preaching led to Augustine's conversion and baptism. As with his other contemporaries, Ambrose was engaged in stopping the corrupting influence of Arianism. His works, therefore, were aimed at refuting Arian heresy, paying special attention to the exposition and defense of the divinity of Christ and the Trinity. Ambrose formulates his arguments according to Nicaean orthodoxy, quoting direct statements from the creed in his treatises. The principal work from which we will extract his theological concepts of the doctrine of God is *The Exposition of the Christian Faith*, or *De fide* as it will be cited in our study. This work was written at the request of the emperor Gratian, specifically wanting a treatise that proved the divinity of Christ, to repel the Gothic invasion and Arian heresies. *De fide* is comprised of five books and presents an exposition of Christian doctrine. It emphasizes the full divinity of Christ, asserting his equality in substance, wisdom, power, and glory with God the Father, in constant appeal to the Scriptures, elucidating the plain sense of the text. Additionally, Ambrose confronts new objections from the Arians and refutes their false interpretations.

Book I

Ambrose begins *Book I* with the underlying presupposition, "the declaration of our Faith," that "God is One." The oneness of God is declared in Scripture, in that he is the Lord Almighty, who beholds all things and is demonstrated as such through his works (*De fid.* 1.1.6–7). Ambrose sets out to prove the deity of the Son, demonstrating his oneness with the Father and the Spirit, in the blessed Trinity. The Arians asserted the oneness of God. Ambrose leveraged this shared fundamental biblical principle to illustrate the inseparability of Christ from the Father. He demonstrated that the scriptural designations of divinity attributed to Christ, proper to the Father, effectively maintain the unity of God.

Ambrose appeals to the baptismal formula, the NT revealing of the triune God in Matthew 28:19, in which God is "one in name" and "one in power," of the Trinity. The difference between the Persons is observed, but their unity of essence is demonstrated, as Christ himself testifies that he and the Father are One (Jn 10:30), in which there is "no separation of power and nature." Quoting the Athanasian Creed, clause 4, Ambrose writes, "The Father and the Son are One, not by confusion of Person, but by unity of nature." Ambrose moves into the classic texts and expressions in the Gospel of John, pointing the reader to the power and works of God displayed by the Son as the validation of his full divinity same as the Father (Jn 5:19, 30). God is eternal, good, almighty, true, and perfect, and it is in Christ whom all the fullness of the Father dwells (Col 2:9), thus the eternality, goodness, almightiness, truthfulness, and perfection dwell in him (*De fide*. 1.2.13). And "seeing that Christ is God," Ambrose writes, "He is, by consequence, good and almighty and eternal and perfect and true; for these attributes belong to the essential nature of the Godhead" (*De fide*. 1.2.15).

The Son is related to the Father through generation, not procreation, which is the typical erroneous assumption of the heretics. Through generation—the Father is begetter, and the Son is begotten; the Son is one with the Father, one in eternality and divinity, yet distinct by relation. Ambrose points out that we do not use mere names to make the distinction but rather through "signs of power manifesting itself in works." And in Scripture's designation that God is Father, he then must have a Son, and the Son does the same works as his Father, which testify that "there is no difference either of substance or will" (*De fide*. 1.2.16–18).

Ambrose refers to OT passages that show the unity of operation and of name (Ps 45:6–7; Ge 19:24), whereby we do not speak of two individual Gods but rather the unity of the Godhead. The Pauline formula in First Corinthians 8:6, where Paul specifically modifies the Shema (Dt 6:4), lexically extends the unique identity of the one God to consist of God the Father and the one Lord the Messiah—*through whom all creation exists* (cf. Is 42:5; 44:34; 45:12). Paul's concern was monotheistic worship, in which eating food offered to idols and participating in temple banquets to anyone or anything other than God is an abomination. Therefore, to mitigate any confusion in Corinth as to what Christ is (i.e., is he an idol?), Paul incorporates Christ into the Shema, *the highest* confessional statement of monotheism in all of Scripture.

In chapter 7, Ambrose takes up his proof of the divinity of Christ by examining Paul's statement that the Son is the image of the Father, "the image of the invisible God" (Col 1:15). Others before Ambrose have referred to this passage to defend the deity of the Son, but I think Ambrose's treatment has a certain analytical clarity I find particularly helpful that boxes in his opponent, resulting in the incontrovertible truth that the Son is equal to the Father.

Ambrose remarks on Hebrews 1:3, which says, "The Son is the radiance of God's glory and the exact expression of his nature." Coupled with Colossians 1:15, Ambrose builds his argument against Arius who denies the Son's sameness in essence with the Father. In looking at these passages, we must ask what is meant by *image*, especially image of that which is invisible. Ambrose cites Psalm 36:9, in which the Psalmist writes, "For the wellspring of life is with you. By means of your light we see light." Therefore, Ambrose concludes, "In the Son the Father's glory shines clearly." When Christ says to Philip, he who sees me sees the Father (Jn 12:45), Christ as the image of the invisible Father cannot mean that Christ is the physical representation of God. Rather, he is the image "simply derived from God, coming out from the Father, drawn from the fountainhead." Ambrose continues, "he who looks upon the Son sees, in portrait, the Father." And what must entail from this statement? If you look upon your portrait, who do you see? Yourself. And because God is invisible, without form, what do we see in the portrait of the Father in Christ? Ambrose writes: "Truth, Righteousness, the Power of God: not dumb, for it is the Word; not insensible, for it is Wisdom; not vain and foolish, for it is Power; not soulless, for it is Life; not dead, for it is the Resurrection" (*De fide.* 7.48–50).[49]

John 1:1 is given special attention as proof for the eternality of the Son like the Father but the indivisible unity of the eternal Godhead, demonstrating that in the Word being "with God," the Word abides in God, "not confounded or mingled" (according to Nicaean orthodoxy), "but is distinguished by the perfection unblemished." And Ambrose concludes, "the Word is God," "not as an utterance of speech but of celestial excellence" (*De fide.* 1.8.57). In chapter 9, Ambrose directly challenges the heretics' assertion that the Son existed before all time yet is not co-eternal with the Father. He grounds his argument in the scriptural teaching that Jesus is the agent of creation. And as such, he is the Creator of time; therefore, as the ruler of his own work, he "cannot have begun to exist after His own work." God is immutable, and so if he is unchangeable, then he has had to always be "Father." Therefore, to be called "Father," and unchangeable, God must have had a generation of the Son that is not in time, thus the Father and *necessarily* the Son are co-eternal, thus suffering no change. Ambrose's forceful argument shows the folly of the heretics if they hold to the view that the Son is not

---

[49] Ambrose finishes the chapter with the typical exposition of Gen 1:27 to demonstrate the shared image of the Son with the Father.

eternal: "The Father is mutable," which they strictly deny—"the Father begets impassibly" (*De fide.* 1.8.58–61, 67).

In chapter 16 (1.16.100–04), Ambrose addresses the error of confusing uncreated and created, particularly the Arians' blasphemy of Christ in assuming that "created" and "begotten" are the same. He looks to the Apostle Paul who forbade creature worship yet professed to be a servant of Christ (Ro 1:1), asking why Paul would call himself a servant of Christ if he were a created being. And how could there be any created nature in God, for he is uncompounded? God alone is divine; nothing can be added to him; he fills and penetrates all things, yet nothing can fill or penetrate him; he is present everywhere, which means he is fully present to every part of his creation every moment of its existence (which he sovereignly sustains).

Explaining that the Son is *from* the Father, Ambrose writes, that his proceeding from God is not an act of creation but of relation and oneness of the Divine essence. He cites John 8:42, a classic text yet not overly explicative of a doctrine of procession. My modern translation says, "Jesus said to them, 'If God were your Father, you would love me because I came from God and I am here. For I didn't come on my own, but he sent me.'" Many can read this passage and assume that Jesus' words meant he was sent from the Father, which is what he states at the end of the passage. But the phrase *I came from God,* has a particular nuance, which becomes more distinct in John 16:28, which says, "I came from the Father and have come into the world." In looking at both passages, we have a distinction between the coming from the Father and coming or being sent into the world. The Greek is helpful to see this more clearly. The word Jesus uses when speaking of his coming from the Father is the Greek word *exēlthon,* which means *to go out* or *come out of.* And this is particular of Jesus in Johannine usage (cf. Jn 13:3; 16:27, 30; 17:8). Elsewhere in the Gospels and Acts we see this word used to refer to spirits that come or go out of persons (cf. Mk 1:25f; 5:8; 7:29; 9:25; Lk 4:35; Mt 12:43; 17:18; Lk 4:35 twice, 41; 8:29, 33, 35, 38; 11:24; Ac 16:18; Mk 5:13; 7:30; 9:26, 29; Lk 4:36; Ac 8:7).[50] Ambrose's argument, exegetically speaking, is sound, demonstrating that if God has nothing created in his nature and Christ comes from the Father, then Christ is not a created being (*De fide.* 1.16.106).

---

[50] "ἐξέρχομαι," in BDAG.

Ambrose remarks on the works the Son does, which belong properly to divinity. These works the Son does because he sees the Father doing them. Since he does the same works that the Father does, then he is equal in power, and, importantly, Ambrose writes, "the Godhead is proper to each Person, and freedom lies not in any difference, but in unity of will" (*De fide.* 1.17.112).

Book II

We now move into *Book II*. Chapter 2 in this book is instructive for us in that Ambrose takes interpretive liberties that we do not see in modern historical-critical hermeneutics. In the previous chapters, and the first *Book*, Ambrose demonstrates that the Son carries out divine operations, as the Father does. Attributing the works of God to Christ can only mean he is divine. Now, in chapter 2, Ambrose makes the lexical move to place Christ in the OT, to show the Son's goodness proved from his works, "namely, His benefits He showed towards the people of Israel under the Old Covenant, and to Christians under the new" (*De fide.* 2.2.2.). Ambrose places Christ at the Red Sea (Ex 14), demonstrating his goodness making the waters "flow around the faithful." He places him standing on the rock at Horeb, Exodus 17 (1Co 10:4), showing "the handiwork of the true Creator," causing the rock to stream forth water. He places him in the wilderness, bringing manna from heaven so that Israel does not perish due to famine, sustaining them, even down to imperishable shoes on their feet (Dt 8) (*De fide.* 2.2.21–4). The whole sweep of the Bible reveals Christ; therefore, Ambrose (and all premodern interpreters of Scripture) sees that the work of God is a work of the triune God in every divine action we see in the text, whether the Old or the New.

Ambrose shifts the discussion to the oneness of the Son as God. The essence of the Son is the same as the Father. God is one, which means there are no other gods. So, if God is in Christ (Jn 17:22–3), we have two distinct persons of the Godhead, but there is "no division of their Godhead" (*De fide.* 2.3.33). And in the oneness of the Son and the Father—the Godhead—the Son is omnipotent. Ambrose bases this on the authority of the Old and New Testaments. The Son is Lord, the Lord is Almighty, therefore, the Son of God is Almighty. The Almighty one is the Alpha and the Omega, who is, who was, and who is to come (Re 1:8). Christ is "Almighty, Lord, and God" (*De fide.* 2.4.34–5).

In showing the unity of the Son with God, in that he is God, Ambrose addresses the challenging doctrine of the incarnation, specifically the Son assuming a human will and affections, clarifying the distinctions between his deity and humanity. The unity of Christ with the Father is identified in their "unity of working." God's "will issues straightway in actual effect." The human will of Christ is observed in his fear of death, but the passion of the Son, to suffer for us, depended on the Divine Will. The Scripture says he bore our grief and sorrows, as the prophet Isaiah declared (53:4). His death, therefore, "made an end of death" (*De fide.* 2.7.52–55). In taking on human nature, he "took the affections of a human soul" because "God could not have been distressed or have died in respect to his being God." Only human nature would cry out in being forsaken, being man; therefore, Ambrose writes, "He is distressed, as man He weeps, as man He is crucified" (*De fide.* 2.7.56).

Ambrose cites Paul and Peter, affirming this distinction, who said "They have crucified the flesh of Christ" (Ga 5:24) and "suffered according to the flesh" (1Pe 4:1). The Godhead is "secure from death." In conclusion, Ambrose notes that when the text says the Lord of Glory was crucified (1Co 2:4), it is because he who is man is also God. It is by virtue of his divinity that he could take on humanity in the man Christ Jesus. In possessing both natures, "He endured the Passion of His humanity, in order that without distinction He who suffered should be called both Lord of glory and Son of man, even as it is written: 'Who descended from heaven' (Jn 3:13)" (*De fide.* 2.7.58).

In the following chapter, Ambrose aims to address a difficult passage that some interpret as suggesting that the Son is inferior to the Father— "The Father is greater than I" (Jn 17:28). Ambrose follows the Great Tradition in his interpretation, making the proper distinction between the *oikonomia* and the *theologia*. The error is taking texts that are proper to Christ's humanity and inferring it to his divinity. The *skopos* of Scripture is the revelation of God in Christ. The revelation is accommodated to humanity, in that the *Divine essence* is revealed in *human essence*. Revelation is not a transformation or mutation of the Divine essence. Therefore, a consistent interpretation must apply a canonical understanding of God, which reveals that his essence is not creaturely. So, when God takes on human nature, we must be careful to avoid interpreting passages in a manner that places human properties in the Godhead. And that is what Ambrose does; he reminds the reader about what is proper to the Divine essence: God is always present in every place and does not pass from place to place. Therefore, Christ is not speaking of his divinity but of his humanity, being lower than the Father. The unity of will and display of divine work demonstrates his deity.

Ambrose takes us to Psalm 22 to prove his point through a prosopological reading of the text. This interpretive tool, as mentioned earlier, situates Christ in the Old Testament in the first person. Christ is speaking in the *character* (Gk. *Prosopon*) of David, engaging in a divine dialogue with the Father. Ambrose's point is to further strengthen his argument regarding the distinction between Christ's humanity and divinity. To do so, he draws our attention to *Christ's words* in Psalm 22 (and buttresses it with Isaiah 53:7) that Ambrose puts in parallel fashion to John 17:28, *lexically extending* the New Testament into the Old and vice-versa. Ambrose writes:

> How, indeed, can He be a lesser God when He is perfect and true God? Yet in respect of His humanity He is less—and still you wonder that speaking in the person of a man He called the Father greater than Himself, when in the person of a man He called Himself a worm, and not a man, saying: "But I am a worm, and no man;" and again: "He was led as a sheep to the slaughter." (*De fide.* 2.8.61)

The Scripture does not speak of his inferiority of his begottenness; rather, he was "'made lower,' that is, *made* inferior." In his taking the form of a servant, Christ did not part with what he was; rather, "he took up what he was not"—a servant (*De fide.* 2.8.62). Ambrose notes that categories of greater and lesser lose their meaning when we are speaking of the Divine essence. Such categories are "proper to corporeal existences; one who is greater is so in respect to rank, or qualities, or at any rate of age" (*De fide.* 2.8.64). He was made lower, *according to creaturely distinction*, so that he "might taste death for everyone" (He 2:9). In an absurd tone, Ambrose states that if we do not affirm this distinction, then "lest we should suppose the Godhead, not the flesh, to have endured the Passion!" (*De fide.* 2.8.65).

While the Jews were in grave error for rejecting Christ as the Son of God, their error proves to be instructive for us, thus an implicit biblical argument for the divinity of the Son. The Jews were in error because they understood the implications of Jesus' *outlandish* claims—

Yahweh in human form. Ambrose points out that the apostle John testifies that the Son is not lower than the Father, just *by reason* of being the Son. When Christ said in John 5:17, "My Father is still working, and I am working also," his words incited the Jews to want to kill him because they understood his claim meant he was "making himself equal to God" (Jn 5:18). And how does Jesus respond? He further proves his divinity stating, "For whatever the Father does, the Son likewise does these things" (Jn 5:19).

In chapter 10, Ambrose takes up the objection that the Son is inferior because he disobeyed God and obeyed his mother. Surely this is a strange objection, but it provides Ambrose with the opportunity to demonstrate the unity of power in the Godhead. Interestingly, Ambrose notes that the events in and after the Passion are exemplary of the oneness in the power of the Trinity. He writes:

> Thus, we have learnt that the power of the Trinity is one, as we are taught both in and after the Passion itself: for the Son suffers through His body, which is the earnest of it; the Holy Spirit is poured upon the apostles: into the Father's hands the spirit is commended; furthermore, God is with a mighty voice proclaimed the Father. We have learnt that there is one form, one likeness, one sanctification of the Father and of the Son, one activity, one glory, finally, one Godhead. (*De fide.* 2.10.85)

What we observe in Ambrose's Trinitarian theology is a constant reference back to the unity of the Godhead. Even in an event where Scripture seems to speak most clearly of the *separation* of the Son from the Father, Ambrose sees it as a marvelous display of the unity and oneness of the triune God.

Book III

We are jumping ahead to *Book III* to briefly look at a few texts in chapter 14. In this section, Ambrose considers the question of the Son's substance, which he argues is one with the Father. Scripture teaches that the Son is the image of the Father's substance, indicating that there is nothing of the Godhead that the Son does not share with the Father. Ambrose cites John 16:15, where Christ says, "Everything the Father has is mine." In his interpretation of this passage, Ambrose does not suggest that "everything" is material, or that "something" is given to the Son by an act of giving. Rather, it is in virtue of his likeness with the Father that he has everything of the Father. Ambrose writes, "We cannot, then, deny substance to God, for indeed He is not unsubstantial, who hath given to others the ground of their being, though this be different in God from what it is in the creature. The Son of God, by whose agency all things endure, could not be unsubstantial" (*De fide.* 3.14.109). The heretics err because they interpret this passage by way of *oikonomia* rather than *theologia*.

Book IV

In *Book IV*, Ambrose continues to refute Arian heresies, specifically showing their inconsistent interpretations and applications of scriptural passages that distort the oneness of the Son with the Father. He considers the Arians' interpretation of Ephesians 5:23–5, which they assert teaches that God being the head of Christ, therefore, makes him inferior to God. As we can see, their mistake is blending or blurring the lines between *theologia* and *oikonomia*. Ambrose outlines the distinction in the context of the passage, clarifying that God is the head of Christ, "in so far as His form of a servant, that is, of man, not of God, is considered." And this taxonomy is proper in the context of *oikonomia*. According to the reality of Christ's assuming of flesh, he is likened unto men, therefore, accordingly, God is the head. It has no bearing on the *theologia*, as it pertains to the Son of God, regarding his Godhead, he is one with the Father; "we do not take his sovereignty but attribute compassion to him" (*De fide.* 4.3.33).

While the *oikonomia* reveals a distinction between the persons, the persons share in the Divine Substance. Therefore, there is no separation in power or wisdom. The Father is in the Son, not to sanctify but according to their mutual indwelling, the Word, the Son is in the Father, the Father in the Son (Jn 15:11; 17:21), and the Spirit in the Father (Ro 8:9, 14; Jn 4:11) and the Son (Ro 8:9). In the oneness or "Unity of the Divine Substance," Ambrose writes, "Nor . . . is the power of the one increased by the power of the other, for there are not two powers, but one Power; nor does the Godhead entertain Godhead, for there are not two Godheads, but one Godhead" (*De fide.* 4.3.36). Ambrose then notes the distinction when it comes to the indwelling of God in man, in that power received comes from the one Christ dwelling in us, but also the Father and the Spirit. And while the unity is common in the Divine essence, "the Substance of God and the substance of man are different."

Therefore, Ambrose writes, the unity that we have with the triune God "shall be one by grace" (*De fide.* 4.3.37).

Ambrose aims to delineate the ontological categories the Arians fail to maintain between the Son and the Father, and in their examples or analogies from Scripture (e.g., they use First Corinthians 3:8 to show that the Father and the Son are one as Paul and Apollos are one in nature and faith). The distinction is noted in Jesus' prayer in John 17:21, where he says, "May they all be one, as you, Father, are in me and I am in you." Ambrose points out that Jesus did not say "You in us, and we in you," but "You in me, and I in you," "to place him apart from His creatures." The full dignity of the Son is that of the Father, which he has "by natural right of His Sonship." We, creatures, have sonship by grace, not by nature (*De fide.* 4.3.38).

In chapter 4, Ambrose responds to the Arians' rejection of the Son as of the Divine Substance when Jesus says, the Son can do nothing of Himself (Jn 5:19). His approach follows the text and its implications, and then he returns to the unity of the Divine Substance, and the implications that follow. Ambrose observes the tenuousness of their arguments, in that in the very next sentence Jesus explains what he means, adding greater force to his argument of the oneness of the Son with the Father. Jesus, qualifying his statement in 5:19, says, ". . . but only what he sees the Father doing. For whatever the Father does, the Son likewise does these things." Ambrose asks: Why is it not written that the Son does "such like things?" If he does the same works the Father does, what does that imply about the Son? He is distinct by relations but one in essence, power, and will. If he does the same works, Ambrose writes, then "let the heretics cease to deny the omnipotence of Him Whom they confess able to do all things that He has seen the Father doing" (*De fide.* 4.4.40–1).

Ambrose wants to take the argument further, grounding it in divine aseity and divine simplicity. He asks the rhetorical question, "Is there anything impossible to God's Power and Wisdom?" His question is a setup. Christ is the Power of God and the Wisdom of God (1Co 1:24). As God's Power and Wisdom, Ambrose, with the understanding that God is Almighty, entails *aseity*, in that his power and wisdom are "not gifts received from another." Rather,

He is the Life, not depending upon another's quickening action, but Himself quickening others, because He is the Life; so also He is Wisdom, not as one that is ignorant acquiring wisdom, but making others wise from His own store; so, too, He is Power, not as having through weakness obtained increase of strength, but being Himself Power, and bestowing power upon the strong (*De fide*. 4.4.43).

While Ambrose does not explicitly deploy a doctrine of simplicity, his argument has all the features of origin, i.e., he makes his argument of the Son's divinity—named the Wisdom and Power of God—from the concept of God's essence as the origin of his being, which means all that he has comes from himself, specifically, he *is* his attributes. Ambrose does not say the Son *has* life, but that he *is* Life; thus, also he *is* Wisdom, he *is* Power. And as the source of Life—he animates, of Wisdom—he gives wisdom, and of Power—he gives power.

Book V

The bulk of *Book V* consists of proofs for the unity of the Father and the Son as demonstrated through divine acts and power. Ambrose considers passages that imply the inferiority of the Son to the Father, which the Arians continually cite to support their argument of the Son's subservient position, by nature, to God.

Throughout *de Fide*, Ambrose, with relentless resolve and great precision, successfully excises the heretical arguments foisted by the Arians, asserting that the Son is a creature. He has applied rigorous exegesis of the specific passages (or rather proof-texts) on which the Arians base their claims. His approach is consistent, in that he does not isolate passages from their immediate context or the canonical context as the heretics do.

In the last segment of *Book V*, Ambrose masterfully handles the quintessential go-to passage heretics use to support their claim that the Son is a creature—Mark 13:32, where Jesus says, "Now concerning that day or hour no one knows—neither the angels in heaven nor the Son—but only the Father." In defending the deity of the Son, exegesis guided by an *oikonomia–theologia* approach proves most formidable and instructive, in that it maintains consistency and clarity *of Scripture as a whole*, unlike interpretations that prioritize one aspect over the other.

Responding to the *misreading* of Mark 13:32, Ambrose writes, "For how could the Son of God be ignorant of the day, seeing that the treasures of the wisdom and knowledge of God are hidden in him?" (Col 2:3) (*De fide.* 5.16.193). Now, Ambrose could have simply left it there, allowing this passage to expose the inconsistency in their interpretation. However, he takes the opportunity to refute their erroneous claims.

First, Ambrose inquires about the nature of knowledge that Paul attributes to Christ in Colossians 2:3. He asks, by what nature (i.e., *how* and /or place of origin) does he have this "knowledge of God"? Does he have it "by reason of His being or by chance?" Creatures have certain aspects of knowledge by nature of their creatureliness and some by learning. Horses can run due to knowledge of nature as do fish swim. Humans, however, can only swim by learning to do so. So then, what do we say of this "knowledge of God" that the Son has? If he has this knowledge through learning, then we cannot call him, as Scripture does, begotten as Wisdom and gradually became perfect, implying he was once not perfect. However, if he has it by nature, "then he was perfect from the beginning. He came forth perfect from the Father; and so, needed no foreknowledge of the future" (*De fide.* 5.16.194).

Ambrose refers to the priciple pattern of Christian truth that Christ is the "the Wisdom of God." Therefore, as *the* Wisdom of God, the Son could not be ignorant of the "day or the hour." And since Scripture tells us that the Son created all things, how could he be ignorant of some thing or some aspect of his creation? Ambrose's attention to this point is significant. It is often misunderstood that, although God created the world with time, *time*, particularly the future, appears to operate independently from God. This view implies that time exists outside of God's sovereign rule until a specific moment *comes* into existence. Hebrews 1:2–3 says, "In these last days, he has spoken to us by his Son. God has appointed him heir of all things and made the universe through him. The Son is the radiance of God's glory and the exact expression of his nature, sustaining all things by his powerful word. After making purification for sins, he sat down at the right hand of the Majesty on high." The Greek word translated as *universe* (or *world* as found in many English translations) is *aiōnas*, which is *ages*. It is the *ages*—past, present, and future—that the Son created and sustains. Ambrose writes,

> How then were those made which are future, unless it is that His active power and knowledge contains within itself the number of all

the ages? For just as He calls the things that are not as though they were [Ro 4:11], so has He made things future as though they were. It cannot come to pass that they should not be. Those things which He has directed to be, necessarily will be. Therefore, He who has made the things that are to be, knows them in the way in which they will be (*De fide*. 5.16.198).

Ambrose's point concludes that if the Son made and sustains the *ages*—past, present, and future—we must believe that he is not ignorant of the day of judgment because that day, though future to us, nevertheless, "the Son of God has knowledge of it, as being already made by him" (*De fide*. 5.16.198).

Next, Ambrose lexically extends the depiction of God as the Creator in the OT to include the Son, stating, that if the Creator—the Son with the Father—has numbered all the stars in the sky and has given them names (Ps 147:4), how could he be ignorant of some things in his creation? Scripture says that the Father made all things in wisdom (Ps 104:24), through his Son, who is the Virtue and Wisdom of God (1Co 1:24) (*De fide*. 5.16.195–96). Would we dare say that there is something in or about creation that the Father does not know?

Ambrose makes a clever move, calling the heretics' attention to Matthew 11:27, where Jesus says, "All things have been entrusted to me by my Father. No one knows the Son except the Father, and no one knows the Father except the Son and anyone to whom the Son desires to reveal him." Therefore, Ambrose asks, if the Son is the only one who knows and can reveal the Father, how is it possible that he does not know the day? (*De fide*. 5.16.200). Demonstrating beyond a doubt that the Son knows the day, Ambrose points us to the Son's words in Luke 17:20–31. In this section, Christ speaks of the day when the Kingdom comes, mentioning the signs, the time, places, or persons, all leading up to that day. He says, "On that day, a man on the housetop, whose belongings are in the house, must not come down to get them. Likewise, the man who is in the field must not turn back." How then, Ambrose exclaims, could he be ignorant of the day? He continues recalling the times and signs that will pass as that day closes in. Therefore, he who is Lord of the Sabbath, how does he know all these events yet *not* know "the day"? (*De fide*. 5.16.202–07).

Ambrose continues to display the continuity of Scripture, by examining passages that show *discontinuity*, answering the question of why Christ was unwilling to state the time of that day. Simply put, "it was not to our advantage to know; in order that we, being ignorant of the actual moments of judgment to come, might ever be as it were on guard, and set on the watch-tower of virtue, and so avoid the habits of sin" (*De fide.* 5.17.208). This follows suit with what Scripture has prescribed, as a means for sinners to keep a close eye on their manner of conduct, knowing that the judgment will come on them when they least expect it. If they knew the day and the hour, then there is no fear of punishment. "For impurity generally spurs them on, but fear is irksome to the end" (*De fide.* 5.17.209). But again, the question is asked, "Why did Christ not refuse his disciples as one who knew, but would not say; and why did He state instead that neither the angels nor the Son knew?" Ambrose draws his answer from other texts that speak about God or the Godhead, not specifically of the Son because he does not separate or isolate passages specific to the person to demonstrate deity; rather, he argues from the unity of will and power of the persons and then examines passages that speak of one person as pertaining to all the persons—all for one, and one for all.

In answering this question, Ambrose offers a *reductio absurdum* argument. He looks to Genesis 18:20–1, in which it appears that God is ignorant of sinful human activity. The text says, "Then the Lord said, 'The outcry against Sodom and Gomorrah is immense, and their sin is extremely serious. I will go down to see if what they have done justifies the cry that has come up to me. If not, I will find out.'" Ambrose remarks, that when God says he will go down to see if Sodom and Gomorrah's sin is so heinous, deserving of God's immediate judgment, does this mean that God was ignorant of the sins they were committing? And then in the Psalms when the psalmist writes that the Lord looked down upon the children of the earth to see if any of them understand and seek for God (Ps 53:2), does this imply that God was ignorant of their merits? (*De fide.* 5.17.213). The answer to both questions is no; God did not have to go down to man to learn of man's ways. The language of Scripture is accommodated to mankind's understanding, so that man can grasp the things of God, in the unfolding of his will and revealing of his nature.

Ambrose takes the reader through a few other passages that seem to imply ignorance or lack of power in God (cf. Lk 20:13; Mt 21:37; Mk 12:6). Ambrose responds by applying the Arians' interpretive logic (i.e., whereby they deny the true deity of the Son due to passages of ignorance applied to him) to passages of ignorance or being deceived that pertain to God the Father, which both sides would never understand imply a denial of divinity (*De fide.* 5.17.213–18). Ambrose's approach is brilliant, by deploying an *oikonomia–theologia* hermeneutic, he destroys the validity of their arguments.

In Ambrose's theology, there is a clear coherence in his interpretation of Scripture, maintaining the unity of the Godhead as the governing rule in how he interprets the Bible. Because of this guiding principle, the essence and nature of God override any notions of creaturely properties that Scripture posits of God (i.e., anthropomorphic language). Doing so promotes continuity in the will and decree of God, which would be lost if an overly literal interpretation, as the Arians applied, had the upper hand in one's interpretation. The outcome of such an approach is that we will end up denying the very doctrines about the essence and attributes of God that the Bible professes about him. In Ambrose we see a continuation of a Nicene-Trinitarian classical metaphysics (spiritual exegesis, dogmas, and metaphysics), forming the basis of his interpretive approach to Scripture, becoming the hallmark of the Great Tradition.[51]

John Chrysostom

John Chrysostom (c. 347–407) was the archbishop of Constantinople. Being the most prolific of all the Eastern fathers, he fought against the ecclesiastical and political leaders for their abuse of authority. He was given the name *Chrysostom* (meaning "golden-mouthed") for his eloquent sermons.[52] This most distinguished of Greek patristic preachers excelled in spiritual and moral application in the Antiochene tradition of literal exegesis, largely disinterested, even untutored in speculative and controversial theology.[53]

---

[51] Carter, *Interpreting Scripture*, 61–91.

[52] Micah Wierenga, "John Chrysostom," in *Lexham Bible Dictionary*.

[53] D. F. Wright, "Chrysostom, John," in Earle E. Cairns, J. D. Douglas, and James E. Ruark, eds., *The New International Dictionary of the Christian Church* (Grand Rapids,

On the Incomprehensible Nature of God[54] (*De incomp.*) will be the text of exposition. As mentioned, Chrysostom did not have an affinity for speculative theology. But it will be interesting to observe how he goes about formulating his thoughts on such a topic. *De incomp.* is a polemical and apologetic work aimed at a new uprising of Arian followers. This new crop of extremists was known as the Anomoeans. They maintained that God is simple and one; unbegotten and not produced. No being, therefore, could be begotten or produced, thus no being could be of the same substance (*homoousios*), of similar substance (*homoiousios*) nor like (*homoios*) God; but it must be dissimilar and unlike (*anomoios*) God—hence the name Anomoeans.[55] While man cannot know the essence of God, the Anomoeans call the Divine essence *agennetos*, "ungendered." The Anomoeans argued that if we do not know God's essence, then we do not know what we are adoring. But Chrysostom responds, stating we are not required to know *what* God is just *that* he is. We can know who he is without needing to know *what* his essence is; thus, speculation of his essence is not expected of us.[56]

De incomp. is divided up into twelve homilies, with the first five dealing with the incomprehensible nature of God, the sixth is an interruption of sorts, with seven through twelve focused on the Son's substance being the same (*homoousios*) as the Father. Chrysostom does not write with the theological depth we find in Basil, Gregory of Nyssa, or Gregory of Nazianzus. His audience is made up of laymen, orthodox and heterodox, whom he is trying to edify and sway from error.[57]

In *Homily 1*, Chrysostom begins with a confession of his own (humble) ignorance, regarding his knowledge about God though he cannot explain it. He writes,

> I know that God is everywhere, and I know that he is everywhere in his whole being. But I do not know how he is everywhere. I know that he is eternal and has no beginning. But I do not know how. My reason fails to grasp how it is possible for an essence to exist when that

---

MI: Zondervan Publishing House, 1978), 225.

[54] Saint John Chrysostom, *On the Incomprehensible Nature of God*, The Fathers of the church (Washington, D.C.: Catholic University of America Press, 1984). *De incomprehensibili Dei natura homilae 1–12.*

[55] "Introduction," in John Chrysostom, *On the Incomprehensible Nature of God*, 18.

[56] "Introduction," in John Chrysostom, *On the Incomprehensible Nature of God*, 26.

[57] "Introduction," in John Chrysostom, *On the Incomprehensible Nature of God*, 28.

essence has received its existence neither from itself nor from another. I know that he begot a Son. But I do not know how. I know that the Spirit is from him. But I do not know how the Spirit is from him. (*De incomp.* 1.19)

His intention is to divert his opponents from "meddling" with the essence of God. He believes that such inquisitiveness is the very height of folly, pointing out that even the inspired prophets of Scripture were unable to fully grasp the vastness of God's wisdom, which comes from his essence. Therefore, how foolish and mad it is that the Anomoeans think "that they could make his very essence subject to their power and processes of reasoning?" (*De incomp.* 1.23). Chrysostom quotes the prophet of grace, David, who, in speaking of God's omnipresence, is dumbfounded at the realization that whether he goes up to heaven or down to hell, God is there (Ps 139:8). And while God has revealed secret and hidden things to David, he says God's wisdom is inaccessible and incomprehensible, having no limit (Ps 147:5). Again, Chrysostom is rebuking and exhorting the Anomoeans to let go of their arrogant assertions, thinking they can limit God's essence and greatness (*De incomp.* 1.26).

Chrysostom addresses the Anomoean's interpretation of First Corinthians 13:12, which says, "My knowledge is imperfect now; then I shall know even as I was known." For some strange reason, the Anomoeans state Paul is talking about God's governance of the universe. Chrysostom replies that Paul is saying his "present knowledge of God is imperfect and in part." And then we see Chrysostom invoke the normative assumption about God's essence. He continues, "Paul did not say 'imperfect' because he knows one part of God's essence and does not know another part—for God is simple and has no parts" (*De incomp.* 1.32). God's essence is unknown to us; therefore, though we know he exists, is wise, is great, is omnipresent, and provides and cares for his creation, we do not know the extent of these attributes nor how he does all the things in the governance of his creation (*De incomp.* 1.33). God is simple and has no parts . . . . Chrysostom's reference to the simplicity of God is intriguing because modern theology views simplicity as a speculative doctrine; however, Chrysostom, who deliberately avoids speculative theologizing, refers to simplicity as *the standard principle* of divine contemplation.

One reason why divine simplicity is often perceived as counterintuitive to a formative biblical doctrine of God is the common modern misconception that it describes something about God. Properly understood, simplicity is a *negative* statement; it tells us what God *is not*. God, as Chrysostom states, does not have parts. He is what he is *through* himself, thus his *true essence*, his divine constitution, is simple. While Chrysostom aims to confine his doctrinal formulations to the biblical text (not in a Biblicist fashion, however), he employs the specific nomenclature of *divine simplicity* in his theology. Chrysostom takes simplicity for granted because of the implications derived from the biblical revelation of God. He sees that the God of the Bible is transcendent and incomprehensible, and apophatic language provides an appropriate framework to speak about the God we cannot comprehend.

In *Homily II*, Chrysostom continues his response, rebuking the Anomoeans' for their blasphemous assumption that they can know God as God knows himself. In their "meddling" of God, the Anomoeans *bring down* the Divine essence to fit their own understanding. Chrysostom cites Isaiah 40:22, who was engaged in a similar discourse of demonstrating the transcendence of the one true God as the Creator and Lord of the universe to idol worshipers. Isaiah directs his audience's attention to God as Creator, demonstrating how he surpasses anything we can comprehend. He spoke the universe into existence, above which God sits enthroned and considers as nothing. His unfathomableness is demonstrated in that Scripture and our senses show the vastness of God's creation, nevertheless, God created it with ease (*De incomp.* 2.25). All the nations, Chrysostom notes, though expansive and many, Scripture says are "like a drop in the bucket before him" (Is 40:15). The myriads of angels, thrones, dominations, and principalities, "God made all these powers with such ease that no words can explain it. The mere act of God's will was enough to make them all" (*De incomp.* 2.28, 30). God's act of willing brought forth the universe. Chrysostom with great pity, says to the Anomoeans, "Tell me. When you hear this, do you not weep for yourself, do you not bury yourself in the earth because you have lifted yourself to such a pitch of madness that you are playing the busybody and striving to meddle with God?" In bringing down God to creaturely apprehension, the Anomoeans are "treating him as something worthless," when he is inestimable (*De incomp.* 2.30, 31).

As with Isaiah, and all the other prophets and authors of Scripture—Old and New Testaments, the distance between God and man is the dialectic of debate. So too in contemporary theology the dialectic of distance, the ontological otherness, is always in tension. Paul shows this distinction between God and man using a potter and clay analogy, showing the vast distinction between God and creatures. But even then, Chrysostom notes, "The distance between the essence of God and the essence of man is so great that no words can express it" (*De incomp.* 2.37). The implication in Paul's potter-clay analogy is to show us that we are clay in the Potter's hands, who has the power and the right to turn, shape, and form as he pleases. Paul's intentions, Chrysostom writes, are not to "deprive us of our freedom" nor "destroy our power to choose. Rather, he spoke so that he might do more and more to curb the arrogance of our tongues" (*De incomp.* 2.37).

Chrysostom notes the arrogance that Paul addressed was not as great as the Anomoeans. Paul's audience was inquisitive of God's will, and his governance—why is one man punished, one finds mercy, or one escapes vengeance? But they were not "meddling" with the essence of God (*De incomp.* 2.38). The Anomoeans' actions are antithetical to the way of faith. Not that we show faith blindly; rather, we are called to show faith in that which we cannot comprehend, trusting God as Abraham did, "fully convinced that what God had promised, he was also able to do" (Ro 4:21), even if we cannot comprehend *how*. The resurrection is the pinnacle of mystery. No power of reasoning can understand it, which is what the ultimate demonstration of faith is: to know the power of his resurrection, which Paul makes as his aim and goal (*De incomp.* 2.45).

For Chrysostom, the glory of God is untarnished whether man praises him to his best ability or dishonors him, as the Anomoeans. "God always abides in his own glory" (*De incomp.* 3.3). God's glory is brought down by the Anomoeans in the "madness and folly" of their arrogance to claim they can grasp the ineffable God "who is beyond our intelligence, invisible, incomprehensible, who transcends the power of mortal worlds" (*De incomp.* 3.5). In their extravagant boasting, they have reduced themselves to "creatures who crawl on the ground." Chrysostom's sharp tone may seem inappropriate, but for him, such claims jeopardize one's salvation and thus must be denounced as blasphemy.

To further expose the radical disparity in the Anomoeans' claims, Chrysostom poses another challenge to them. Citing Paul, who says, the Lord dwells in "unapproachable light" (1Ti 6:16), he asks the "heretic" What does this mean? It does not say the one who is in unapproachable light but rather it is the *light* that is unapproachable. By way of *argumentum a fortiori*, Chrysostom observes, if the light is unapproachable, how much more so is the one who dwells in it? To be unapproachable means that one cannot investigate or come near to it (*De incomp.* 3.11, 12). The Seraphim must cover their faces because the light, the very essence of God, is beyond their ability to see and comprehend. What they could behold was "a condescension accommodated to their nature" (*De incomp.* 3.15). God accommodates his revelation in relation to the weakness of vision in creatures. While Isaiah stated he saw the Lord sitting on a high and lofty throne (Is 6), the essence of God does not "sit." He is not enclosed, encompassed, or circumscribed by any limit, for he is the one who determines limits. The Seraphim are around him, not locatively speaking, but because they are nearer to God than man because "their nature is far more pure, wise, and clear-sighted than man's nature" (*De incomp.* 3.17). In coming to the end of this homily, Chrysostom laments about his weariness that has arisen from making numerous arguments about the incomprehensibility of God. But he is not tired; rather, he writes, "My soul shudders and has become frightened since it has dwelt too long on speculations about heavenly matters" (*De incomp.* 3.30).

Homily IV continues pressing in on the Anomoeans. Again citing Paul, who refers to the "unfathomable riches of Christ" (Ep 3:5–7), Chrysostom exclaims, "What does he mean by 'unfathomable'?" It means the riches of Christ cannot be discovered, or searched out, nor can we even find a trace (*De incomp.* 4.14). Chrysostom looks to the Apostle John to expand the cloud of support against the Anomoeans. He expounds on the implications in John's statement that "No one has ever seen God" (Jn 1:18). He recalls the previous examples given so far, whereby humans and creatures have "seen" God, however, this was merely an act of accommodation and condescension to the weakness of creatures. "No one," writes Chrysostom, "of those prophets saw God's essence in its pure state from the fact that each one saw him differently. God is a simple being; he is not composed of parts; he is without form or figure" (*De incomp.* 4.19).

Chrysostom evidences his statement by the fact that all the prophets saw different forms and figures when they beheld God. Again, it is fascinating to note that the simple essence of God is a normative touchstone of his theology. However, this begs the question, "What then did they see?" As to the "powers above" (i.e., angels, Seraphim, and Cherubim), Chrysostom qualifies that "sight" is knowledge. They do not have material eyes like creatures have. So, when Scripture says they turned their eyes away, the intention is to demonstrate that not even the "powers above" can endure and comprehend God with a pure and perfect knowledge. To look "fixedly" on God "means to know" (*De incomp.* 4.22, 23).

The Apostle John understood that knowledge of God is beyond all comprehension, which is why he references "the Son" who is seated at the right hand of God (Jn 1:18; cf. Ps 110:1). And while this should be enough to silence the Anomoeans, the Son is called the one Lord (1Co 8:6) and the unique Son. In finishing his prologue, John makes the unquestionable assertion that while no one has seen God, "the only begotten Son, who is in the bosom of the Father, has revealed this."

Chrysostom notes that John gives the Son "special excellence" in designating the title "only begotten" to him. Therefore, we see he stands out from all the earthly notions of a son, in that among men the name *son* also belongs to us by analogy. But the "title *only begotten* is Christ's alone and belongs to one else, even by analogy" (*De incomp.* 4.25, 26). And if this is not enough to persuade the Anomoeans, Chrysostom *crassly* asks, "Would the Father let himself have the Son in his bosom unless the Son were of the same essence?" Furthermore, "could the Son endure to dwell in the Father's bosom if the Son were of a nature inferior to the Father's?" (*De incomp.* 4.28). The manner of expression we see from the Apostle John means we must understand that *bosom* equals *knowledge.* How else are we to understand the nature of Christ's sonship to the Father if he does not have a body? Chrysostom notes that we have two incontrovertible truths: God is the "I am who I am," from which we understand he is eternal and "Who is in the bosom of the Father," teaches us that the Son is in the bosom of the Father from all eternity" (*De incomp.* 4.30). And here we see Chrysostom's proof that the Father and the Son are of the same essence, glory, majesty, and power, which the Arians and the Anomoeans deny.

Chrysostom, having thoroughly demonstrated from Scripture that the essence of God is incomprehensible to *every* creature, proceeds to expound that only the Son and the Holy Spirit possess "full and perfect knowledge" of God (*De incomp.* 4.31). After a detour, he returns to where he left off (the subject matter in 4.24–30), resuming his discussion regarding John 1:18, "No one has ever seen God. The only begotten Son, who is in the bosom of the Father, himself declared him" (*De incomp.* 5.4). John 6:46, where John noted Jesus' reply to the Jews, stating "Not that anyone has seen the Father except the one who is from God. He has seen the Father" informs Chrysostom's interpretation. He understands "see" as "know." He asserts that Jesus' intention in stating "Nobody" and then adding "except the Son" is to exclude all created beings. Some ask why he excludes the Spirit. The Spirit is not excluded; "nobody" qualifies creatures only, the Spirit is not a creature. Chrysostom notes that "the word, 'Nobody', always is used to express the exclusion of creatures alone . . . in the very matter of knowledge" (*De incomp.* 5.6). To prove his point, Chrysostom looks to Paul to support two particular arguments: 1) If the question is about the Father, it does not exclude the Son. And 2) If it is about the Son, it does not reject the Spirit. His qualifiers show a normative assumption of interpretation: God is triune; therefore, whatever is designated about the incarnation pertains to all three, thus the being of God.

In First Corinthians 2:11, Paul writes, "For who knows a person's thoughts except his spirit within him? In the same way, no one knows the thoughts of God except the Spirit of God." In comparing these two *inspired* statements, if we understood that both writers were excluding the Son (Paul) and the Spirit (John) from "knowing" God, then we have a contradiction. Either "no one" does *not* pertain to the Spirit and Christ (but refers specifically to creatures) or it does, and then the biblical writers are incoherent. Chrysostom demonstrates a serious problem if we follow such logic, noting that "the word 'one' is used in the same way as 'no one,' and has the same force and power." He continues:

> Consider this. Paul says: "One God, the Father from whom are all things, and one Lord, Jesus Christ, through whom are all things." If the Father is said to be one God, it excludes the Son from being God; if the Son is said to be one Lord, it excludes the Father from being Lord. But surely the Father is not excluded from being Lord because of

Paul's words: "One Lord, Jesus Christ." Therefore, neither is the Son excluded from being God because of the words: "one God, the Father." (*De incomp.* 5.8)

The specific designations of the Father as "one God" and Jesus as "one Lord" do not exclude either person from the Divine essence; rather, Chrysostom writes, that the very addition of the word "Father" designates a "personal reality" in God. If "'God' can belong to and denote only that personal reality, the addition of the name 'Father' would serve no purpose" (*De incomp.* 5.10). The name "God" is common to both the Father and the Son, so Paul's statement would be unclear if he did not specify the personal reality of the person he was referring—the Father is the "first and unbegotten personal reality" (*De incomp.* 5.11).

Chrysostom looks at two specific passages (Mt 22:42–44; He 1:7–8) where both the Father and the Son are listed together as being called "Lord" and "God." In Matthew 22:42–44, Jesus cites David (Ps 110:1), speaking in the Spirit, who says, "The Lord said to my Lord: Sit at my right hand." And Jesus puts his audience to the test: "What do you think about the Messiah? Whose son is he?" "David's," they say. And Jesus replies, "If David calls him 'Lord,' how then can he be his son?" Chrysostom asks, "Do you see how both Father and Son are called Lord?" (*De incomp.* 5.18). Showing the Father and the Son together are called "God," in Hebrews 1:7–8, citing David (Ps 104:4), the author attributes to the Son, writes, "Your throne, O God, stands forever and ever . . . therefore, God, your God, has anointed you with the oil of gladness beyond your fellows" (*De incomp.* 5.19).

Chrysostom goes on to show scriptural proofs from the OT demonstrating that the word "God" is not greater than the name "Lord" (Ex 20:2; Dt 6:4, 13; Ps 83:19; 147:5), and then he observes OT and NT passages where the Son is called God (Is 7:14; 9:6; Ps 83:19; in *De incomp.* 5.17, Jn 1:1; Ro 9:5; Ep 5:5; 2 Ti 1:10; Ti 2:13) (*De incomp.* 5.13, 15). Chrysostom notes, that for the biblical writers to *not* give the impression that they were just "referring to the Father when they spoke of God, they first made mention of the divine plan of salvation. For surely, the Father was not born of a virgin nor did he become a little child" (*De incomp.* 5.15). His charge, or rather an interpretive rule of thumb, to the Anomoeans, and all other heretics, is that when hearing *"the words 'one' and 'no one,' do not diminish the glory of the Trinity but, by these terms, learn the distance which separates the Trinity from created beings*" (*De incomp.* 5.24, emphasis added). This distance is infinitely vast. He writes, "For an inferior essence would never be able to have clear knowledge of a superior essence (i.e., traverse the infinite distance), even if the difference between them were slight" (*De incomp.* 5.25). Therefore, we must conclude the full divinity of the Son as the Father because Scripture says the Son is in the bosom of the Father, that no one knows the Father except the Son, and no one has seen the Father except the Son. And, also, we conclude the same regarding the Spirit, in that no one else knows the depths of God but the Spirit of God (*De incomp.* 5.24, 25).

Jumping to *Homily VII*,[58] Chrysostom moves into his "second stage of wrestling with the heretics," where he addresses the question as to whether "the Son and the Father have the same power and might, whether they are of the same essence" (*De incomp.* 7.7). While Chrysostom expresses his embarrassment of sorts in having to "prove" the Son is of the same essence, power, and might of the Father, nevertheless, there are those who "shamelessly oppose these truths" (*De incomp.* 7.7). In fact, he remarks (humorously) that such notions are obvious in the very nature of things as observed in animals or even trees.

The Anomoeans claim it is evident that in stating the Son is of "the same substance (*homoousios*) with the Father because he is called the Son, we, too, can be of one substance with the Father. For, surely, we, too, are called his sons." The Psalmist, quoting the Father, writes: "I have said: You are gods, and all of you are the sons of the most 'High'" (Ps 82:6) (*De incomp.* 7.10). Chrysostom decries their antics, in that not only do they claim to have a knowledge of God as he has of himself, they now bring the glory of the Son down to their level, positing that they are also sons of the Most High. But he rebuts them for violating the rules of analogy, in that Christ is the Archetype, the begotten, *the Son*, which alone is proper to him; whereas the Anomoeans are sons only in word; they are not the only begotten. Only *the* Son lives in the bosom of the Father (Jn 1:18), is the brightness of his glory, is the exact representation of his being (He 1:3), and is in the form of God (Ph 2:6) (*De incomp.* 7.11).

---

[58] The second stage is the last stage with the first, homilies I–V, dealing primarily with the incomprehensibility of God's nature, and homilies VII–X, moving the discussion to the consubstantiality of the Son with the Father.

Chrysostom shows how the Son demonstrates that he is of the same essence and power as the Father. To show the same likeness, in essence, the Son says, "he who has seen me has seen the Father" (Jn 14:9) and "I and the Father are one" (Jn 10:30). To show the same likeness in power, the Son says, "For as the Father raises the dead and grants life, so the Son also grants life to whom he wishes" (Jn 5:21). To show that the Son is to receive identical worship as the Father, Jesus says, "So that all men may honor the Son as they honor the Father" (Jn 5:23). And to show that the Son has the same authority to amend the law, he says: "Father works, and I work" (Jn 5:17).

Heretics struggle with the concept of the hypostatic union because they perceive weakness in the Lord Christ, especially in his desire to avoid the cup of wrath and his shedding of blood during his prayer (Lk 22:42–4). Chrysostom follows the interpretive rule of the *oikonomia-theologia* distinction, stating that if the Son only showed what was proper to man, then people would have thought he was just a man; and if he only did what was proper to divinity, then no one would believe in the plan of redemption (*De incomp.* 7.53, 54). Brilliant! The Anomoeans are mistaken because they have stretched the rules of interpretation.

In contemporary theology, we would note their error of *biblicism*. Chrysostom defines the subtle, yet gaping, distinction between a biblical and biblicist interpretation. He writes, "Today I warn and advise you not to go merely to what is written but to search out the meaning of what is said. If a person should busy himself with nothing more than what has been written, he will fall into many errors" (*De incomp.* 8.4). This theologically "grave" error stems from a rigid anthropomorphism. I have said this often and will continue to do so, the interpreter falls into great error, distorting the plain meaning of the text when, for example, Psalm 17:8 says, "You will protect me in the shadow of your wings," are we to assume that God's "spiritual and indestructible essence" (*De incomp.* 8.4) has wings like a bird, a duck, or a flying squirrel? No, rather, the metaphor provides a composite view of that which is incorporeal to communicate to us a true, metaphysically, and/or moral, statement about God. Chrysostom looks at other example texts where one passage says God sleeps (Ps 44:24) and another says he does not (Je 14:9, LXX). To interpret rightly, Chrysostom emphasizes the importance of reason when "searching into the treasure house of the divine Scriptures." He reiterates his warning: "If we listen to words only, if we do not think but take the words as they come, not only will those absurdities follow but many a conflict will be seen in what has been said" (*De incomp.* 8.5).

It is instructive for us to observe in Chrysostom's theology the metaphysical framework *behind* and thus *leading* his interpretation. We see this in how Chrysostom interprets these two supposedly conflicting passages, he writes:

> One man says that God sleeps, and another says that he does not sleep. Yet both statements are true if you understand the words in the proper way. The man who says that God is sleeping is pointing out God's forbearance and patience; the one who says he is not sleeping makes clear that God's nature is pure and undefiled. (*De incomp.* 8.6)

Chrysostom's approach embodies the Great Tradition, where the theological norm is based on a classical Trinitarian framework.

In *Homily IX*, Chrysostom addresses objections from Jews of Antioch (Messianic Jews who have joined the Anomoeans), who deny the divinity of Christ. He easily deflates their arguments, showing their incompetence in interpreting the biblical text. For example, one piece of evidence the Jews give to show that Jesus cannot be God is from John 11:34, where Jesus does not know where dead Lazarus was lying. In mocking fashion, the Jews say: "Do you see that he did not know? Do you see his weakness? Is this man God? He did not even know the place!" (*De incomp.* 9.4).

A beginner or novice in biblical interpretation might be stumped by such an argument. But Chrysostom turns the tables. He says, that if Jesus' not knowing where Lazarus was buried means that he cannot be God, then we must strip the Father of his deity since he too failed to know where Adam was hiding in the garden (Ge 3:9). Did not God say, "Adam, where are you?" Or, when God asks Cain where his brother is (Ge 4:9), should we infer that God is ignorant of Abel's whereabouts? Another example, in Genesis 18:20–1, God tells Abraham of the cries he hears against Sodom and Gomorrah and that he must go down to see if their actions measure up to the outcry against them. Did God have to "go down" to Sodom and Gomorra? Did he not know? Chrysostom writes, "The one who knows all things before they come to pass, the God who searches hearts and minds, he who knows the thoughts of men is the one and only one who has said: 'Therefore, I shall go down and see whether or not their actions match the outcry against them which comes to me, so that I may know'" (*De incomp.* 9.6, 7).

The Jews have fallen into error because, as Chrysostom warned earlier, they are making theological judgments based on "what is written" not from the "meaning of what is said." They are taking the words as they come and are quickly drawing conclusions without giving attention to whether their conclusions are *canonically consistent* regarding the being of God. It is a failure to understand the literary modes employed in Scripture, where one must look at the *meaning* being conveyed in the mode of expression, rather than letting the mode dictate one's theological presumptions. Chrysostom's interpretation of Genesis 18:20–1 demonstrates an acuity to the corpus of the Bible, notably the nature and character of God. Chrysostom writes, "What the Father is saying is this:

> 'A report came to me. But I wish again to test this rumor more exactly in the light of the facts. I do not do this because I do not know. I do it because I wish to teach men not to heed words alone nor to believe them recklessly if someone speaks them against another.' Men must believe what they hear only after they have first made an exact search and considered well the proof in the light of the facts. And this is why God said in another Scriptural passage: "Believe not every word" [Sirach 19:15] For nothing is so destructive of men's lives as for a person to give quick credence to whatever people say. The prophet David was proclaiming a divine revelation when he said: "Whoever slanders his neighbor in secret, him have I banished and pursued" [Ps 101:5]. (*De incomp.* 9.8)

Chrysostom interprets this passage (Ge 18:20–1) from a canonical approach, in that he understands the essence and character of God as revealed in Scripture (and in general revelation). When he encounters a passage that clashes with the teachings of Scripture regarding the essence of God, he places theology proper at the forefront. His interpretation is steered by his metaphysical axiom of the essence of God, serving as the fundamental principle driving his understanding. Why is that? Otherwise, as noted already, we lose continuity in the will and decree of God. If God claims to judge men by the secrets and intentions of their hearts (Ro 2:16), then he must have perfect, complete knowledge of the secrets and intentions of every human being—past, present, and future. If he cannot, then Solomon's closing statement of Ecclesiastes loses its thrust to instill fear of the Lord but also provides comfort and hope: "For God will bring every act to judgment, including every hidden thing, whether good or evil" (Ec 12:14).

In Chrysostom's reading of Genesis 18:20–1, if he "takes the words as they come," interpreting them "off the cuff," and concludes that the being of God must "go down" to "see" and "learn" about the wickedness in Sodom and Gomorrah, his interpretation would conflict with Psalm 139:7–8, which teaches us that the Divine essence is omnipresent. David writes, "Where can I go to escape your Spirit? Where can I flee from your presence? If I go up to heaven, you are there. If I make my bed in Sheol, you are there." Or, in Jeremiah 23:23–24, God, condemning the false prophets who think their deception will go unnoticed, says, "'Am I a God who is only near'—this is the Lord's declaration—'and not a God who is far away? Can a person hide in secret places where I cannot see him?'—the Lord's declaration. 'Do I not fill the heavens and the earth?'—the Lord's declaration." But why should those passages have priority? For the text from Ecclesiastes to be true, Psalm 139:7–8 and Jeremiah 23:23–24 must be true. These passages tell us about the manner in which the Divine essence subsists—everywhere present, all at once. For God to bring every act to judgment, including every hidden thing, whether good or evil, his essence *must* be everywhere present all at once, as Proverbs 15:3, employing anthropomorphic language, tells us: his "eyes are everywhere observing the wicked and the good" (Prov 15:3). Therefore, these passages must have priority; in fact, they must guide our interpretive decisions as we formulate theological judgments about the triune God.

In *Homily X*, Chrysostom addresses the claim that Christ is inferior to the Father because he took on flesh. He addresses this assertion on the heels of demonstrating that Christ is the same essence of the Father as observed in his authority to forgive sins and cast into hell, to make laws of his own, heal the sick, restore limbs, restore sight to the blind man with mud just as God took dust from the earth and formed man, and calling the dead to life (*De incomp.* 10. 24–30). All these examples, writes Chrysostom, "surely make it clear that Christ is the same essence as the Father who begot him" (*De incomp.* 10. 24). The enemies of the truth posit that if he were of the same essence as the Father, why didn't the Father take on flesh? He must have assumed the form of man because he was the inferior one. Chrysostom refers to Paul's words in Philippians 2, observing that if Christ put on flesh as an act of humility but was inferior, then the thrust of Paul's exhortation to look to Christ as the example of humility dissipates. It "is an act of humility when an equal obeys an equal." Philippians 2:6 is a powerful creedal imperative, in that we have one of the rare instances of a direct, explicit statement of the deity of Christ. Chrysostom writes, "What does it mean when he says: 'He did not consider it robbery to be equal with God, but he emptied himself, taking the nature of a servant'?" Christ has no fear of losing a possession that cannot be taken away from him, even though his possession is hidden away (*De incomp.* 10. 52). He expounds further, noting that the equality he had with the Father was solely his; a glory that "was truly and genuinely his by nature."

Chrysostom emphasizes that the incarnation demonstrates the Son's equality with the Father, keeping the same glory that alone belongs to God. If Christ were not of the same glory and essence as the Father, the incarnation would lose all significance (*De incomp.* 10. 55–56). It is dumbfounding that the God of the universe would become part of that universe, in the most lowly and humble manner among the very creatures he commanded to rule over.

Homily XI considers the glory of the Son and the equality and consubstantiality he has with the Father, demonstrated in his display of power. Chrysostom chooses to begin his fight with the "weapons taken from the Old Testament." His purpose is to strike down the heretics of his day, along with the likes of Marcion, Manichaeus, Valentinus, and all Jewish communities. Chrysostom begins with the creation account, summarizing all the days of divine *fiat*, whereby the command of creation is carried out by *the only begotten*. He aims to refute the notion that the Son is merely a servant of God. Chrysostom notes that when man was formed (Ge 1:26–7), God did not give the command of "Let there be"; rather, he says, "'Let us make,' so that from the character of the consultation indicated by his words, he might reveal the equality of honor which belonged to him to whom he spoke" (*De incomp.* 11.13).[59] In God saying, "Let us make man," he denotes that there is *one* image, not

---

[59] Chrysostom provides a clear example of a master/servant relationship in the dialogue observed in Matthew 8:8–9, when the centurion perceives the honor due to the Son because of his unique power, and he pleads with him to heal his servant. He makes a comparison of his position with the Lord's, in having those under him that he commands to "Go," "Come," "Do this," and "he does it" (*De incomp.* 11.19–20).

images, nor one image unequal to the other image; but rather, the *same* image.[60] And while God does not need a counselor (Is 40:13), Scripture shows the honor and equality of the Son with God by calling the Son "Wonderful Counselor" (Is 9:6). Chrysostom's christological import in Genesis and Isaiah is indicative of a *Trinitarian* license of interpretation.

Homily XII continues his discourse of the glory of the Son from the Old Testament texts but Chrysostom shifts to the New Testament to demonstrate his glory. A standout example is drawn from Jesus' healing of the paralytic. Not only did he heal him, but he also told him to pick up his bed and walk, showing a complete restoration to health. Chrysostom comments on the reason why Jesus had him do this. He writes, "Unless his limbs had been made solid and his joints held fast, he would not have been able to support the weight on his shoulders. In addition to all this, he also showed that, when Christ gave the command, everything happened in a single moment—he was both free from his disease and returned to health" (*De incomp.* 12.26–27). When a physician helps a patient, he is unable to bring him back to immediate, perfect health. It takes time, with the patient slowly regaining his strength back. But not with Jesus; "in a single moment he both frees from disease and restores to health" (*De incomp.* 12.28). At this point, Chrysostom addresses those he calls "busy-bodies." That is the pejorative term he uses when speaking of the Anomoeans. Their folly, and ultimate demise, is that they inquire about God's essence, particularly *how* he brought about complete restoration, health, and strength to the paralytic's body. Chrysostom, in step with the title of his treatise, says, "[M]arvel at what was done. Do not be inquisitive about the way it was done" (*De incomp.* 12.30).

Chrysostom concludes this treatise by presenting evidence of the Son's equality with the Father from the Gospel of John, chapter 5. In this passage, Jesus asserts his authority over the Sabbath while performing a healing miracle. Chrysostom notes a salient point for the reader to pay attention to, which "is the crux of the whole struggle" (*De incomp.* 12.41). "This is why they kept persecuting him, because he did these things on the Sabbath." The stakes are high on this claim because how Jesus

---

[60] Chrysostom says, "This is why the Son is said to sit at the right hand of the Father—that you may learn that they are the same in honor and exactly alike in power. For a subordinate does not sit with his superior but stands alongside him" (*De incomp.* 11.24).

responds will conclusively demonstrate he is either a servant or in command. According to the Law of Moses, a man would be stoned to death for carrying wood on the Sabbath. Even though the Jews observe a miracle—an act beyond human power, they are infuriated with him because he did it on the Sabbath. How does Christ respond to this charge? He says, "My Father is still working, and I am working also" (Jn 5:17). Chrysostom contends that if Christ were inferior, his response was "grounds for a more serious charge." He did not say he does this *because* the Father does, which would be a heinous violation of the law. Rather, his claim situates him *with* and *equal* to the Father, which the Jews understood he was asserting and is why they wanted to kill him. Chrysostom offers an example, stating that an emperor or king is the only one allowed to wear the crown and pardon criminals (*De incomp.* 12.42–44). If a mere commoner were pardoning criminals, and he defended his unlawful actions by stating he wears the crown, just as the king does, he would be put to death. Important to remember is that Christ was sinless, keeping the law completely. Therefore, "he would not have used this kind of plea to defend himself." When confronted about his actions, Christ defends himself with authority, establishing he is of the same dignity as the Father, in that when he is accused of breaking the Sabbath, asserting he does these things because he works as the Father is working, Chrysostom writes, "It is altogether necessary that Christ be equal to the Father, who also acts with authority" (*De incomp.* 12.48).

Conclusion

In Chrysostom, we see a theologian who reads Scripture with the utmost attention to developing theology *from* the biblical text. He seeks to be theologically responsible, avoiding, as much as possible, any speculative discourse. He carefully and patiently argues his position with stunningly rich exegesis, well-grounded in revelation, with a fully systematic scope of vision. Interestingly as it pertains to a key theme of investigation in this book, Chrysostom assumes the doctrine of divine simplicity as normative in the Christian doctrine of God. It is telling about the immensely important role of metaphysics, notably the metaphysics that purports divine simplicity, in that one such as Chrysostom adopts it as properly basic in his doctrine of God.

Augustine

To much of the Western world, Augustine (354–430) has no rival. He is the preeminent—uninspired—theologian of the Christian faith. When reading the titans of the church—i.e., Aquinas, Luther, and Calvin—Augustine's theology and ideas are voluminously parroted throughout *their* writings. His influence is unparalleled. Even the secular world sees Augustine as a mammoth figure in the shaping of human history. Our study of Augustine will proceed through an exposition of his most well-known works, *City of God*, *Confessions*, and his *Letters*. Augustine's dogmatic account of the Trinity will conclude the study.[61]

The Immutable Essence of God

Augustine's doctrine of God is classical, through and through. He writes, "There is One invisible, from whom, as the Creator and First Cause, all things seen by us derive their being: He is supreme, eternal, unchangeable, and comprehensible by none save Himself alone" (Aug., *Ep.* 232.5). When reading his works, the doctrine of immutability is paramount, coming forth repeatedly.

In his *Confessions*,[62] Augustine begins with his very first sentence with extolling the Creator. The Lord of heaven and earth, with inscrutable wisdom, Augustine asks if any praise is worthy of his majesty (*Conf.* 1.1). He speaks of the unfathomable Divine essence that is everywhere present, of which heaven and earth cannot contain him; rather, "You contain all things in yourself and fill them by reason of the very fact that you contain them" (*Conf.* 1.2). However, the ineffable Lord

---

[61] Books *I–VIII* of his (*De Trinitate*) *The Trinity*, trans. John E. Rotelle, English Translation. (New City Press, 1991). The remaining Books (*XI–XIV*) make up Augustine's constructive psychological or mental image of the Trinity. Though very profound and instructive, trying to cover that material here would detract from my intentions in this work. Noting what Edmund Hill says, the translator and contributor of the Introduction, Forewords, and notes in the edition of Augustine's *De Trinitate* I will be using, in his foreword to Books *IX–XIV*, writes, "In the dogmatic sense, Augustine's doctrine about the divine processions has already been given [in Books *I–VIII*]." And therefore, the remaining books are Augustine's investigation of the processions of the persons seen through a mental conceptualization of memory, understanding, and will in the human mind the appropriates to the Father, the Son, and the Spirit.

[62] English Translation cited: Saint Augustine, *Confessions*, trans. R. S. Pine-Coffin (Harmondsworth, Middlesex, Engl: Penguin Classics, 1961).

God, "has condescended to accept the worship of men's mouths and has desired us through the medium of our own words to rejoice in His praise" (*De doctr. christ.* 1.6.6).

Augustine is awe-struck in contemplating the presence of God in his creation. He ponders: Are you present to all things and are you present in all things at once (*Conf.* 1.3.)? He asks, "What, then, is the God I worship? He can be none but the Lord God himself, for *who but the Lord is God? What other refuge can there be, except our God?*" (Ps 18:31) (*Conf.* 1.4.). Augustine's conception of God is directly tied to the revelation of God as *Lord* and *refuge* in the biblical text. He understands that the declarative statements regarding God's divine acts for his creatures lead him to conclude that the Lord God *must* be "supreme, utmost in goodness, mightiest and all-powerful, most merciful and most just" (*Conf.* 1.4). For Augustine, immutability, or his unchangeableness, is consequential of divinity. Creatures are mutable; "the Nature which is immutable is called Creator" (*Ep.* 18.2). As the unchangeable one, "he changes all;" "he is never new, never old, and yet all things have life from him." As the unchangeable one, he is "ever active, yet always at rest." And while he gathers all things to himself, he is never in need of them; rather, he desires to nourish his creatures, "and bring them to perfection." Augustine does not see an inconsistency (and there is none) in saying God is unchangeable and loves his creatures yet can be angry with them (*Conf.* 1.4).

In God's working and in his resting, Augustine writes, he is not affected. If he is affected by something, "then it implies that there comes to be something in His nature which was not there before" because "whatever is acted upon is changeable" (*De civ. Dei* 12.17). And because he is unchangeable, and "the source of all good" (*Conf.* 1.6), his goodness is never idle; he did not "awaken from inactivity" in eternity past to create; rather, "by one and the same eternal and unchangeable will He effected regarding the things He created, both that formerly, so long as they were not, they should not be, and that subsequently, when they began to be, they should come into existence" (*De civ. Dei* 12.17). Time is a creature; thus, God is not bound by it, for he is "Himself eternal, and without beginning, yet he caused time to have a beginning," having made man in time according to "his unchangeable and eternal design" (*De civ. Dei* 12.14.1). God's infinity means for him, "'today' ever comes to an end:

and yet our 'today' does come to an end in you, because time, as well as everything else, exists in you. If it did not, it would have no means of passing. And since your years never come to an end, for you they are simply 'today.'" (*Conf.* 1.6).

As already mentioned in the *Introduction* of this work, before Augustine's conversion, he was a Manichean. The Manichean's ontological conception of God did not distinguish between created and Uncreated being. Augustine thought God was a material thing, "entirely physical" (*Conf.* 4.2). He struggled to formulate a conception of God that was real but distinct from the material world. While he knew God could not have a bodily shape, he could not free himself from thinking that God "was some kind of bodily substance extended in space, either permeating the world or diffused in infinity beyond it" (*Conf.* 7.1).

However, his philosophical intuition understood that bodies change and decay, and if God had a body, it means he is inferior because bodies decay. God is free from corruption, mutation, and any degree of change. It was not until he came to understand the Platonic concept of a spiritual substance that his eyes were opened to the "unseen," Uncreated *metaphysical* reality in which all things live, and move, and have their being" (Ac 17:28). At one time Augustine did not know that "God is a spirit, a being without bulk and without limbs defined in length and breadth" (*Conf.* 3.7), "encompassing [creation] on all sides and penetrating it in every part, yet yourself infinite in every dimension" (*Conf.* 7.5). But his reading of the Platonists prompted him "to look for truth as something incorporeal," having "*caught sight of your invisible nature, as it is known through your creatures*" (*Conf.* 7.20). Paul's words finally became clear to Augustine. It is through creation, as the Apostle Paul writes, that we can "catch sight of the Truth." This "Eternal Truth, true Love, beloved Eternity—all this, my God, you are" (*Conf.* 7.10). Augustine could now grasp that "God is Spirit, unchangeable, incorporeal, present in his whole Being everywhere" (*Ep.* 148.1.2).

Augustine's affirmation of God as the Creator of all things posed a problem regarding the existence of evil.[63] How could God create evil since he "is not only good but Goodness itself" (*Conf.* 7.3; 12.16)? While he contemplated deep and wide on such matters, Augustine could not traverse the gulf of the Divine essence. Regardless of the impasse at

---

[63] Augustine's approach to the problem of evil will not be addressed in this work.

which he arrived, Augustine's starting point in contemplating God is that the divine nature was incorruptible, "supreme, the perfect Good." We see Augustine's assumption of God's perfections as being *the* Divine essence, in that God's nature is insufferable because it cannot be compelled to change by anything against his will because "the will and power of God are God himself" (*Conf.* 7.4).

Scripture reveals the otherness of God's essence from created being, as Augustine saw God's substance as "the Light that never changes casting its rays over the same eye of my soul, over my mind. . . . It was above me because it was itself the Light that made me, and I was below because I was made by it" (*Conf.* 7.10). Citing James 1:17, as the "Father of lights, who does not change like shifting shadows," his knowledge does not differ from that which it ever was nor shall be because variations in creaturely reality, that of time, past, present, and future, do not affect his knowledge as they do us. God's unchangeability, or immutability, entails that his knowledge is not derived through "transition of thought, but beholds all things with absolute unchangeableness" (*De civ. Dei* 11.21.1). As "perfect being, so you alone have perfect knowledge" (*Conf.* 13.16). For "all things which He knows are at once embraced. For as without any movement that time can measure, He himself moves all temporal things, so He knows all times with a knowledge that time cannot measure" (*De civ. Dei* 11.21.1).

Augustine posits that that which is in time is a "lower order" than God's "absolute being," which he signifies as "real being." He writes, "They are real in so far as they have their being from you, but unreal in the sense that they are not what you are. For it is only that which remains in being without change that truly is" (*Conf.* 7.11; cf. Ex 3:14). God's perfect "being knows and wills unchangeably; and your will is and knows unchangeably" (*Conf.* 13.16). And the one who truly is "can never change, because you alone are absolute simplicity, for whom to live is the same as to live in blessed happiness, since you are your own beatitude" (*Conf.* 13.3).

For Augustine, the fact that the earth and the heavens exist demonstrates they were created. They are subject to change and variation, in that there was nothing before, and "the meaning of change and variation is that something is there which was not there before" (*Conf.* 11.4). How did they get there, Augustine asks? Because nothing exists apart from God, "it must be that *you spoke and they were made*. In your Word alone you created them" (*Conf*. 11.5). And God's "speech was expressed through the motion of some created thing" (*Conf*. 11.6). Augustine intimates an incomparable difference between divine speech and human speech, in that human words are "sound in time," are spoken, are heard, die away, and are lost; whereas the Word is "silent," "uttered eternally," and "uttered at one and the same time." The eternal utterance of the Word entails immutability, otherwise, it would not be truly eternal nor truly immortal (*Conf*. 11.7). And "mutability belongs to all things that are subject to change" (*Conf*. 12.6).

Augustine addresses the question that asks if God is eternal, and the will of God "is part of his substance," and creation is a product of the divine will, why isn't creation likewise eternal? (*Conf*. 11.10). Such questions or objections arise due to a lack of understanding divine immutability. Such people err because "their thoughts still twist and turn upon the ebb and flow of things in past and future time." They need to revel in the "splendor of eternity," seeing that time, in contrast to eternity, "derives its length only from a great number of movements constantly following one another into the past, because they cannot all continue at once." However, "in eternity, nothing moves into the past: all is present. Time, on the other hand, is never all present at once" (*Conf*. 11.11).

He reflects further on time and eternity, purposing to quell misconceptions about God's relation to time. Because our language is couched in creaturely notions, our expressions always come forth in relation to time—then, when, before, after, etc. And all expressions are notions of change. But God "is unchanging, your years never change" (*Conf*. 11.13; Ps 102:27). God cannot be considered "idle" *before* creation, as many object, regarding immutability because "there was no time" thus "there was no then." God's years are present all at once, in a "permanent standstill." Augustine continues this line of thought to demonstrate the eternality of the Son. He writes, "Your years are one day, yet your day does not come daily but is always today, because your today does not give place to any tomorrow nor does it take place of any yesterday. Your today is eternity. And this is how the Son, to whom you said *I have begotten you this day* (Ps 2:7), was begotten co-eternal with yourself" (*Conf*. 11.13).

Creatio ex nihilo, to use the term anachronistically, is the creation doctrine imbibed from Augustine's ontological framework. Because God is *before* all things and is not subject to change, when God is said to have "made something in the Beginning," this "something" Augustine writes, "is of yourself, in your Wisdom, which is born out of your own substance, and you created this out of nothing." But when Augustine says creation was out of God's own substance, he does not mean that the heavens and the earth "were made out of your own substance" (*Conf.* 12.7). There was nothing apart from God that God used to bring the world into existence; otherwise, he would be a craftsman, not the Creator. Rather, Augustine writes, God created "from matter which you created at one and the same time as the things that you made from it, since there was no interval of time before you gave form to this formless matter" (*Conf.* 13.33). Augustine offers a formulaic expression of the simple Trinitarian essence of God to support his argument, writing, "But besides yourself, O God, who are Trinity in Unity, and Unity in Trinity, there was nothing from which you could make heaven and earth" (*Conf.* 12.7). For Augustine, creation, and the works of God, "are very good, because it is you who see them in us and it was you who have given us the Spirit by which see them and love you in them" (*Conf.* 13.34).

In our brief survey of Augustine's views of the Divine essence, it is strikingly obvious that divine immutability occupies the chief place in his theology. Why is it such a powerful driving force for Augustine? *Peace.* Augustine can only find rest and peace in the eternal God (cf. Ps 4:8). He writes, "For, when the saying of Scripture comes true, and death is swallowed up in victory (1Co 15:54), who shall withstand us? You truly are the eternal God, because in you there is no change and in you we find the rest that banishes all our labor" (*Conf.* 10.4).

Augustine's comprehension of spiritual substance was shaped by Platonic thought, while the initial claims about God's unchanging essence were made in Scripture. Although Platonic thought offered conceptual tools and a divine grammar, it did not encompass the revelation of the triune God. Augustine writes, "Believing that my God is a Trinity," provided him the lens to see him as the personal Creator, in the scriptural witness of the Trinity's divine acts in time and space. And therefore, when he "searched for this truth in the sacred words" and "found where it says that your Spirit moved over the waters. Here, then, is the Trinity, my God, Father, Son, and Holy Ghost, the Creator of all creation" (*Conf.* 13.5). Next, we will proceed to explore Augustine's Trinitarian theology.

Book I

In the beginning chapter of *De Trinitate*, Augustine begins by expressing the equality of the Divine persons. Central to his theological framework is the concept of God's timeless existence and unchanging nature, in that he who is "without any change in [him]self makes things that change, and without any passage of time in [him]self creates things that exist in time" (*De Trin.* 1.1.3). And the unchangeable and eternal Divine essence is shared by the Father, the Son, and the Spirit (*De Trin.* 1.1.4). The essence of the triunity of God is equally a unity. Augustine confesses this truth from those before him, who have derived this understanding from the Scriptures, which teaches that "Father and Son and Holy Spirit in the inseparable equality of the one substance present a divine unity; and therefore, there are not three gods but one God" (*De Trin.* 1.2.7). As an express article of the Faith, Augustine offers the formulaic idiom of the distinction of the persons:

> The Father has begotten the Son, and therefore he who is the Father is not the Son; and the Son is begotten by the Father, and therefore he who is the Son is not the Father; and the Holy Spirit is neither the Father nor the Son, but only the Spirit of the Father and of the Son, himself coequal to the Father and the Son, and belonging to the threefold unity" (*De Trin.* 1.2.7).

Retaining the threefold unity, Augustine offers a few passages from Scripture, demonstrating that the divine acts of the triune God bring about creaturely effects that terminate in the individual persons properly or distinctly. For example, it is the Son who is born of Mary, not the Father nor the Spirit. It is the Spirit that took the form of a dove, not the Son nor the Father. And nor was it the same three that spoke from the heavens, stating, "You are my Son," at Jesus' baptism; rather, it was the Father (Mk 1:11). Nevertheless, "just as Father and Son and Holy Spirit are inseparable, so do they work inseparably" (*De Trin.* 1.2.7).

As Augustine concludes, the inseparable operation of God is fundamental to the catholic faith. It is an indisputable conclusion that the Divine essence and attributes are identical. Augustine will elaborate on this later. In short, God *is* his essence *and* attributes, as divine simplicity entails; therefore, he is also *his actions*. When the *oikonomia–theologia* framework is overlooked or conflated, it leads to ontological and categorical errors. Augustine is tasked with providing hermeneutical corrections.

Those who reject the full deity of the Son do so because they metaphysically stumble over the incarnation. They understand and affirm that the Divine essence is not subject to change, but they err in assuming the incarnation is a change and conclude that the Son cannot be the immutable Divine essence. Unfortunately, those who make this mistake, Augustine writes, "have been confuted by the utterance of the clearest and most consistent divine testimonies," the apostle John's words in the opening verse of his Gospel (1:1): "In the beginning was the Word, and the Word was with God, and the Word was God" (*De Trin.* 1.2.9). Bringing in John 1:14 ("the Word became flesh") and 1:3 ("all things were made through him, and without him was made nothing") into the discussion, Augustine offers a straightforward exegesis of these passages, concluding in the Son's full divinity. His logic is sound when he writes:

> For every substance that is not God is a creature, and that is not a creature is God. And if the Son is not of the same substance as the Father he is a made substance; if he is a made substance then not all things were made through him. But all things were made through him; therefore, he is of one and the same substance as the Father. And thus he is not only God, but also true God. (*De Trin.* 1.2.9)

A few paragraphs later, Augustine substantiates his conclusion with other NT passages, First Corinthians 8:6 and Romans 11:33–6. He then brings the focus back to the inseparability of the three persons, emphasizing the divine operations in the one act of God manifested in the *oikonomia*, as observed in the prepositional phrases (*ek*, *dia*, and *eis*) of these passages.

Augustine notes the utterance of the divine act in Scripture shows distinct attribution of the effect to the divine persons, *from* him, *through* him, and *to* him. The common error is to see these prepositions in an instrumental form, whereby God the Father creates *through* the Son, with the Son functioning as the Father's instrument of creation. And therefore, *instrumentality* implies a "lesser than God" status of the Son. However, as the *telos of classical theism is the doxology of God*,[64] we see Paul's theology of the three orients to God's glory in the singular

---

[64] Quote from J. L. Steffaniak.

expression, *to him* be the glory forever and ever. We must therefore conclude that all three are the *one* God (*De Trin.* 1.2.12).

The testimony of the apostolic witness conflicts with Augustine's opponents who want to ascribe creation to the Father only. Because, as Augustine identifies, how can all things be made *through* the Father, as Romans 11:36 intimates, yet, as noted in John's Gospel (1:3), all things were made *through* the Son? Augustine answers, referring to the inseparable operations of the *one* God, manifested in the *triune* persons of the *oikonomia*. He writes, "If some things were made through the Father, others through the Son, then it cannot be all things through the Father nor all through the Son. But if it is all things through the Father and all through the Son, then it is the same things through the Father as through the Son. So, the Son is equal to the Father, and the work of the Father and Son is inseparable" (*De Trin.* 1.2.12).

Augustine focuses on specific passages that present interpretive challenges when it comes to affirming that Scripture teaches that the Son shares the same essence as the Father. The key to maintaining consistent interpretation is to uphold the *oikonomia–theologia* distinction when approaching the text. Augustine notes errors are made when one tries "*to transfer what is said of Christ Jesus the man to that substance of his which was everlasting before the incarnation and is everlasting still*" (*De Trin.* 1.3.14, emphasis added). When it comes to "the Father is greater than I" passage in John 14:28 (cf. 1Ti 2:5), the answer and the rule, Augustine writes, where the distinction is set out, is in Philippians 2:6: "who, though he was in the form of God, did not count equality with God a thing to be grasped, but emptied himself, taking the form of a servant, being born in the likeness of men" (Ph 2:6–7, RSV).

The rule established from this passage is that "the Son of God is God the Father's equal by nature, by condition his inferior. In the form of a servant which he took, he is the Father's inferior; in the form of God, the Word *through whom all things were made* (Jn 1:3).... [I]n the form of God he made man, in the form of a servant he was made man" (*De Trin.* 1.3.14). In the incarnation, the immutability of God is maintained, in that "neither of them [God/man] changed into the other by that 'take-over'; neither Godhead changed into creature and ceasing to be Godhead, nor creature changed into Godhead and ceasing to be creature" (*De Trin.* 1.3.14). Augustine notes that when Christ told his disciples that he was going to the Father, who is greater than I, he did so because, in his human form, they assumed he was inferior to the Father, thus their focus was aimed at his creatureliness, his "adopted condition," not realizing he enjoys full equality with the Father (*De Trin.* 1.3.18).

In the rest of *Book I*, Augustine works through First Corinthians 15:24–28, expounding other judgment texts along with it (i.e., Mt 25:31, 32; Jn 5:22, 24, 26, 27, 28; 8:50; Re 1:7), arriving at a theologically consistent interpretation, whereby he concludes that the reason for the Son taking on flesh and judging as the Son of Man, with full authority from the Father, is "because the wicked cannot see the Son of God in his equality with the Father in the form of God" (*De Trin.* 1.4.30). Those born again receive the Son of God as God in the form of man. The wicked do not. So, in the form of man, all authority is given to him, so that "both good and bad may see him judging, as Son of man—the form in which he can be seen by all; by some however to their undoing, by others to eternal life" (*De Trin.* 1.4.30).

Book II

In *Book II* Augustine examines passages that refer strictly to the Son's being, his co-eternal equality from the Father. Passages such as John 10:30 and Philippians 2:6 indicate the equality and unity of substance between the Father and the Son. Augustine intends to bring precision to the discussion, whereby highlighting an important rule when interpreting christological passages. Many have erred when it comes to "less-than" passages (e.g., Jn 14:28; cf. Ph 2:7), extracting from them the sense that the Son is inferior to the Father (*De Trin.* 2.1.3). Others look at passages judging that the Son is neither less nor equal to the Father (i.e., Jn 5:19, 26), seeing that the Son is from the Father. If we follow such thinking, Augustine opines, it implies that in the Son taking on a creaturely form less than the Father, then we would have to conclude that it was the Father walking on water and performing healing miracles, which nobody, Augustine says, "even out of his wits, could have such an idea" (*De Trin.* 2.1.3).

How are we to interpret these passages about the Son in relation to the Father? Augustine says we are to conclude that "the life of the Son is unchanging like the Father's, and yet is from the Father." The works done can only be a work of God; therefore, when Jesus says, "Whatever the Father does, the same the Son does likewise" (Jn 5:19), the "likewise" does not mean similar to or something he does after seeing the Father do it; rather, "the working of the Father and of the Son is equal and indivisible, and yet the Son's working comes from the Father. That is why the Son cannot do anything of himself except what he sees the Father doing" (*De Trin.* 2.1.3). And from this understanding we derive "the rule," when it comes to interpreting such passages, which purposes to show "not that the person is less than the other, but only that one is from the other." But more precisely, the rule affirmed is that the Son is not less than Father; rather, he is from the Father, "his birth in eternity" (*De Trin.* 2.1.3).

Augustine's rule reflects the *oikonomia–theologia* interpretive approach, or, as he refers to it: "the form-of-a-servant rule" and "the-form-of-God rule." Properly applied to the text, we then understand John 7:16, which says, "My teaching isn't mine but is from the one who sent me," that the Son and the teaching are simply the Son's life and the Son's teaching (*De Trin.* 2.1.4). And the same goes for the Spirit, Augustine writes. He has what is the Son's because he takes what is the Son's and declares it. And the Son has everything of the Father. No creature can take what is the Father's.

Further grounding his ontological understanding of the Spirit in the Divine essence, Augustine takes John 15:26 as parallel with John 5:19, whereby he reasons that both the Son and the Spirit are from the Father but neither are of ontological inferiority to the Father. Augustine's statement reveals a "pro-Nicene picture of the Son and the Spirit as dependent on the Father."[65] To further strengthen his argument for the ontological equality of the Son and the Spirit with the Father, Augustine observes that the Spirit and the Father are said to both glorify the Son (Jn 16:14; 17:5). And so, he offers a concession; granted, the one "who glorifies is greater than the one he glorifies," but "let them at least grant that those who glorify each other are equal" (*De Trin.* 2.1.6).

In chapter 2, Augustine begins by refuting a Homoian objection: "The one who sends is greater than the one sent" (*De Trin.* 2.2.7). He dabbles in it a bit now, but he will expound further in *Book IV* on MISSIONS as God's revealing in time the processions of the persons. The Homoian objection is bereft of logic. Why is that? The Son and Spirit are already in this world. So, why is the sender greater than the sent, considering "where he [the Son and/or the Spirit] was sent to is where

---

[65] Lewis Ayres, *Augustine and the Trinity* (Cambridge University Press, 2010), 179.

he already was" (*De Trin.* 2.2.7)? Augustine asks, if both and Son and Spirit are already in the world, what then does it mean to say the Father (who is never said to have been sent) sends the Son or the Spirit? Augustine concludes from Galatians 4:4 that in God sending his Son, it was "in being made of woman that the Son was sent" (*De Trin.* 2.2.8).

Augustine reminds us that the Father and the Son have one will and operate indivisibly, so every divine work manifested in time is one work of the Father, the Son, and the Spirit. But this point presents another (possible) challenge Augustine wants to address. According to the preceding statement, one could say that the Son sent himself. How then could the Father have sent him if the Son sent himself (*De Trin.* 2.2.9)? In response, Augustine asks: "In what manner did God send his Son?" An order? A command? Well, "whatever way it was done, it was certainly done by word." The following elaboration on what Augustine means needs to be quoted in full. He writes:

> But God's Word is his Son. So when the Father sent him by word, what happened was that he was sent by the Father and his Word. Hence it is by the Father and the Son that the Son was sent, because the Son is the Father's Word. Would anyone adopt so blasphemous opinion as to suppose that it was by a word in time that the Father sent the eternal Son to appear in the course of time in the flesh? Though it is true that in the Word of God which was in the beginning with God and was God, that is to say in the Wisdom of God, there was timelessly contained the time in which that Wisdom was to appear in the flesh. So while without any beginning of time *in the beginning was the Word and the Word was with God and the Word was God* (Jn 1:1), without any time there was in the Word the time at which the Word would become flesh and dwell among us (Jn 1:14). And when this *fullness of time came, God sent his Son made of woman* (Ga 4:4), that is made in time, in order that the Word might be shown to men incarnate; and the time at which this should happen was timelessly contained within the Word. The whole series of all times timelessly contained in God's eternal Wisdom. Since then it was a work of the Father and the Son that the Son should appear in the flesh, the one who so appeared in the flesh is appropriately said to have been sent, and the one who did not to have done the sending. (*De Trin.* 2.2.9)

The inseparable divine act of the Father and the Son, the eternal Father speaking his eternal Word, not by command but by the one will of God, with the Word as the Wisdom of God, the Word was sent in the fullness of time, to be made manifest among men. Augustine makes an important distinction, giving the proper nuance regarding the Father sending the Son. The invisible Father sent the invisible Son, who was made visible. Augustine writes that if the Son's substance changed into something visible, then we could think of the Son as simply being sent by the Father "and not also as sending with the Father." The distinction retains the inseparability of the divine persons, with the manifesting of the invisible Son in the human form of Jesus as the outward sign of the divine act. And likewise with the Spirit; his action in Acts 2:2, "*tongues of fire*," Augustine writes, "visibly expressed and presented to mortal eyes is called the sending of the Holy Spirit" (*De Trin.* 2.2.10).

Book IV

In *Book IV*, Augustine delves deeper into his understanding of the missions of the triune God. It's important to grasp Augustine's doctrine of eternal processions and his definition of missions. As mentioned before, for him, being sent does not imply being less than the sender. Instead, the Son being sent means he is from the sender, like light is from light. The Father sending the Son and the Spirit is the act of making known the eternal processions in the economy. The sending of the Son is for the purpose of being known by men that he is from the Father. And thus the mediating benefit of the Son in reconciling humanity to God, thus giving eternal life to mortals, is *knowing* that the Son is from the Father (Jn 17:3). Comprehension of this aspect is crucial for understanding Augustine's Trinitarian theology.[66]

Chapter 5 is where Augustine will flesh out some of the important aspects noted in the previous paragraph. Augustine makes the qualifier that the sender and the one sent, Father and the Son, only have a distinction of relation, not a substantial one (*De Trin.* 4.5.27). They are both fully divine, sharing the same essence. The Son is the Father's Word, who was sent to become flesh; he was sent to become man. Augustine cites the Book of Wisdom 7:27, which speaks of a pure outflow of the

---

[66] Material for this paragraph was drawn from Hill's, "Introductory Essay on *Book IV*" in *The Trinity*, 148.

glory of almighty God, to express that the glory of the Son outflows from one and the same substance of the Father. He writes, "It is not like water flowing out from a hole in the ground or in the rock, but like light flowing from light" (*De Trin.* 4.5.27). Augustine interprets John 16:28, "I came from the Father and have come into the world," to indicate that the Son flows out from the Father, as the brightness of eternal light. His *birth* from the Father means "he is from eternity to eternity . . , but that he is sent ["and have come into the world"] means that he is known by somebody in time" (*De Trin.* 4.5.28). The Word of God, as the begotten, is sent by the begetter, the Father who sends.

A few paragraphs later, Augustine offers speculation about John 7:39 regarding the giving of the Spirit that occurs once Jesus is glorified. His ruminating thoughts lead him to an interesting elucidation about the essence of the Trinity and our finite comprehension of the Divine persons using a psychological analogy. As it pertains to John 7:39, Augustine asks, in what sense is the Spirit given? We see other texts that speak of the Spirit working or being "given" before Jesus' glorification (i.e., Lk 1:15, 46, 67; 2:25). He remarks that it must be some unique quality yet not observed. While he is not completely sure about what to conclude, he does say,

> with absolute confidence that the Father and Son and the Holy Spirit, God the creator, of one and the same substance, the almighty three, act inseparably. But they cannot be manifested inseparably by creatures which are so unlike them, especially material ones. . . . In their own proper substance by which they are, the three are one, Father and Son and Holy Spirit, without any temporal movement, without any intervals of time or space, one and the same over all creation, one and the same all together from eternity to eternity . . . . But in my words Father and Son and Holy Spirit are separated and cannot be said together, and if you write them down each name has its own separate space. (*De Trin.* 4.5.30)

Here is when Augustine's now famous psychological analogy makes its first appearance, which he formulates into a theory of the divine image, expounded further in *Book X*. His intends to demonstrate how the inseparable *Three* manifest separately in creaturely things, yet the *Three* are inseparably at work in each of the creaturely things, though having the proper function of manifesting *one* of the *Three*. He writes, "When I name my memory, understanding, and will, each name refers to a single thing, and yet each of these single names is the product of all three; there is not one of these three names which my memory and understanding and will have not produced together. So too the Trinity together produced both the Father's voice and the Son's flesh and the Holy Spirit's dove, though each of these single things has reference to a single person" (De Trin. 4.5.30).

Augustine ends *Book IV* by expressing his satisfaction with his demonstration of the co-equality of the Son and the Spirit with the Father, and that purpose in the visible manifestation of the Son and the Spirit is so that man could see that "the Father is the source and origin of all deity" (De Trin. 4.5.32). In *Books V, VI,* and *VII,*[67] Augustine is focused on using reason to address the Arians. In these three books, we see Augustine's approach to divine discourse, specifically *how to* talk about the triune God. As we have often observed in this study, the Son's equality with the Father (and the Spirit) while maintaining proper distinctions is the battling ground during this time.

In *Book V,* Augustine explains how to predicate about God's nature and attributes, making distinctions within an Aristotelian categorical framework of accidents. Such distinctions frame our language, so when we say something of God, we refer to his very being or essence, not as an accident that is merely added to him.[68] Therefore, we would say God's goodness is not an accident as something added to God's nature; rather, God's goodness is properly his Divine Substance. Augustine attributes all accident words as substance words when he predicates something about God.

In *Book VI,* Augustine considers an exception to this rule of predication in the form of relationship words, such as Father and Son. These words are different than accident words in that they signify relationships within God not indicative of his substance. In this way, the divine equality of the persons, although relationally distinct, is established. However, the words of the Apostle Paul present a challenge to this manner

---

[67] The following summary of *Books V, VI,* and *VII* is a paraphrase of Hill's ,"Foreword to *Books V, VI, VII,*" 186–8.

[68] In metaphysics, an *accident* is something that has its being in dependence on something else. For example, "whiteness could not exist in reality except through a body that is white." Joseph Owens, *An Elementary Christian Metaphysics*, Reprint edition. (Houston, TX: Center for Thomistic Studies, 1985), 155.

of thinking when he states, "Christ is the power of God and the wisdom of God" (1Co 1:24). Because in this context, and throughout the NT, we see substance words used as relationship words, in that they seem to have the same manner of expression in phrases such as "Son of the Father" and "Word of the Father." Augustine prematurely concludes that we must see all words about God as relationship words, except when we say "God" or "substance," which also are proper to the Godhead only.

In *Book VII*, however, the logic of this approach will reduce God himself to relationship status, thus also making such words as "substance" and "being" relational terms as well. Therefore, Augustine backtracks to his substance and accident word categories, whereby words like "wisdom" and "power" are predicated of the Divine Substance equally and identically in each of the persons. And so, the persons, though relationally distinct, can each have the substance words predicated to them. However, there is an improper manner to avoid, whereby, going back to First Corinthians 1:24, one would appropriate "wisdom" to be of the Son and "God" to the Father, to then say the Father is not wisdom and the Son is not God.

Lastly, Augustine considers the terms "person" and "hypostasis," which are translated as substance, noting that these words cannot be reduced to relationship-only words, because we would never say "three Gods" or "three wisdoms" but one God. To avoid the problems as he sees from the East, Augustine maintains that the distinction between *substance* and *person* is linguistic, not substantive about God; the terms function to keep our divine speech coherent.

Book V

Before getting into the first chapter of *Book V*, Augustine sets the mental tone for the mammoth task ahead:

> Thus, we should understand God, if we can and as far as we can, to be good without quality, great without quantity, creative without need or necessity, presiding without position, holding all things together without possession, wholly everywhere without place, everlasting without time, without any change in himself making changeable things, and undergoing nothing. Whoever thinks of God like that may not yet be able to discover altogether what he is but is at least piously on his guard against thinking about him anything that he is not. (*De Trin.* 5.1.2)

In Chapter 1, Augustine considers the Arians' categorical error by assuming substance distinctions between the *unbegotten* Father and the *begotten* Son, seeing that the *unbegotten/begotten* terms are not strictly relational but as substance modifications between the Father and the Son, employing the rule that "whatever is said or understood about God is said substance-wise, not modification wise." In response to this assertion, Augustine writes, "If everything that is said about God is said substance-wise, then *I and the Father are one* (Jn 10:30) was said substance-wise. So, the substance of the Father and of the Son are one" (*De Trin.* 5.1.4). The terms *unbegotten* and *begotten* are relational, thus denoting no change or modification of substance in the persons because the substance is not changeable (*De Trin.* 5.1.6). Therefore, the substance predicated of the persons is the same in each, with the term *unbegotten* purposed to say what the Father is *not* and *begotten* to say what the Son *is*. Augustine writes, "Being son is a consequence of being begotten, and being begotten is implied by being son" (*De Trin.* 5.1.8). The relationship words have no bearing on the substance words, so in saying the Son is *not* the Father (or unbegotten) that denial of relation is not a denial of substance.

In Chapter 2, Augustine delves further into substantive predication, beginning with the *chief point* that we must maintain, which is that whatever "the divine majesty is called in reference to itself is said substance-wise; whatever is called with reference to another is said not substance- but relationship-wise . . . therefore, whatever is said with reference to self about each of them is to be taken as adding up all three to a singular and not to a plural" (*De Trin.* 5.2.9). That means we call each of them God, but they are not three Gods. We call each of them "great," but they are not three "greats." And then Augustine draws an example from Scripture to support his point, writing,

> When the Lord Jesus was accosted just as a man by the young man who said *Good master*, he did not want to be taken for just a man, and so he significantly said, not "No one is good but the Father alone," but *No one is good but the one God* (Mk 10:18; Lk 18:19). The name "Father" signifies only the Father in himself, but the name "God" includes him and the Son and the Holy Spirit, because the one God is a trinity. (*De Trin.* 5.2.9)

Augustine elaborates further regarding the language used to talk about the being and persons of God. He notes that when he refers to the *being* of God, he means *ousia* as what the Greeks use, which he understands as *substance*. The term *hypostasis* is obscure and is too translated as *substance*, but because we lack the vocabulary to express the divine Trinity, we normally use the expression one being or substance, three persons, so *hypostasis* is *not* translated as *substance* in this expression. So, when someone asks, "Three what?" we say three persons, not to be precise, "but in order not to be reduced to silence" (*De Trin.* 5.2.10).

Augustine concludes Chapter 2 with a brief exposition on divine simplicity. He returns to the point he was discussing earlier about the greatness of God, noting the differences in the term *greatness* as it is predicated of various things, which when used of such things are not equally understood to be great in the same manner as others. We call things great in which they "partake of greatness." Therefore, those things that partake of greatness are not as excellent as those where greatness is primary in them.

But God's greatness is not something he participates in; rather, "he is great with a greatness by which he is himself this same greatness." Here Augustine is speaking substance-wise about God. The greatness of God is therefore not predicated of God as three "greatnesses," "for God it is the same thing to be as to be great." Augustine's ontology stresses the oneness, thus the simplicity of God as primary. And therefore, God's greatness is great "because he is his own greatness." This can be said as well for all predication of God, his goodness, eternity, omnipotence, etc., all absolute in his substance, in that he *is* properly these things (*De Trin.* 5.2.11); they are not appended to his Divine essence as accidents, as they are in created things.

Chapter 3 continues the discussion of predication, looking closely at the relative terms, notably the term "gift" regarding the Holy Spirit, the divine names referred to the persons, and the names as they are also referred to in creation. Augustine begins by restating that "the triad, the one God is called great, good, eternal, omnipotent, and can also be called his own Godhead, his own greatness, his own goodness, his own eternity, his own omnipotence" (*De Trin.* 5.3.12). Then he contrasts these substance terms with the relative terms, noting that the triad cannot be called Father, except metaphorically so, in reference to creation because of our adoption as sons. However, there is no denoting any accidents in God using these terms.

Augustine notes more examples of relation-wise terms of the Father and the Son, such as the Father being called *origin*, *Father* in relation to the Son, and the Son is called *Word* and *image* relation-wise, but none of these terms are attributed to the Father. The Holy Spirit is called *the gift of God* (Ac 8:20; Jn 4:10), specifically of the Father and the Son "because on the one hand, he *proceeds from the Father* (Jn 15:26), as the Lord says; and on the other, the apostle's words, *Whoever does not have the Spirit of Christ is not one of his* (Ro 8:9), are spoken of the Holy Spirit" (*De Trin.* 5.3.12). Augustine sees the Spirit as "a kind of inexpressible communion or fellowship of Father and Son," and as "gift" and "giver," the Father and the Son are both *spirit* because it is common to them, and are one only God, and all *is* good, great, eternal, and omnipotent. Other terms such as *origin* are also said of the Spirit concerning creation because, along with the Father and the Son, they are the one Creator God.

But as it relates to the inner being of God, in which the distinctions of persons are denoted by their relations, the Father is origin in reference to the Son, since "he produced or begot him." Augustine, however, asks about the Spirit, stating whether the Father is origin in respect to him because he is said to proceed from the Father (Jn 15:26). Getting this accurate, Augustine notes, has been a common problem because the question arises as to why the Holy Spirit is not a son, in that he too comes from the Father. Augustine sees the relational name of the Spirit as *gift*, so his coming forth is not an eternal birth, as the Son is from the Father; rather, *he is given* from the Father and the Son, and he is *given to* us. Therefore, he is properly called the Holy Spirit and is also "called the Spirit of the Father and the Son who gave him, and also our Spirit who received him" (*De Trin.* 5.3.15). But do we then see the Father and the Son as two origins if the Spirit comes from both? This issue created a wedge between the East and the West.

The East asserts that this makes the Father and the Son two origins, thus losing monotheism. But Augustine says they are not two origins because, "just as the Father and the Son are one God, and with reference to creation one creator and one lord, so with reference to the Holy Spirit they are one origin; but with reference to creation Father, and Son, and Holy Spirit are one origin, just as they are one creator and one lord" (*De Trin.* 5.3.15). Does this serve as the final say on the matter?

Augustine moves into deeper waters as he brings chapter 3 to a close, raising the question concerning the how the Spirit acquired his being, and whether he acquired it in the same manner as the Son's being. If the Spirit gets his being as "gift" receiving his being, did he have his being before being given? How could he have the Divine Substance if his being only proceeds when he is given? Augustine resolves the issue by stating that the Holy Spirit always proceeds as gift from eternity, proceeding "as to be givable," thus it is a gift before it is given, and only at a point in time is he a "donation" (*De Trin.* 5.3.16).

In Chapter 4, Augustine discusses the concept of divine immutability, which concludes *Book V*. The central issue pertains to the potential of modification in God, particularly in relation to the Spirit's bestowal of the title "lord" at the moment of creation within time. Augustine reasons that God cannot be everlastingly *lord* otherwise we would be forced to say that creation is eternal (*De Trin.* 5.4.17). So, how do we resolve the issue? Augustine says we will be able to maintain that nothing is said of God by way of modification because in these instances the *substance* of God doesn't change. A coin, for example, has a relationship to other things by way of price, but it doesn't change in its form or value. Therefore, Augustine writes, "How much more readily should we be to accept a similar position about the unchangeable substance of God?" (*De Trin.* 5.4.17).

Augustine emphasizes that relationship status doesn't produce ontological change; rather, the change is in the creature. For example, when we consider Psalm 90:1, Augustine adduces that in the Lord becoming our refuge, he becomes our refuge by relationship; "the name has reference to us. And he becomes our refuge when we take refuge in him." It is not God who has now become better off in being our refuge; rather, "we were worse before we took refuge in him, and we become better by taking refuge in him. But in him, no change at all." Augustine comments that when we become children of God by his grace (Jn 1:12), our substance changes for the better in being made his sons, but he, though becoming our Father, does not undergo change in his substance. Regarding God's love for the saints, Augustine writes,

> it is unthinkable that God should love someone temporally, as though
> with a new love that was not in him [in God] before, seeing that with
> him things past do not pass, and things future have already happened.
> So he loved all his saints *before the foundation of the world* (Jn 17:24;
> Ep 1:4), as he predestined them; but when they are converted and find
> him, then they are said to begin to be loved by him, in order to state
> the thing in a way that can be grasped by human feeling. (*De Trin.* 5.4.17)

The manner in which creatures perceive God's dispositions is contingent
upon their relationship with him, rather than his relationship with
them. God is analogous to light, which may be harsh for weak eyes but
pleasant for the strong.

Book VI

This book is short—nine pages. Here, Augustine considers the problem
of **APPROPRIATION**. Using First Corinthians 1:24, *Christ the power of
God and the wisdom of God*, as his pretext for the discussion, he briefly
addresses Arius' well-known statement about the Son—if he was born,
then there was a time he was not. As we have seen throughout this study,
Arius and his ilk do not understand the Son's birth is an everlastingly
birth (i.e., filiation), denoting the Son's relationship to the Father (i.e.,
paternity), thus he is coeternal with him. First Corinthians 1:24 is a key
proof text to refute this claim because the Nicene tradition understands
wisdom and *power* to be substance-wise terms, which are predicated of
God's very essence. Therefore, if the Son *is* the wisdom and power of
God, "and it is crazy to say" God could have been without those, then, we
conclude that he could never have been without his Son; therefore, there
was no time when the Son did not exist (*De Trin.* 6.1.1).

Augustine must tackle a problem he discerns in the appropriation of
terms. The issue is whether such appropriation means that the Father
can "only be wise by having the wisdom which he begot, not by being
himself very wisdom" (*De Trin.* 6.1.2). Augustine wonders if the Son
can be wisdom from wisdom, as, the Nicene creed states, he is God from
God, light from light. And if wisdom is something the Father begets,
then why can't he beget his own power, wisdom, goodness, etc.? Is the
Father only called what he is in reference to the Son, so he would only be
great in begetting greatness in the Son, *just* in begetting justice in the
Son, *powerful* in begetting power in the Son, and so on and so forth, and
likewise, in-turn for the Son? If this is so, Augustine writes, "Then it

follows that whatever they are called with reference to themselves, neither is called without the other; that is, whatever they are called to indicate their substance they are both called together" (*De Trin.* 6.1.3).

Augustine concludes that the Father and the Son are not God apart from each other; "they are both God together." Therefore, he says we must interpret John 1:1, *In the beginning was the Word*, to mean "in the Father was the Word" because, though the Son is the Word, the Word is the image of the Father and both cannot be the image. The Son is the Word *alone* and was with God; however, the Father is not the Father alone, but the Father and the Son are both God together. So how do we address this difficulty? Augustine makes a mind/body analogy to solve the dilemma. He writes, "You could say 'the mind was with the man,' that is in the man, though the mind is not body, while man is both mind and body together. So, we could understand what follows, *and the Word was God* (Jn 1:1), meaning that the Word which is not the Father was God together with the Father" (*De Trin.* 6.1.3). But how does this reconcile with the creedal phrase "God from God, light from light"? Augustine concludes that the creedal affirmation is a "nutshell" statement of the Son's coeternality with the Father. And so, only the terms uniquely appropriated to the Father and the Son cannot be phrased in the same way as in the Creed. The purpose is to denote the relationship of the Son with the Father to make a distinction in the Divine essence, which is eternal. "The begetter did not precede what he begot." The Father cannot be called Word from Word or Image from Image because those terms are appropriated to the Son only. The Father and the Son are not both Word or Image together; therefore, when we look at the passage of John 10:30, *I and the Father are one*, Augustine says, "'Are one' means 'What he is, that I am too by way of being, not by way of relationship'" (*De Trin.* 6.1.3).

Augustine aims to demonstrate that the Son is equal to God, and in looking at the attributes, greatness, wisdom, power, eternity, etc., belonging properly to the substance, which the Father and the Son share, then none of these attributes can be any more or any less in the Son or the Father. The Father cannot be greater than the Son because his greatness *is* the Son, who, however, cannot be greater than the one who begot him (*De Trin.* 6.1.4). His point is to say that if the Son is not equal in any one thing, then he is not equal at all. However, his opponent says,

"But the Scripture cries out, *He did not think it robbery to be equal with God* (Ph 2:6, emphasis added)." But Augustine puts his adversary in a trap; if he affirms the authority of the Apostle Paul, then he must affirm that the Son is at least equal with God in one thing. And if equal in one, then he must be equal in *all*, as it pertains to this substance (*De Trin.* 6.1.5).

Augustine provides further elaboration on the distinction between human essence and the Divine essence. He emphasizes the concept of simplicity as constituting the divine being of God, while noting that human essences are composite. This underscores the notion that a human being possesses a human nature without being synonymous with the human nature itself. In contrast, God is not characterized by the possession of a Divine essence; rather, he is the Divine essence, indeed, the very embodiment of existence. To press his point further, Augustine notes that the human spirit has human virtues, which vary in each person, such as courage, wisdom, justice, etc. A human can have one or none of these virtues, but it does not mean he is no longer human or that his humanness diminishes or goes out of existence. Having all these virtues, equally, is not necessary for a human being to exist. God created human nature to have such virtues accidentally not properly to their natures. In the Divine essence, however, "it is the same thing to be powerful or just or wise or anything else that can be said about his simple multiplicity or multiple simplicity to signify his substance." That is the difference between composite beings, as created essences are, and simple being, as the Uncreated essence is. Therefore, Augustine concludes, in the apostle calling the Son equal to God, then "the Son is equal to the Father in every respect and is of one and the same substance" (*De Trin.* 6.1.6).

Regarding the Holy Spirit, he too shares in the same substance. And as the love of God, which the Spirit is, so also God is love (1Jn 4:8), the Spirit too is God's substance, and the Spirit has all the attributes fully, equally, and completely as proper to the Divine essence. Therefore, Augustine writes,

> just as it is substance together with the Father and the Son, so it is great together and good together and holy together with them and whatever else is said with reference to self, because with God it is not a different thing to be, and to be great or good etc. . . . So the Holy

Spirit is equal too, and if equal, equal in every respect, on account of
the total simplicity which belongs to that substance. (*De Trin.* 6.1.7)

In chapter 2, the last chapter of *Book VI*, Augustine examines further
divine simplicity, aiming to reconcile it with the triunity of God. He
first explains how a created substance "is multiple and in no way truly
simple," (*De Trin.* 6.2.8) in that it has size, color, and shape (parts), of
which any one of those can change while the other parts can remain
the same. All parts can change, or individual parts can change without
the others. However, a "spiritual creature such as the soul," while it is
simple in comparison to a created substance, nevertheless it is still
multiple. The reason it is considered simple compared to the body,
Augustine writes, is because it "has no mass spread out in space, but in
any body, it is whole in the whole and whole also in any part of the
body." And the soul's wholeness means that when the body is affected
the whole soul is aware of it, just a little part of it. With that said, in
the soul, there are parts, in that it can be ingenious, unskillful, have a
good memory, fearful, joyful, sad, etc., and all these things can be in the
soul without the other quality; "countless qualities can be found in the
soul in countless ways," thus "its nature is not simple but multiple.
Nothing simple is changeable; everything created is changeable" (*De Trin.*
6.2.8, emphasis added).

So, in Augustine, we have a definition of simplicity with the
necessary corollary of immutability inherent in that which is simple.
And that which is created is mutable; therefore, all creatures are
multiple. However, God is called multiple in the sense that his ways are
great, good, wise, blessed, true, and any other perfection proper to him.
While he is multiple in his ways, which he manifests to us in his
external acts or effects (*ad extra*), in his essence (*ad intra*) Augustine
says each of these qualities is identical to each other. So, his wisdom is
identical with his greatness; his goodness with his wisdom and
greatness; his truth identical with them all. Augustine then explains
how his triunity doesn't entail multiplicity, while we can talk of each
person individually, each of the persons is inseparable from one
another and are "always in each other and neither is alone" (*De Trin.*
6.2.9). And so, when we speak of one of the persons, we do so to
indicate their distinction from each other, not separation from one
another.

Book VII

In this book, Augustine revisits and solves the problem he spoke of in the previous book, which is the appropriation of *wisdom* and *power* as predicated of the Son, which he determined are substance-wise predications. More specifically, Augustine addresses whether we can predicate these attributes to each person by himself or only in the Trinity (*De Trin.* 7.1.1). He notes the linguistic and the logical problem that we run into: are we to conclude that God is the Father of his wisdom and his power in the eternal begetting of the Son? Can the Father be said to be wise "singly" and is indeed his own wisdom? If the Father is only wise or powerful because of his begetting of the Son, "then the Father is not anything with reference to himself" (*De Trin.* 7.1.2).

Augustine wants to avoid being cornered by the language he has used to express the inexpressible. The language blurs the predication, leading to unexpected and untenable conclusions. This forces us to assume that the Son is called *being* in relation to the Father (and vice versa). Therefore, *being*, then, is not *being*; rather, it is relationship. If relationship, then we cannot predicate *being* properly nor anything as proper to anyone or anything because we lack an origin from which we can reference. For example, if we were to say a man is a master, we point to his relationship to a slave. But man is predicated as man with reference to himself (*qua man*). And so, if the relationship is being, then being is not being (*De Trin.* 7.1.2) Augustine must untie the substance–relation Gordian knot. So, what is the way forward?

Augustine makes a deductive move. He notes that what is called by relationship with something must be something in reference to itself otherwise we do not know what the relationship is predicating. So, then, as the Father is called father in relationship to the Son, that which is Father must be something with reference to himself, otherwise "there is absolutely nothing there to be talked of with reference to something else" (*De Trin.* 7.1.2). But Augustine qualifies the uniqueness of this situation, in that it is not the same as the color of something. A color is only a color of that which is predicated of the color (i.e., the man's body is white). With that said, a body's color is not its being; "body signifies its being" and whiteness a quality therein, "since it is not the same for it to be and to be white." But "wisdom is both wise and wise with itself," in that "a soul becomes wise by participating in wisdom, but if it then becomes unwise, wisdom remains in itself" (*De Trin.* 7.1.2). Color simply ceases to be when a body changes to another color.

Because of the simple being that God is, to say the Father begets wisdom to then become wise with it would mean he is not the same as his wisdom because the Son (*the begotten*) would be a quality of his, not his offspring. And if for God it is the same for him to be and to be wisdom, then if the Father begot wisdom, it is wisdom that begot him. And then the cause of his being wise is the cause of him being at all, and such a conclusion is absurd, nor would anyone even consider thinking such a thing. Augustine concludes, therefore, that for God to be wise he must be his wisdom; thus,

> the Father is himself wisdom, and the Son is called the wisdom of the Father in the same way as he is called the light of the Father, that is, that as we talk of light from light, and both are one light, so we must understand wisdom from wisdom, and both one wisdom. And therefore also one being, because there to be is the same as to be wise. What being wise is for wisdom, and being powerful for power, and being eternal for eternity, being just for justice, being great for greatness, that simply being is for being. And because in that ultimately simplicity to be is not different from to be wise, there wisdom is the same as being. (*De Trin.* 7.1.2)

Augustine resolves the problem. While he has deduced the attributes in God to God's being, and thus are the same as being (in God), the linguistics of the Father and the Son as denoted by relationship are not the same. The Father and the Son are not the Word because the Father is not the Son; however, they are both wisdom and they are both power, which can be predicated of each singly. The Son is not the Word as he is wisdom because he is only Word by "relationship to whose Word he is" (*De Trin.* 7.1.3). The Word is a relation-wise term and wisdom is a substance-wise term. In closing, addressing the *unbegotten/begotten* problem of predication (in the Arians that is), Augustine writes, "It does not follow that because the Father is not the Son nor the Son the Father, one is unbegotten, the other begotten, that therefore they are not one being; for these names only declare their relationships" (*De Trin.* 7.1.3).

I heard one church historian say, "If you get into Augustine, you will never get out." And he was speaking to the massive amounts of literature Augustine produced. I say that because our brief look at Augustine's doctrine of God just scratches the surface of his corpus. Hopefully, I distilled key aspects of his theology from some of his important and well-known writings. Augustine was and still is a towering figure in the Christian tradition. His influence spread far and wide, along with the classical doctrines of that tradition, a tradition he carried on from those before him, adding more depth and rigorous development to the Tradition's doctrine of God.

Cyril of Alexandria

Cyril of Alexandria (370–444) was a towering figure of his time. As the patriarch of Alexandria (in 412), the tradition of leaders before him elevated the Alexandrian see to a position of great influence, rivaled only by Rome, Constantinople, and Antioch. Cyril is most famous for his christological works, formulating a doctrine of the hypostatic union grounded in Nicene theology that articulates two natures in Christ, a human and divine, which are hypostatically united in one person. His key writings were preserved in the Councils of Ephesus and Chalcedon, moving the church's theology of Christ forward against heretical notions, most acutely in the influential writings of Nestorius, the bishop of Constantinople, who taught that the human person and the divine person were united in a manner making them indistinguishable. However, Cyril's doctrine lacked precision as it pertains to "person" and "nature," so the Council at Chalcedon (451) modified it, making the distinction that affirmed Christ's two natures indivisibly united, without confusion, in the single subject of the person of Jesus, with both natures contributing to his enhancement and development.

When reading Cyril's commentaries and treatises, one will quickly take note of his profound biblical and theological depth. His commentary on John, which will be the primary text of exposition, is a rigorous work articulated according to the *skopos* of the Bible. His elucidations show a mastery of the text and a proper appropriation of theological and metaphysical terms as developed in the Nicene Tradition. Because of his theologically tumultuous context, Cyril particularizes his arguments toward dispelling heretical assumptions and teachings, notably those advanced by the Arians (i.e., the *Homoians*).

As mentioned, Cyril's *Commentary on John*[69] (*Comm. Jo*) will be our primary text of study, with his well-known work *On the Unity of Christ*[70] (*Unity*) and his not-so-well-known *Festal Letters*[71] (*Fest.*) as supplemental literature. While the focus of this study is to highlight a metaphysical grammar, Cyril's works are mostly christological. However, the developed divine grammar from those before him enables him to establish a robust and theologically rigid christological framework.

Cyril's Christology follows the theological footprint of Athanasius. Jesus is the Son of God, the Son of the Father, the second person of the Trinity, as framed through a Nicene construct. When a believer is adopted and brought into fellowship with the triune God, "Cyril insisted that in Jesus the believer encountered none other than the second person of the Trinity himself."[72]

The Gospel According to Cyril

The Christ, Cyril writes, the prophets of Old declared his appearance to come. He sees this uttered in the Psalms, "Send your light and your truth!" (43:3); "Lord, part your heavens and come down!" (144:4). And he came. Cyril's Christology is supported by key passages, Hebrews 1:3, Philippians 2:7, and Acts 2:24 when he writes, the "Only-Begotten Word of God came to stay, therefore, he who is the exact impress of the Father's substance, who put on our likeness, and, having become a human being, 'appeared on earth and lived among human beings,' as one of the wise has said" (*Fest. L.4*). The chief aim of Cyril's doctrine of Christ is to constantly bring to the fore that the Son is "from the Father's substance." (*Fest. L.5*). As the Word, "the Father's Only-Begotten," he is, like the Father, "passionless and immortal" (*Fest. L.7*).

Paul's letter to the Philippians provides the basis of Cyril's high Christology, due to the distinction set forth regarding the Son's *kenotic*[73]

---

[69] Cyril, Joel C. Elowsky, and David R. Maxwell, *Commentary on John: Volume 1*, Ancient Christian Texts (Downers Grove, IL: IVP Academic, 2013); Cyril, David R. Maxwell, and Joel C. Elowsky, *Commentary on John: Volume 2*, Commentary on John (Downers Grove, IL: IVP Academic, 2015).

[70] English translation cited: Cyril of Alexandria, *On the Unity of Christ*, trans. John Anthony McGuckin (St Vladimirs Seminary Pr, 1997).

[71] St. Cyril of Alexandria, *Festal Letters 1-12*, Fathers of the Church (Washington, D.C.: Catholic University of America Press, 2009).

[72] McGuckin, "Introduction," in Cyril of Alexandria, *On the Unity of Christ*, 28.

[73] *Kenosis* is the Greek word that means "self-emptying." *Kenoticism* refers to the self-

event. The Word who was in the form of his Father, did not consider what we were; rather, he considered *us* so that in taking on flesh, putting it to death, and rising from the grave, he might make us like him. However, his taking on flesh did not mean his form was no longer; rather, it was because of his divine form, as "the One who possesses all power" (*Fest. L.*8), that he was able to take on human form, conquer sin and death, thus "being the basis for our salvation" (*Fest. L.*7). Cyril writes, "he despoiled all of hell at once, opened the inescapable gates to the spirits of those asleep, left the devil there solitary and alone, and then rose on the third day" (*Fest. L.*7). The Word is "called Jesus because he saves his people;" he is called "Christ because he was anointed for us" (*Fest. L.*8). While the incarnation was the manifestation of the person of Jesus Christ, the Word has always been with the Father, as Scripture says: "he was the same yesterday and today and forever" (He 13:8) (*Fest. L.*8).

In the revealing of the Word from the Father and the outpouring of the Spirit, Cyril tells us the simple message of the church: "We have been baptized, that is, in the Father and the Son and the Holy Spirit. And by believing that the Holy Trinity is consubstantial, we worship one Godhead in it, thanking God the Father for having sent from heaven his own Son for the sake of our salvation and life" (*Fest. L.*12).

Exposition of John's Gospel

The festal letters we observed above were written with the layperson in mind. Cyril's commentary on John is a percipient piece of work. Though lucid, Cyril is relentless in his argumentation, as he dismantles every "lofty" argument raised against the truth of the Son's full, shared essence with the Father. We won't examine the entire commentary; we will look at Cyril's exegesis of some key passages and the theological insights he derives from them.

Chapter I. *In the beginning was the Word.* What is "the beginning"? Cyril writes, "There is nothing older than the beginning, as long as one does not violate the definition of beginning" (*Comm. Jo.* 1.1.17). His obvious point is crucial for one to affirm if John's Gospel is to make any

---

emptying of Christ, who, in the form of God, took on the form of man. Some have greatly erred saying that Christ emptied himself of his divine properties. A more consistent kenosis doctrine teaches that God the Son added humanity to himself. The Divine essence cannot "lose" properties of divinity.

metaphysical and theological sense at all. And in *the beginning*, John writes, *was* the Word. We must assume that John has the beginning of time in mind. If the beginning has another beginning, then we will continue into infinite regress (*Comm. Jo.* 1.1.17). It is incomprehensible to think of what is before "the beginning." Logic and reason restrict us to a beginning point. Therefore, we must contend that John's beginning implies the beginning point of created reality. And at this beginning point, *the Word was there*. The Word did not come to be *in the beginning*. Rather, the Word was—. No matter how far back that beginning is, "the Son will be found to have come to be not in time but rather to exist eternally with the Father" (*Comm. Jo.* 1.1.17). He exists before all ages. In fact, "his divine nature exempts him from having an end because he will always be the same" [Ps 102:27] (*Comm. Jo.* 1.1.18).

Cyril explains that the Word's eternal relationship exists "in his Father as in a source according to his own statement, 'I came from the Father and have arrived'" [Jn 16:28] (*Comm. Jo.* 1.1.18). Following the Nicene Tradition, Cyril understands the Word's *ad intra* relations with the Father is "because the Word was his wisdom, power [1Co 1:24], imprint, radiance, and image [He 1:3]." And because the Word is these things, and the Father could never have been without them, then the Son must be eternal with the Father. Cyril is precise in stating that the Son "*is* these things" for the Father (*Comm. Jo.* 1.1.18). Utilizing an analogy from nature, Cyril notes that we are to think of the Son as existing from the Father as water comes from a spring. While the common mistake is to see the Son as inferior because of this relation, one must understand that the Son "exists in the substance of the Father. He radiates out from that substance like beams from the sun or heat from a fire" (*Comm. Jo.* 1.1.19). While it seems that beams and sun are different or that water and source are different, both are inseparable. "The one cannot exist in itself apart from the other if the integrity of its own nature is truly preserved" (*Comm. Jo.* 1.1.19). Our creaturely minds struggle to grasp the importance of this necessary distinction. It is necessary because we believe in the one, true God. And while we believe God is one God, we believe there are three divine persons or distinct modes within the one being of God. An important rule when it comes to retaining a consistent monotheistic Trinitarianism is: *Distinctions do not diminish divinity.*

The Son's eternal relationship to the Father, Cyril writes, "will always be in [the Father] and with him and radiating from him according to the ineffable mode of divine generation" (*Comm. Jo.* 1.1.19). The Father is the *arche* or origin of the Son and the Spirit. Cyril says the "Father is the beginningless beginning of the Son's nature, so to speak, but only in the sense of source because the Son's existence is 'from' the Father." What are the entailments of this christological understanding? The Son "will possess with the Father the beginning (or dominion) that transcends all things" (*Comm. Jo.* 1.1.20).

Chapter II. *And the Word was with God.* In this chapter, Cyril advances the discussion into the matter of the Father and the Son having an individuated existence termed *hypostasis.* The term denotes the Word is a concretely existing individual. Cyril writes, "The Son is of the same substance as the Father, and the Father is of the same substance as the Son. Therefore, they ascend into an exact likeness so that the Father is seen in the Son, and the Son is seen in the Father, and the one shines in the other" [Jn 14:9–10] (*Comm. Jo.* 1.2.25). It may sound like Cyril is being redundant or maybe even pedantic. However, too many have made doctrinal errors, so getting the divine grammar accurate is of the utmost importance.

The Father and the Son each have their own subsistence. While they are the Divine essence, the Father is not the Son and the Son is not the Father. Along with the Spirit, each one has its distinct identity or *hypostasis* in the Holy Trinity (*Comm. Jo.* 1.2.25). If Cyril doesn't emphasize that there is a real distinction between the Father, Son, and Spirit, then the names have no meaning when it comes to reading and interpreting Scripture. What is the point, Cyril writes, "of ordering believers to be baptized not into the Unity but into the Trinity? [Matt 28:19]" Scripture reveals "each one of those numbered is in his own hypostasis. But because there is no change in nature, each hypostasis ascends to one divine nature and receives the same worship" (*Comm. Jo.* 1.2.28).

Chapter III. *And the Word was God.* Here is a pivotal section in Cyril's exegesis, as he merges all his arguments regarding the deity of the Son. Starting with the common ground (even among heretics) that the Divine nature is one, the Trinity must "completely possess identity of nature" in the one being of God. Therefore, the Word *was* God. He did not come to be God later. John's use of the word *was* in attributing the divine nature to the Word, Cyril notes, implies his eternality because the one divine being is eternal, which, Cyril writes, "is a strict consequence of being God" (*Comm. Jo.* 1.3.32). Now, Cyril proceeds to demonstrate that the Son's consubstantiality with the Father means complete equality with the Father. Following the classic pattern in patristic proofs for the deity of the Son, Cyril cites First Corinthians 1:24, Christ is the power and wisdom of the Father. He cites a handful of Psalms, establishing the integral unity of the Son to the Father in his divine actions, whereby the Son is "light and truth" (Ps 43:3) sent by the Father, the "righteousness" (Ps 119:40) of the Father in giving life in Christ to those who believe in him, and "the counsel" of the Father to lead his people (Ps 73:24; 33:11). The Son and Father inseparably act according to the one will of God. The divine acts demonstrate the divinity of the persons.

Again, Cyril has a theological axe to grind. With ardent opposition to Arius and his followers, Cyril asks, how can the Son who is all things to the Father be less than him? If so, then we would have to say that the Father is less than perfect—an impious assumption indeed. To conclude, Cyril writes, "Therefore, it is clear that the Son—the wisdom and power, the light and truth, the righteousness and counsel of the Father—is also perfect. How could he who supplies perfection to his own Father be considered inferior?" (*Comm. Jo.* 1.3.33).

Cyril continues his argument regarding a superior/inferior distinction. He provides a litany of questions and answers to drive home the point that it is madness to think that the scriptural testimony expresses that the Son is less than the Father. I will quote a few of them in full. Take notice of the logical rigor in his argumentation. Cyril writes:

> If the Son is fullness [from John 1:16], how can anything inferior be in him? Opposing attributes cannot be in the same subject at the same time.

> If the Son, who is lesser, fills all things, where will the greatness of the Father go? I am speaking in a corporeal way for the sake of example. Lesser and greater have different senses when applied to incorporeal objects.

> If the divine nature is not subject to quantification but whatever is inferior admits of degrees, how could the Son, who is God by nature,

be considered inferior? If, as they say, he is inferior to the Father, he will be subject to quantification. (*Comm. Jo.* 1.3.34)

And in this last one, Cyril incorporates the Holy Spirit into his argument. See how Cyril considers each of the persons in the one divine operation.

> If the Son is inferior and the Father is superior, then they will clearly act differently in our sanctification in proportion to the measure that each one has. The Father will sanctify more and the Son by himself will sanctify less. There will also be a twofold Spirit who is inferior in the Son and superior in the Father. Those who are sanctified by the Father will be sanctified perfectly, and those who are sanctified by the Son will be sanctified imperfectly. But this line of reasoning is totally absurd. The Holy Spirit is one, and sanctification is one and perfect, supplied from the Father through the Son by nature. Therefore, the one who has the same activity as the perfect Father is not inferior to him. He has the Spirit of the one who begat him, a good of his own nature, living and hypostatic,[74] just as the Father has. (*Comm. Jo.* 1.3.34–5)

Cyril continues his proofs for many pages. Some might say overkill. But heresy cannot be killed enough because it will rear its ugly head again and again. We will jump to chapter 5 in Cyril's commentary, where he exposits John 1:3: "All things came to be through him, and without him, not one thing came to be."

The Son as Creator

Cyril begins noting the polytheistic errors of the Greeks, being devoted to the wisdom of the world. And others, he notes, "pursued a more refined error," worshiping the creation instead of the Creator (Ro 1:25) (*Comm. Jo.* 1.5.66). The Theologian (the Apostle John) must correct such idolatrous thinking and "introduce the Only Begotten to us as the

---

[74] "Cyril here uses the word [*enhupostaton*] to describe the Spirit. This does not mean the Spirit is enhypostatic in the sense he exists only 'in' the hypostasis of another and has no hypostasis of his own. That is how the term later comes to be used to describe Christ's human nature. Here it means that the Spirit exists concretely as his own person." Translation notes from *Commentary on John: Volume 1*, 14. Enhypostasis literally means *inpersonality*; "having one's subsistence of another, normally employed to safeguard the union of the two natures through affirmation of the oneness of Christ's person: his person is divine and not the sum of the two natures." Richard A. Muller, *Dictionary of Latin and Greek Theological Terms: Drawn Principally from Protestant Scholastic Theology*, 2nd ed. (Baker Academic, 2017), 106.

creator and craftsman by nature." The Word as Creator is the *key* identifying mark of the transcendent God. Therefore, we have another argument demonstrating that the Son is equal to the Father. The Word as Creator puts him above all creaturely reality because he is completely distinct from his creation; he is *sui generis* [unique]. And as Creator, the Word, "By his ineffable power," Cyril writes, "brought all things into existence from nonexistence" (*Comm. Jo.* 1.5.66).

The Son's power to create was not given to him, as the heretics would say. As the wisdom and power of God, he *is* the wisdom and power that proceeds "by an altogether ineffable mode of generation from the Father." Reason being, writes Cyril, "so that the wisdom and power of the Father is understood to be the truly existing Son" (*Comm. Jo.* 1.5.67). And being the power and wisdom of God, all things that exist, came to be *through* the Son. God creates through his wisdom, in *conceiving* what to create; God creates through his power, in *executing* what he determines to create. Cyril ensures to maintain his creation doctrine within the confines of the Trinity. He writes, "Of course, the Father and the Holy Spirit also work with him and accompany him . . . . [T]he Son is completely in [the Father] on account of the immutability of his substance and the utter proximity and unmediated character of the Son's procession from him by nature" (*Comm. Jo.* 1.5.68).

Cyril provides an example from nature to help explain the Son's procession, writing, "It is as though one were to say that the flower itself is with its fragrance by the operation of the sweet smell since the fragrance proceeds from the flower by nature." Cyril comments on the lackluster effect this illustration has in that the divine nature "surpasses this example, so these ideas barely scratch the surface" (*Comm. Jo.* 1.5.68). Nevertheless, as with the patristic habit, such examples from creaturely reality to explain the ineffable are helpful, though limited in manner and form.

Cyril jumps ahead to comment on John 5:17, "My Father works until now, and I also work." It is a helpful move for Cyril to address this passage here. How are we to understand this passage if we claim the Son and the Father are one in creative work? Is the Father idle when the Son works? But that cannot be the case since the Son says, "I am in the Father, and the Father is in me" (Jn 14:10). Otherwise, Cyril writes, "The Father would receive the ability not to have the Son always in himself, and the Son likewise would be seen not to have the Father always in himself" (*Comm. Jo.* 1.5.68).

Cyril elaborates on the metaphysics of John 14:10. He writes,

> When we see the Son (as imprint) in the Father and the Father (as archetype) in the Son, we should certainly not understand that to indicate a mere similarity of substance. Rather, we hold that the Son shines forth begottenly from the Father's substance and that he is and subsists on his own in and from that substance as God the Word (*Comm. Jo.* 1.5.69).

Cyril purposes to emphasize the exactness of the Son to the Father and the inverse. They are distinct or separate by relation to each other but in having the same nature, they are in one another. And with this truth, "and the Holy Spirit [who] clearly comes with them, the number of the holy Trinity arrives at one and the same divine nature" (*Comm. Jo.* 1.5.69).

However, an objection follows. Can we have a proper sense of any of the persons if "each one withdrew into complete individuality, and though separated in every respect from the shared nature of the other and from any essential relationship, they were each called God?" Cyril raised this question because he anticipated the problem. And to answer: we do affirm the individuality of the persons but we "do not mix up the difference *of persons or names* with the position each one has" (*Comm. Jo.* 1.5.69. Emphasis added). In doing so, we refer to the persons as the one divinity when it comes to their nature; thus, in each having the same nature and each one is in the other when each one works, they all work in one *divine* working.

To solidify this point, Cyril brings us back to the Son as the wisdom from the Father's mind, noting that in the "interpenetrating" of the Son and the Father, there is no distance between them; therefore, "the mind can be seen in the Word and wisdom, and the Word, in turn, in the mind." This is profound for our understanding of the inseparability of the divine will and actions in the persons so that we can say they are distinct as modes in the being of God yet are *the one* being of God. And I will let Cyril expound further:

> And there is nothing intervening or separating one from the other. He is also power since power resides, without distance, in those who are naturally capable of it. It cannot be separated from them, the way an

accident can, without the destruction of the subject. He is also the imprint since an imprint is always naturally with and cannot be separated from the substance whose imprint it is.

Therefore, since each one is in the other by nature and by necessity, it is clear that when the Father works, the Son will work since he is his natural, essential and hypostatic power. Likewise, when the Son works, the Father works as well, since he is the source of the creating Word, and he is by nature in his own offspring just as the fire also is in the heat that proceeds from it. (*Comm. Jo.* 1.5.70)

In this *interpenetration*, or in theological terminology, *perichoresis*,[75] which the Son and the Father have by nature, thus by necessity, the Son is the glory of the Father, in that he is the agent of creation, through whom all things came to be. And as the agent of creation, the wisdom and power of God, God the Father is then glorified as Creator because it is through the Son that "he works all things, and he brings into being things that are not" (*Comm. Jo.* 1.5.71). Cyril points out that in the decree of God to create mankind in "our image and likeness" the Father does not command the Son to "Make mankind!"; rather, the interpenetration of the Father and the Son means there is no distance between them, whereby the Son would be an instrument or derivative cause in creating. Rather, the Father "shares his will for humanity in common with the Son" since the Son is in the Father by nature, as "the imprinted Word who is in him" (*Comm. Jo.* 1.5.71). Cyril is careful to note that we shouldn't see the Father and Son as individuated in bringing about creation, as if there were two gods, nor does one envelope or contract in the other. He writes, "But we understand it in this way: as if one were to grant that light exists with the rays that it emits." So, Cyril brings us back to a common analogy of Trinitarian expression. The Father and the Son are inseparably one in nature and essence, but there is a distinction between them (Sun/Sun rays) that must be retained (*Comm. Jo.* 1.5.71).

Concluding chapter 5, Cyril responds to those "insane people" who will claim the Son is second rate or less than the Father in substance,

---

[75] *Perichōrēsis*, synonymously termed in Latin, *Circumincessio*, "refers primarily to the coinherence of the persons of the Trinity in the divine essence and in each other, in such a way that each person is fully possessed of the entire divine essence." Muller, *Dictionary of Latin and Greek Theological Terms*, 64.

equality, and likeness because Scripture employs the prepositional phrase *through whom* when speaking of God's creative agency. He attends to various passages of Scripture (1Co 1:9; 2Co 1:1; Ga 4:7) where we see the divine economy manifesting in redemptive activity, such as Paul being called to God in fellowship, apostleship, and sonship *through* the person of God the Father. Cyril critically asks, "Would we then impugn the very glory of the Father with the name and status of an underling, just because the word *through* is applied to him also?" Such thinking is absurd. Therefore, we must be reminded of the fact that human language is weak "when it comes to a precise explanation of the ineffable and God-befitting glory" (*Comm. Jo.* 1.5.73), and we must not let feeble words insufficient for the task of speaking of that which is incomprehensible demur our conception of any person of the Holy Trinity. Rather, "we must concede supremacy to the divine and inexpressible nature over the power of language and the sharpness of every mind. In this way, we will be pious in no small degree" (*Comm. Jo.* 1.5.73).

We are going to skip ahead to Cyril's exegesis on John 5, starting at v. 17. At this point in John's Gospel, Jesus healed a sick man on the Sabbath, which was reported to the Jews resulting in their persecuting Jesus. In response to them, Jesus says, "My Father is still working, and I am working also." Therefore, the Jews sought to kill him because Jesus' statement implied that God was his own Father, thus making himself equal to God (v. 18). It is fascinating that the Jews' (though unable to perceive who the Son is) response to Jesus' words provide one of the most precise statements in Scripture about Jesus' relationship to the Father. They understood that Jesus calling God his own Father implied that he shared the same essence of the Father. Cyril provides a lengthy paraphrase of what he thinks Jesus is trying to communicate:

> It is as though he wants to say something like, If you believe, my friend, that God, who by his will and counsel crafted everything and set it in place, also rules creation even on the sabbath day, so that the sun rises, rain-bearing fountains are likewise let loose, fruit springs up from the ground, not refusing to grow on account of the sabbath, and fire performs its own work, ministering to human needs without being prevented, then know and admit with certainty that the Father does what is God-befitting even on the sabbath. Why then, he says, do you ignorantly blame the one through whom he works all things? For God

the Father will work in no other way than through his power and wisdom, the Son. That is why he says, "I am also working." (*Comm. Jo.* 2.5.314–15)

Jesus words are damning to them because they claim to honor the Father in keeping the Sabbath but show they do not know him because they dishonor the Son. Jesus continues to speak about his works, in that he can only do what he sees the Father doing. By doing the same works as the Father, he demonstrates that he is from the Father, thus sharing the same "identity of substance with him." If he only does what the Father does, who is incomprehensible divinity by nature, then the Son, likewise is incomprehensible divinity by nature because "the things that have the same nature as each other will act in the same way" (*Comm. Jo.* 2.6.318). And Cyril teases this out further, noting that the Son's working all things after the Father, in sustaining the world on the Sabbath (i.e., healing a man), is not because the Father taught him how to act; rather, it is according to the "laws of uncreated nature" in that "he ascends to the same will and action as God the Father" (*Comm. Jo.* 2.6.318).

In verse 19, Cyril logically concludes that the Son is of the same essence as the Father because if the Son does whatever the Father does, how then is the Son inferior to the Father? To argue his point from an earthly analogy, Cyril asks, "Could the offspring of fire have a different activity than fire without changing its activity?" So then, the Son's ability to do "likewise" implies he is of the same nature and power as God the Father (*Comm. Jo.* 2.6.319). Cyril understands the difficulty in grasping the implications of this passage, so he examines it again under greater scrutiny so that we can understand it according to godliness.

He writes, "Do you see how through the exact identity of their works, the Son shows himself to be like the Father in all things so that he might be revealed through this to be the heir of his substance as well?" (*Comm. Jo.* 2.6.324). Cyril's exposition draws out the *oikonomia*, the revealing of the triune nature and persons of God in creation through Jesus Christ. And because he is the Son made flesh, he speaks in a language that attributes aspects proper to both natures. In the Son's expressing that "he is not able to do anything on his own, but only what he sees the Father doing" (Jn 5:19), he is speaking of the divine nature, not the human nature. "He was, after all, really both in the same" (*Comm. Jo.* 2.6.325). But his saying that he is unable or cannot, is not indicative of weakness in the Son; rather, it denotes the capability of what is proper to one of the natures. The Divine essence cannot eat grapes; it is unable to, just as the human essence cannot part the Red Sea; it is unable to.

Getting back to the context of the passage—the Jews persecuting him on the Sabbath, Cyril understands when Jesus says he only does what the Father does, he means to say that as the Father extends mercy on the Sabbath since the Son is compassionate all the time as the Father is, then the Son likewise will extend mercy all the time. Thus, the Son carries out the works of the Father in every way since he is from him (*Comm. Jo.* 2.6.326–7).

Before moving on to examine Cyril's Christology in more detail, I thought examining Cyril's interpretation of John 5:22 would prove quite instructive, not just for understanding Cyril, but as an exegetical tool in our theological interpretation (i.e., *skopos* and *oikonomia; economy*). In John 5:22, Jesus says, "The Father, in fact, judges no one but has given all judgment to the Son." Heretics cite this passage as a key proof text to demonstrate that the Son is not truly God by nature. Cyril interprets this passage according to the *economy*, whereby the Father is giving the authority to judge to the Son according to his human nature. Jesus according to his human nature has to *play by the rules*, if you will, thus we can only attribute what is proper to humanity, even though it is Jesus Christ. Therefore, while the Word, has all the fullness of the divine nature, and thus has all things that belong to the Father, the Word *made* flesh receives what he has *from* God as is proper to humanity. Cyril cites First Corinthians 4:7, "What do you have that you did not receive?" And so, "[the Son] confesses that it was fitting for him to receive that authority" (*Comm. Jo.* 2.7.331).

Next, Cyril takes up the position of his opponents, who will look at this passage and say, "See! The Son explicitly says that he has received 'judgment' from the Father. Clearly, one who receives does not have. How then could the one who gives with authority not be greater and of a superior nature than the one who must receive?" Cyril isn't intimidated one bit. Why is that? The argument is "unskillfully constructed," in that it "perfectly fits the *oikonomia* with the flesh when he was called a slave and when we humbled himself, being made in our likeness" (*Comm. Jo.* 2.7.332). Cyril's response is superb. I quote him in full:

First let us say, the one who is said to give something does not necessarily or in every case grant it to someone who receives because they do not have, nor is the giver always greater than the receiver. Otherwise, what will you do when you see the holy psalmist saying in the Spirit, "Give glory to God"? [Ps 75:7] Shall we think then that God stands in need of glory or that we who are commanded to offer it to him are greater than the creator because of this? But not even you, who do not shrink from blasphemy, will dare to say this, since the divine nature is full of glory even though it does not receive it from us. That which has something inherently and receives it as an honor could never be considered inferior to those who offer glory to it as a gift. One may then see that very often the one who has received something is not inferior to the giver, and the Father is not of a superior nature to his own offspring just because "he has given all judgment" to him . . . .

Judging is an activity and nothing else. What then has the Father given the Son? He does not give something additional as from his own nature when he entrusts all judgment to him, but rather he gives him an activity over against those who are judged. How then will he be greater because of this or be of a superior nature because he added something that was not in the Son, since the Son says, "Everything that the Father has is mine"? [Jn 16:15]

So, listen to how giving must then be understood. Just as God the Father has the ability to create and creates all things through the Son as through his own power and strength, so also he has the power to judge, and he will exercise that power through the Son as through his own righteousness [1Co 1:30]. Just as though fire were said to supply a certain "burning" to the activity that is from it by nature, so also if we reverently interpret "he has given" along the same lines, we will escape the snare of the devil. But if they shamelessly persist in asserting that glory is added to him from the Father because of his appearing as judge of the earth, let them teach us how he could still be considered the "Lord of glory," [1Co 2:8] if he is crowned with this glory in the end times? (*Comm. Jo.* 2.7.332–33)

Cyril's interpretation is consistent, in that he does not stray away from the *oikonomia*. Heretics stray from the *skopos*, the governing rule of scriptural interpretation that Christ is fully human and fully divine. And they stray from it because it is a revealed rule; it is only through divine revelation that we can receive the glorious truth that the incomprehensible God took on flesh. And applying that revealed rule ensures our interpretation aligns with the meaning the divine Author intended for his people to know.

There is much more to be examined in Cyril's writings. In the brief review thus far, we notice in Cyril a tenacious consistency in maintaining the unity of the Father and the Son, whereby he operates within his interpretive parameters with the understanding that the distinction between the Father and the Son is only by relation, not essence. Cyril's interpretive conclusions fulfill the texts' intention to convey two equal truths. Misinterpreting the texts with a rigid dichotomy can distort the meaning, potentially leading to mythology or incoherency.

On The Unity of Christ

The text of exposition, noted already, is his work On the Unity of Christ. The treatise comprises a dialogue through which Cyril meticulously expounds his doctrine of the hypostatic union, integrating theological and philosophical principles with precision and rigor. His main opponent is Nestorius, bishop of Constantinople (c. 345), who entered the spotlight for his rejection of the term Theotokos ("God-bearer") for the Virgin Mary. He rejected it because he thought no human woman could bear the eternal God. That debate will not be examined here. But it has relevance for his doctrine of Christ in that as he could not affirm a human being could bear the eternal God, the incarnation, likewise, could not be a true union of divinity and humanity. Nestorius saw that God and man were radically different. Jesus was truly human, experiencing all that pertains to humanity. But in the incarnation, the fully divine Logos was in communion with the human life of Jesus but was not in any way dominated nor subjugated by it.[76] Nestorius thought "the divinity and humanity can only be maintained if the two remain 'two.'"[77]

Cyril thought Nestorian's doctrine of the incarnation was abhorrent. For Cyril the redemptive aim was not about God and man merely having a relationship; rather, it was about full reconciliation of God and man in Jesus. As such, the divine act of reconciliation is a work intended to transform humanity from a mortal fallen creature to an immortal, divinized spiritual creature. Therefore, the incarnation had to

---

[76] McGuckin, "Introduction," 34.

[77] Aaron Riches, Ecce Homo: On the Divine Unity of Christ (Grand Rapids, MI: Eerdmans, 2016), 27.

be a "seamless union."[78] This process was the drawing of humanity into the life of God, termed *theosis* (deification). Far from a pagan conception of this process, *theosis* was the ineffable act of grace whereby the Second Person of the Trinity becomes man so that we might become like God. Cyril slogans this redemptive act: "What he was by nature, we become by grace."

The incarnation is the unfathomable demonstration of God's infinite power, making the invisible Lord visible, in that the Eternal God who cannot be contained, contains himself in human flesh, living among his people, and ultimately going to the cross for them. The challenge the church, and Cyril, faced was the manner of articulating a cogent doctrine of the incarnation that was completely distinguishable from a paganized concept of divinity. As mentioned, this divine act was inexplicable. Nevertheless, it was the event of all events in human history, and Scripture's revelation of this event presses the human intellect to its limits.[79]

The impetus driving Cyril's investigation was to articulate a coherent account of the subjective unity of Christ. If he followed Nestorius, then the incarnational scheme posited two Sons, existing side-by-side. But Cyril could not accept such perversion. This work is his attempt at solving that dilemma in a logical manner that is faithful to biblical revelation, ensuring to avoid any hint of corrupting the gospel.[80] Cyril's task is to develop a doctrine that accounts for the humanity and deity of Christ, a true union of humanity and divinity that is by no means mixed, overlapped, co-habited, or of mere association. Rather, as we will see, Cyril terms his doctrine a *hypostatic union*, whereby, to quote McGuckin's summation of it,

> the person of the Logos is the sole personal subject of all the conditions of his existence divine or human. The Logos is, needless to say, the sole personal subject of all his own acts as eternal Lord (the creation, the inspiration of the ancient prophets, and so on), but after the incarnation the same one is also the personal subject directing all his actions performed within this time and this space, embodied acts which form the context of the human life of Christ in Palestine.[81]

---

[78] McGuckin, "Introduction," 35.
[79] McGuckin, "Introduction," 36.
[80] McGuckin, "Introduction," 39.
[81] McGuckin, "Introduction," 40–1.

Cyril's hypostatic union doctrine was a *mia physis*, a "singularity of the existence of Jesus and not a blurring of the quiddities [i.e., the whatness] of divinity and humanity."[82] The most egregious error would be to propose a doctrine that posits Christ as a *tertium quid*, a third thing.

Cyril begins his treatise, in dialogue form, getting familiar with Nestorius' aberrant views, which stray from orthodoxy. Immediately, he inquires about his rejection of Mary as the *Theotokos*, noting it is because he maintains she has not given birth to God, since the Word was before her, in fact before every age, thus he is coeternal, "ineffably begotten by nature" from God the Father (*Unity*, 52, 53). Cyril shifts his argument toward "they," which seems to refer to a band of Nestorian followers. In their understanding of the Word becoming flesh (Jn 1:14), the Word's becoming human meant he ceased to be what he was before. Taking on flesh signified a change in the Word. But Cyril is put off by their erroneous assumptions, noting scriptural passages that speak of the Lord as our refuge (Ps 90:1; 94:22) by no means implies that he does so by a transformation of his nature into something else (*Unity*, 54). God by nature is immutable, "he remains that which he was and is forever," regardless of his becoming a refuge for us. Cyril will not budge from his formative doctrine of God. He must provide an account of the incarnation that "preserves the immutability and inalterability as innate and essential to God" (*Unity*, 54).

Therefore, the incarnation was not a change, mixing, or blending of the Only Begotten Word into/with human form; rather, Cyril says it was an act of submission, as Hebrews 12:2 reveals: "For the joy that lay before him, he endured the cross, despising shame." Therefore, as God, Cyril writes, "he wished to make that flesh which was held in the grip of sin and death evidently superior to sin and death. He made it his very own, and not soulless as some have said, but rather animated with a rational soul, and thus he restored flesh to what it was in the beginning" (*Unity*, 55). The incomprehensible and ineffable act, Cyril writes, was "for the economy of salvation." In "one single act of generation," the Son is begotten from God the Father, which is then revealed to us in the divine economy. Drawing from Second Corinthians 8:9, Cyril succinctly states: "He took what was ours to be his very own so that we might have

---

82 Riches, *Ecce Homo*, 39.

all that was his" (*Unity*, 58, 59). But his opponents "have turned the mystery of the economy in the flesh completely on its head" (*Unity*, 69).

Cyril addresses his opponents who have strayed from the *skopos* of Scripture, interpreting passages that seem to indicate Christ is not true God of God as the Father. Masterfully, Cyril interprets Scripture with the *oikonomia–theologia* lens, which maintains the unity of the God-man, whereby the person of the Lord is sole subject, experiencing and acting in what is proper to his humanity and also his divinity. When he refers to Christ as the sole subject, Cyril is claiming "that (1) Jesus is a real existent being (*mia physis*); and (2) he is the one Logos existing as incarnate (*tou logou sesarkomeneh*)."[83] All that we see in Scripture about Christ, that which speaks of his eternity as God, and that which speaks of his human birth, pertains to one and the same, as befitting for him as God and befitting him as man (*Unity*, 69). Therefore, Cyril's interpretation of christological passages glides along the spectrum of the *oikonomia–theologia* framework, so that he doesn't deny key teachings found elsewhere in Scripture.

How does he do this? We will examine how Cyril handles a few passages. In Matthew 23:9, Jesus says, "Do not call anyone on earth your father, because you have one Father, who is in heaven." Cyril writes, "And because he came down into our condition solely in order to lead us to his own divine state, he also said: 'I am ascending to my Father and your Father, to my God and your God'" (Jn 20:17). And Cyril writes, "In this case, the Heavenly One is his natural Father; in our case he is our God. But insofar as this true and natural Son became as we are, so he speaks of the Father as his God, a language fitting to his self-emptying" (*Unity*, 69). Cyril avoids the interpretive mistakes his opponents (i.e., the Nestorians) make in that they swerve to the divine "side" of Christ (or the human side), giving it the dominant controlling power in their interpretations. While there is a non-contrastive dichotomy between the natures, there is an undissolvable unity in the one person (i.e., subject) of the Lord Christ. When it comes to these types of "conflicting" passages, Cyril interprets them in a manner befitting of the context.

In Matthew 23:9, Cyril delineates the *economic* entailments, in that because no one is to call a man "your father," since there is only one true Father in heaven, "he," the Son, came down to us to bring us to his own

---

[83] Riches, *Ecce Homo*, 39.

divine state. As the God-man, he is the true form of perfected humanity, who is fully obedient to the Father, as the last Adam. And thus, as the perfect human, he will not call a man on earth his father. But as the God-man, he comes down from heaven, so that he can bring us to the true Father in heaven. Therefore, in referencing John 20:17, in which Jesus tells Mary that he is going to his Father and your Father, Jesus is speaking of the Heavenly one as his Father, befitting of his natural generation as the begotten Son from the Father. But to us, the Father is our God. And in becoming as we are in human weakness, he speaks of the Father as his God, in "self-emptying" language befitting of his humanity (*Unity*, 63). This last point is crucial. For Christ to fulfill the law and redeem humanity, he must live as man in every way as man—in complete *creaturely* submission to God. And on the cross, "the fragility of Jesus' flesh becomes the medium of translucency to the glory of God.... The crucified Son simply 'is' the glory of God."[84]

Conclusion

When we consider the unity of Christ, we have an ontological unity, which maintains both natures unitedly. Between the two natures is a *communicatio idiomatum*, the communication of properties in the one person. This entails a threefold axiom: (1) It is *truly* God the Son who is man. (2) It is *truly man* that the Son of God is. (3) The Son of God *truly is* man.[85] In these axioms, the Lord Jesus is truly and fully divine, truly and fully human, and there is ontological unity between the person of the Son and his humanity. In this synergistic union, the human nature of Jesus does not have its own *hypostasis* apart from the one Lord. The Son is the "singular 'existent' of the human Jesus."[86] In the hypostatic union, "the human nature acquires existence in the existence of God, in the mode of being of the Word."[87] Articulation of the doctrine in this

---

[84] Riches, *Ecce Homo*, 100.

[85] Riches, *Ecce Homo*, 44–5. The three points are direct citations but spaced out in the original. Riches contrasts Cyril's axiom with the metaphysical errors of Nestorianism and Eutychianism, one is dualist (Nest.) and the other monist (Eut.). In the former, the 'proximity' of God does not enhance the integrity of human reality but rather weakens it; in the latter, the 'proximity' of the human to God threatens to corrupt his divine passibility" (p.63).

[86] Riches, *Ecce Homo*, 112.

[87] Karl Barth, *Church Dogmatics*, ed. G. W. Bromiley and T. F. Torrance (Edinburgh: T & T Clark, 1936), I/2, 163.

manner guarded against the idea of a double existence of Christ as Logos and as man. The incarnation has no creaturely analog. Thus, in the hypostatic union what "Christ achieves in the new integrity of human nature, discovered in his theandric energy, is a crucial inversion: divine things are done humanly, and human things are done divinely. . . . 'If he conquered as God, to us it is nothing; but if he conquered as man we conquered in him.'"[88]

---

[88] Cyril of Alexandria, *In Ioannis Evangelium*, 16.33, quoted in Riches, *Ecce Homo*, 106.

COUNCIL OF CHALCEDON
451

hile the previous councils focused on hammering out a cogent
Trinitarian grammar (not *logic*)[89] to speak coherently about the
threeness of God that does not compromise divine simplicity,
the Council of Chalcedon in 451 called for greater precision. Two
traditions, the Alexandrian and the Antiochian, needed to come together
and resolve the tension over the most pressing question: How does the
immutable, eternal God join to a mutable, historical man?[90] The church had
a divine grammar to speak of the Divine essence, but how the Divine
essence *incarnated* was akin to theological quantum theory. Multiple
perspectives circled among the clergy dealing with the two–natures
dilemma. Succinctly stated, they were: *Apollinarianism*: Christ did not have
a genuine human soul. *Nestorianism*: Christ is two distinct persons.
Eutychianism/Monophysitism: A blending of the two natures into one
(*tertium quid*: a third thing). *Dyophysitism/Miaphysitism*: The two natures
unite in the one person of Jesus Christ.

Though Cyril had been dead almost a decade, the Cyrillian formula
(*mia-physis*) already had doctrinal authority going into the Council.
However, leading up to the Council, a few years prior, Eutyches, an

---

[89] Holmes, *Quest for the Trinity*, 109.
[90] Justo L. Gonzalez, *Story of Christianity: Volume 1, The: The Early Church to the Dawn
of the Reformation*, 2nd. Revised and Updated. (HarperOne, 2010), 296.

archimandrite who gained notoriety by heavy-handedly opposing the teachings of Nestorius (Christ was two distinct persons) in the Council of Ephesus (431), though defended the Cyrillian formula, failed to uphold a crucial theological distinction: Christ's consubstantial nature with humanity.[91] His declaration: "I confess that our Lord was from two natures before the union, but after the union, I confess one nature," was his condemnable error.[92] Much more could be said regarding the doctrinal issues leading up to the Council,[93] but ultimately, the Council needed to erect a christological guardrail around the incarnational language. We (the catholic tradition) needed to be able to make statements such as "God died on the cross" and "The Lord Jesus Christ created the world" without anyone running to get rope, wood, and a torch. Again, it was not a logical move but a *grammatical* one.

At the conclusion of the Council, the fathers composed the *Definitio fidei*, or the Chalcedonian Definition, clarifying what the church held to be true, while also utilizing language to counter any extreme Nestorian or Eutychian notions. The Definition needed to cover all the heretical *bases*. In the Definition, the fathers included key adverbs regarding the incarnation: *without confusion, without change, without separation*, and *without division*. The crucial section of the Chalcedonian Definition states:

CHALCEDONIAN CREED

Following therefore, the holy Fathers, we confess one and the same Lord Jesus Christ, and we all teach harmoniously [that he is] the same perfect in Godhead, the same perfect in manhood, truly God and truly man, the same of a reasonable soul and body; consubstantial with the Father in Godhead, and the same consubstantial with us in manhood, like us in all things except sin; begotten before ages of the Father in Godhead, the same in the last days for us; and for our salvation [born] of Mary the virgin theotokos in manhood, one and the same Christ, Son, Lord, unique; acknowledged in two natures without confusion, without change, without division, without separation—the difference of the natures being by no means taken away

---

[91] Riches, *Ecce Homo*, 57–8.

[92] Quote cited from Weinandy, *Does God Change?*, 61.

[93] For detailed treatments on the subject and the important *theotokos* controversy, see Davis, *The First Seven*, 134–206; J. N. D. Kelly, *Early Christian Doctrines*, Revised Edition. (HarperOne, 1978), 280–343; Weinandy, *Does God Change?* (Still River, MA: St. Bede's Press, 2002), 32–66.

because of the union, but rather the distinctive character of each nature being preserved, and [each] combining in one Person and hypostasis—not divided or separated into two Persons, but one and the same Son and only-begotten God, Word, Lord Jesus Christ; as the prophets of old and the Lord Jesus Christ himself taught us about him, and the symbol of the Fathers has handed down to us.[94]

In using the four adverbs, taken directly from Cyril himself, "The result of the Chalcedonian formulation was to realize very clearly that 'the proximity of the divine' does not threaten or compromise 'the integrity of the human,' but in fact *establishes it.*"[95] In a way, the Definition did not actually produce something new; rather, it returned to the incarnational *two-natures-in-one-person* theology of Tertullian, "the original *unitas* of the one Lord Jesus Christ."[96] As stated, *logic* was not the goal. The Definition does not explain *how* the union took place; rather, it gives "the sense of setting the limits [the grammatical guardrails], beyond which error lies."[97]

---

[94] Hardy, *Christology of the Later Fathers*, 373.
[95] Riches, *Ecce Homo*, 61. Emphasis added.
[96] Riches, *Ecce Homo*, 61.
[97] Gonzalez, *Story of Christianity: Volume 1*, 302.

CONCLUSION

The God of the Bible is a speaking God. "Long ago he spoke ... at different times and in different ways" (He 1:1). In the speaking of his Word (Jn 1:1–18), God revealed himself most clearly in his Son (He 1:2). While God's Word is the perfect Statement, that Statement continues to unfold. Soon after the birth of the church, communication barriers emerged as the church was carrying out its mission to disciple the nations. The triune God is not a God of confusion but works his plan through fallen, finite creatures who stumble along the way. By God's grace, his Word continues to move throughout the world, shaping the cultures it enters around God's revelation. God's Word is pure, but creaturely words are not. However, God accommodates to us, giving us the proper grammar so that we can speak truly and clearly about the God who is incomprehensible. And that is what we observed throughout this book. God shows himself to us as a beam of light refracting through a prism, revealing all the beautiful colors contained in it. *Language* is the means God uses to refract his glorious self so that creatures can grasp what we cannot see.

The first four centuries of the Christian Faith were pivotal for the movement of the church. The metaphysical divine grammar that developed during those years, today, some 1600 years later, is still the grammar in theological discourse of the Christian doctrine of God.

However, in modern theology, we have witnessed a trend in theological discourse that shies away from the metaphysical grammar undergirding the foundational doctrines of the Christian Faith. The problem is those trending that way think they can coherently retain the orthodox truths of the Christian tradition while substituting a different metaphysical grammar. However, such attempts prove to be theologically inconsistent. Metaphysics matters. Modern theology needs an *ad fontes* to the metaphysical grammar of the early church. If the church is to move forward, it must look back.

This investigation primarily aimed to validate Richard Muller's claim regarding the normative assumption of divine simplicity within the historic Christian tradition. However, Dr. Muller did not require my validation; he is a leading scholar in his field, known for his meticulous research and providing numerous sources to support his claim. I simply wanted to explore this for myself. I can confidently affirm that I fully agree with Dr. Muller's assertion. Furthermore, this investigation offered much more than validation. Contemplating God alongside the Church Fathers has been a soul-enriching journey, deepening my understanding of the grandeur of the One, Holy, and Blessed triune God. *To Him be all the glory!*

Glossary

Appropriation: involves attributing a common reality, divine action, or created effect to a specific person of the Trinity in a unique way, based on the affinity of this shared reality with the unique characteristics of that person. This is done to better illustrate the distinctions between the divine persons to believers. For instance, power is specifically linked to the Father. The understanding of appropriation requires recognizing the distinct properties of each person of the Trinity.

Begotten: the personal property of the Son is defined by his relationship of origin from the Father, i.e., his mode of being (not to be confused with the modalist heresy) in relation to the Father. The *unbegotten* (see, UNBEGOTTEN) Father *begets* the Son, indicating the Father is the head or source, from whom the Son originates from. The language indicates an eternal relationship, not one of origin of existence.

Consubstantial, Consubstantiality: the sharing of divine substance, which is identical in the three divine persons. Consubstantiality is applied to the Son and the Holy Spirit in relation to the Father.

Economy (*oikonomia*): the works through which God reveals and communicates himself, such as the incarnation of the Son and the gift of the Holy Spirit.

ESSENCE: the attribute that defines a thing and sets it apart from others. The essence of God is his divinity, which is one and identical in the three divine persons.

HYPOSTASIS: the concrete reality that exists individually and subsists through itself. It designates what is distinct in God, connected to a personal property.

MISSION: the sending of the Son and the Holy Spirit in the economy of grace.

MODALISM: a heterodox doctrine denying the real personal distinction of the Father, Son, and Holy Spirit. Equivalent expressions: Sabellianism, Unitarian Monarchianism.

MODE OF EXISTENCE: the distinct manner characterizing each divine person according to their relative property.

NATURE: the internal principle of operation and the essence of a being. The divine nature is one and identical in the three persons.

ORIGIN: the eternal provenance of a divine person, referring to the generation of the Son and the procession of the Holy Spirit.

PERSON: an individual with rational nature, distinguished by personal properties in Trinitarian doctrine. The equivalent word to *person* in Trinitarian theology is *hypostasis*. The personal property of the Father is *paternity*, the Son is *filiation*, and the Spirit is *procession*.

PRINCIPLE: that from which a thing is produced. The Father is the principle of the Son, and the Father and the Son are the principle of the Holy Spirit.

PROCESSION: the origin of the Son and the Holy Spirit, specifically referring to the origin of the Holy Spirit and his relative personal property.

RELATION: traditional Catholic doctrine acknowledges four real relations within the Trinity, which explain the distinction of divine persons: paternity, filiation, spiration, and procession. These relations are defined by their origin, for instance, filiation, the Son's relation, exists in his connection to the Father who begets him. They also involve an "opposition" (the Son is not the Father). Paternity, filiation, and procession are referred to as "personal relations" (St. Thomas Aquinas).

SPIRATION: the Father and the Son both "breathe" the Holy Spirit who proceeds; this reflects the "common notion" of the Father and the Son as the singular principle of the Holy Spirit (meaning, the relation of the Father and the Son to the Holy Spirit).

SUBSISTENCE: being in oneself and through oneself; the unique essence in which it exists independently and not in another; what exists independently and in itself. In Trinitarian doctrine, the term "subsistence" (in Latin: *subsistentia*) translates to the Greek term *hypostasis*: three subsistences.

SUBSTANCE: that which is suitable to exist independently and not in another. The term "divine substance" refers to the actual reality of divinity, the essential nature of God. The substance of the three divine persons is unified and the same. The unity of power and the unity of nature are linked to the unity of substance.

THEOLOGY (*THEOLOGIA*): the mystery of God's innermost life within the Blessed Trinity, the enigma of the three persons in the transcendent reality of their Divine essence.

UNBEGOTTEN: a property of the Father who does not originate from another person that should not be mistaken for "uncreated" or "not having been made" (an attribute shared by all three divine persons).

BIBLIOGRAPHY

Amos Yong. "Divine Omniscience and Future Contingents: Weighing the Presuppositional Issues in the Contemporary Debate." *Evangelical Review of Theology* 26, no. 3 (July 2002): 240–264.

Anatolios, Khaled. *Retrieving Nicaea: The Development and Meaning of Trinitarian Doctrine*. Grand Rapids, MI: Baker Academic, 2011. Accessed February 16, 2021.

Anselm, and Charles Hartshorne. *St. Anselm Basic Writings: Proslogium, Monologium, Gaunilo's In Behalf of the Fool, Cur Deus Homo*. Translated by S. N. Deane. 2nd Revised. LaSalle, IL: Open Court, 1998.

Aquinas, Thomas. *The Summa Theologica of St. Thomas Aquinas*. Translated by Fathers of the English Dominican Province. 5 vols. New York: Christian Classics, 1981.

Aristotle. *Physics*. Translated by Robin Waterfield. 1st ed. Oxford University Press, 2008.

———. *The Metaphysics*. Edited by Roger B. Jones. Translated by W. D. Ross. CreateSpace Independent Publishing Platform, 2012.

Augustine of Hippo. *Tractates on the Gospel of John 1–10. The Fathers of the Church, Volume 78*. CUA Press, 2010.

———. *The Trinity*. Translated by John E. Rotelle. English Translation. New City Press, 1991.

———. *Confessions*. Translated by R. S. Pine-Coffin. Harmondsworth, Middlesex, Engl: Penguin Classics, 1961.

Ayres, Lewis. *Augustine and the Trinity*. Cambridge Books Online. Cambridge University Press, 2010.

———. *Nicaea and Its Legacy: An Approach to Fourth-Century Trinitarian Theology*. Oxford University Press, 2006.

———. "On Not Three People: The Fundamental Themes of Gregory of Nyssa's Trinitarian Theology as Seen in To Ablabius: On Not Three Gods." *Modern Theology* 18, no. 4 (October 2002): 445–474.

Barth, Karl. *Church Dogmatics*. Edited by G. W. Bromiley and T. F. Torrance. 4 vols. Edinburgh: T & T Clark, 1936.

Basil of Caesarea. *Against Eunomius*. Translated by Mark DelCogliano and Andrew Radde-Gallwitz. *The Fathers of the Church*. Washington, D.C: CUA Press, 2011.

Bates, Matthew W. *The Birth of the Trinity: Jesus, God, and Spirit in New Testament and Early Christian Interpretations of the Old Testament*. Reprint edition. Oxford University Press, 2016.

Beckwith, Carl L. "Suffering without Pain: The Scandal of Hilary of Poitiers' Christology." In *In the Shadow of the Incarnation: Essays on Jesus Christ in the Early Church in Honor of Brian E. Daley, S.J*, 71–96. Notre Dame, ID, 2008.

Beeley, Christopher A. "Divine Causality and the Monarchy of God the Father in Gregory of Nazianzus." *Harvard Theological Review* 100, no. 2 (April 2007): 199–214.

Behr, John. *Formation of Christian Theology: The Nicene Faith*. First. Vol. 2. Crestwood, NY: St. Vladimirs Seminary Press, 2004.

———. *Formation of Christian Theology: The Way to Nicaea*. First. Vol. 1. Crestwood, NY: St. Vladimirs Seminary Press, 2001.

Bray, Gerald. *God Has Spoken: A History of Christian Theology*. 1st ed. Wheaton, IL: Crossway, 2014.

Calvin, John. *Commentary on the Epistle of Paul the Apostle to the Romans*. Translated by John Owen. Bellingham, WA: Logos Bible Software, 2010.

———. *Concerning the Eternal Predestination of God*. 1st edition. Louisville, KY: Westminster John Knox Press, 1997.

Carter, Craig A. *Interpreting Scripture with the Great Tradition: Recovering the Genius of Premodern Exegesis*. Grand Rapids, MI: Baker Academic, 2018.

Carter, Craig A., and Carl Trueman. *Contemplating God with the Great Tradition: Recovering Trinitarian Classical Theism*. Grand Rapids, MI: Baker Academic, 2021.

Chrysostom, John. *On the Incomprehensible Nature of God*. *The Fathers of the Church*. Washington, D.C.: CUA Press, 1984.

Clement of Alexandria. *Stromateis, Books 1–3. The Fathers of the Church*, Volume 85. CUA Press, 2010.

Comfort, Philip W., J. D. Douglas, and Donald Mitchell. *Who's Who in Christian History*. Wheaton, IL: Tyndale House, 1992.

Cyril of Alexandria, Joel C. Elowsky, and David R. Maxwell. *Commentary on John: Volume 1*. Ancient Christian Texts. Downers Grove, IL: IVP Academic, 2013.

———. *Festal Letters 1-12. The Fathers of the Church*. Washington, D.C.: CUA Press, 2009.

———. *On the Unity of Christ*. Translated by John Anthony McGuckin. St Vladimirs Seminary Pr, 1997.

Davis, Leo D. *The First Seven Ecumenical Councils*. Liturgical Press, 1990.

Wright, D. F. "Chrysostom, John," in Earle E. Cairns, J. D. Douglas, and James E. Ruark. *The New International Dictionary of the Christian* . Grand Rapids, MI: Zondervan Publishing House, 1978.

Elwell, Walter A., and Barry J. Beitzel, eds. *Baker Encyclopedia of the Bible*. Logos Research. Grand Rapids, MI: Baker Book House, 1988.

Emery, Gilles. *The Trinity: An Introduction to Catholic Doctrine on the Triune God*. Thomistic Ressourcement Series. Washington, D.C.: Catholic University of America Press, 2012

Feldmeth, Nathan P. *Pocket Dictionary of Church History*. IVP Academic, 2008.

Gavrilyuk, Paul L. *The Suffering of the Impassible God: The Dialectics of Patristic Thought*. Oxford University Press, 2006.

Gonzalez, Justo L. *Story of Christianity: Volume 1, The: The Early Church to the Dawn of the Reformation*. 2 Revised and Updated. HarperOne, 2010.

Grant, Richard M. *The Early Christian Doctrine of God*. Richard lectures. Charlottesville: University Press of Virginia, 1966.

Gregory of Nazianzus. *St. Gregory of Nazianzus Select Orations*. Translated by Martha Vinson. Vol. 107. Washington, D.C.: Catholic University of America Press, 2004.

———. *On God and Christ: The Five Theological Orations and Two Letters to Cledonius*. Crestwood, NY: St Vladimir's Seminary Press, 2002.

Grillmeier, Aloys. *Christ in Christian Tradition: From the Apostolic Age to Chalcedon*. 2 Revised edition. Westminster John Knox Press, 1988.

Hägg, Henny Fiskå. *Clement of Alexandria and the Beginnings of Christian Apophaticism*. Oxford early Christian studies. Oxford: Oxford University Press, 2006.

Hallman, Joseph M. "The Mutability of God: Tertullian to Lactantius." *Theological Studies* 42, no. 3 (September 1981): 373–393.

Hanson, R. P. C. *The Search for the Christian Doctrine of God: The Arian Controversy, 318-381.* Grand Rapids, MI: Baker Academic, 2006.

Hardy, Edward Rochie. *Christology of the Later Fathers.* Westminster John Knox Press, 1954.

Helm, Paul. "Understanding Scholarly Presuppositions: A Crucial Tool for Research?" *Tyndale Bulletin* 44, no. 1 (May 1993): 143–154.

Hengel, Martin. *Judaism and Hellenism: Studies in Their Encounter in Palestine During the Early Hellenistic Period.* Fortress Press, 1981.

Henry, Carl F. H. *God, Revelation and Authority.* Logos edition. 6 vols. Crossway, 1999.

Hilary of Poitiers. *The Trinity. The Fathers of the Church.* Washington, D.C.: CUA Press, 2002.

Holmes, Stephen R. *The Quest for the Trinity: The Doctrine of God in Scripture, History and Modernity.* Downers Grove, IL: IVP Academic, 2012.

Josephus, Flavius. *The Works of Josephus: Complete and Unabridged, New Updated Edition.* Translated by William Whiston. Hendrickson Pub, 1980.

Kelly, J. N. D. *Early Christian Creeds.* 3rd ed. A&C Black, 2006.

Kreeft, Peter. *The Platonic Tradition.* South Bend, IN: St. Augustine's Press, 2018.

Letham, Robert. *The Holy Trinity: In Scripture, History, Theology, and Worship.* Phillipsburg, N.J.: P&R Publishing, 2004.

May, Gerhard. *Creatio Ex Nihilo: The Doctrine of "Creation out of Nothing" in Early Christian Thought.* London; New York: T&T Clark, 2004.

Moo, Douglas J. *The Epistle to the Romans.* Grand Rapids, MI: Wm. B. Eerdmans Publishing Company, 1996.

Muller, Richard A. *Dictionary of Latin and Greek Theological Terms: Drawn Principally from Protestant Scholastic Theology.* 2nd ed. Baker Academic, 2017.

———. *Post-Reformation Reformed Dogmatics: The Rise and Development of Reformed Orthodoxy, ca. 1520 to ca. 1725.* 2nd ed. 4 vols. Grand Rapids, MI: Baker Academic, 2003.

"Nicene Creed | Christian Reformed Church." Accessed May 13, 2024. https://www.crcna.org/welcome/beliefs/creeds/nicene-creed.

Origen. *Origen.* Translated by John Behr. New York: Oxford University Press, 2020.

Orr, Brian J. *A Classical Response to Relational Theism: A Reformed Evangelical Critique of Thomas Jay Oord's Evangelical Process Theology.* Eugene, OR: Wipf and Stock Publishers, 2022.

Osborn, Eric. *The Emergence of Christian Theology*. New York, NY: Cambridge University Press, 2005.

Owens, Joseph. *An Elementary Christian Metaphysics*. Reprint edition. Houston, TX: Center for Thomistic Studies, 1985.

Pelikan, Jaroslav. *The Christian Tradition: A History of the Development of Doctrine, Vol. 1: The Emergence of the Catholic Tradition*. Chicago, IL: University of Chicago Press, 1975.

Plato. *Plato in Twelve Volumes*. Translated by R. G. Bury. Cambridge, MA: Harvard University Press; London, William Heinemann Ltd., 1967.

———. *The Republic*. Translated by B. Jowett. New York: Vintage Books, 1960.

Prestige, G. L. *God in Patristic Thought*. Reprint. Eugene, OR: Wipf and Stock Publishers, 2008.

Riches, Aaron. *Ecce Homo: On the Divine Unity of Christ*. Grand Rapids, MI: Eerdmans, 2016.

Runia, David T. *Philo of Alexandria and the Timaeus of Plato*. Philosophia antiqua. Leiden: Brill, 1986.

Silvas, Anna M. *Gregory of Nyssa: The Letters: Introduction, Translation and Commentary*. Gregory of Nyssa: The Letters. Brill, 2006.

Noble, T.A. "Basil of Caesarea," in Sinclair B. Ferguson, and J. I. Packer, eds. *New Dictionary of Theology*. Electronic ed. Downers Grove, IL: InterVarsity Press, 2000.

Kelley, D.F. "Novatian," in Sinclair B. Ferguson, and J. I. Packer, eds. *New Dictionary of Theology*. Electronic ed. Downers Grove, IL: InterVarsity Press, 2000.

Soskice, Janet Martin. "Athens and Jerusalem, Alexandria and Edessa: Is There a Metaphysics of Scripture?" *International Journal of Systematic Theology* 8, no. 2 (April 2006): 149–162.

Stead, Christopher. *Philosophy in Christian Antiquity*. Cambridge University Press, 1994.

Torrance, Thomas F. *The Mediation of Christ*. Revised. Colorado Springs, CO: Helmers & Howers, 1992.

Vaggione, R. P., trans. *Eunomius: The Extant Works*. Clarendon Press, 1987.

Webster, J. B. (John Bainbridge). "Perfection and Presence - 'God with US' According to the Christian Confession." Transcript edited by David M. Goetz, 173. Trinity Evangelical Divinity School, 2007. https://henrycenter.tiu.edu/kantzer-lectures-in-revealed-theology/past-lectures- publications/john-webster-perfection-presence/.

Weinandy, Thomas. *Does God Change?* First edition. Still River, MA: St. Bede's Press, 2002.

———. *Does God Suffer?* Notre Dame, IN: University of Notre Dame Press, 2000.

Whitaker, G. H., Colson, F. H. *Philo of Alexandria, Works (Loeb Classical Library in 12 Volumes)*, Public Domain.

Wierenga, Michah. "John Chrysostom," in Barry, John D., David Bomar, Derek R. Brown, Rachel Klippenstein, Douglas Mangum, Carrie Sinclair Wolcott, Lazarus Wentz, Elliot Ritzema, and Wendy Widder, eds. *The Lexham Bible Dictionary*. Bellingham, WA: Lexham Press, 2016.

Wilken, Robert Louis. *The Spirit of Early Christian Thought: Seeking the Face of God.* Yale University Press, 2005.

Yonge, C. D., trans. *The Works of Philo: Complete and Unabridged, New Updated Edition.* Peabody, Mass: Hendrickson Publishers, 1993.

Young, Frances M., and Andrew Teal. *From Nicaea to Chalcedon: A Guide to the Literature and Its Background.* 2nd ed. Baker Academic, 2010.

Index of Scripture

Index of Subjects

www.ingramcontent.com/pod-product-compliance
Lightning Source LLC
Chambersburg PA
CBHW022118080426
42734CB00006B/168